The Fractured Subject

FOUNDING CRITICAL THEORY

Series editors:

Owen Hulatt, Teaching Fellow, Department of Philosophy, University of York
Darrow Schecter, Professor in Critical Theory, University of Sussex

Editorial Review Board:

Brian O'Connor, University College Dublin, Ireland
Gordon Finlayson, University of Sussex, UK
Werner Bonefeld, University of York, UK
Fred Rush, Notre Dame University, USA
Jay Bernstein, The New School, USA
Lambert Zuidervaart, Institute for Christian Studies, Canada
Deborah Cook, University of Windsor, Canada
Christoph Menke, Goethe Universitat, Germany
Andrew Arato, The New School, USA

This series publishes original research on prominent figures, texts and topics in, and associated with, the first generation of Frankfurt School Critical Theory. The series comprises specialized treatments of topics and thinkers together with new translations of key texts from the period. Emphasis is lent to Critical Theory as an ongoing research project, and both its original research and historical scholarship is articulated in these terms. Critical Theory contains an intrinsic commitment to inter-disciplinary research, and this series attempts to honour this commitment where possible.

The Aesthetic Ground of Critical Theory, edited by Nathan Ross
Communication and Expression, Philip Hogh, translated by Antonia Hofstätter
Freedom and Negativity in Beckett and Adorno: Something or Nothing, Natalie
  Leeder
*Experience and Infinite Task: Knowledge, Language and Messianism in the
  Philosophy of Walter Benjamin*, Tamara Tagliacozzo
Walter Benjamin and the Post-Kantian Tradition, Philip Homberg
The Fractured Subject: Walter Benjamin and Sigmund Freud, Betty Schulz

The Fractured Subject

Walter Benjamin and Sigmund Freud

Founding Critical Theory

Betty Schulz

ROWMAN & LITTLEFIELD
Lanham • Boulder • New York • London

Published by Rowman & Littlefield
An imprint of The Rowman & Littlefield Publishing Group, Inc.
4501 Forbes Boulevard, Suite 200, Lanham, Maryland 20706
www.rowman.com

86-90 Paul Street, London EC2A 4NE

British Library Cataloguing in Publication Information Available

Library of Congress Cataloging-in-Publication Data

Names: Schultz, Betty, author.
Title: The fractured subject : Walter Benjamin and Sigmund Freud / Betty Schultz.
Description: Lanham : Rowman & Littlefield, [2022] | Series: Founding critical theory | Includes bibliographical references and index. | Summary: "An investigation Walter Benjamin's conception of the subject as fractured, via a reading of Benjamin's use of Freud; the topics cover gender, dreams, memory, childhood and mental illness"-- Provided by publisher.
Identifiers: LCCN 2022039807 (print) | LCCN 2022039808 (ebook) | ISBN 9781538163368 (cloth ; alk. paper) | ISBN 9781538163375 (epub)
Subjects: LCSH: Benjamin, Walter, 1892-1940--Criticism and interpretation. | Subject (Philosophy) in literature. | Psychoanalysis and literature. | Freud, Sigmund, 1856-1939--Influence. | LCGFT: Literary criticism.
Classification: LCC PT2603.E455 Z893184 (print) | LCC PT2603.E455 (ebook) | DDC 838/.91209--dc23/eng/20220916
LC record available at https://lccn.loc.gov/2022039807
LC ebook record available at https://lccn.loc.gov/2022039808

Contents

Acknowledgments

No work is ever the result of one author alone. I would like to acknowledge some of the many people who have contributed to the possibility and existence of this text in various ways.

First, to the series editor and my mentor, Darrow Schecter, and the editorial team at Rowman &Littlefield.

I would like to extend my gratitude to my PhD supervisor, Howard Caygill, for his comments and suggestions on the thesis that formed the backbone of this work, as well as his unwavering kindness. Without his close reading of my writing and enriching feedback and support, this work would not have been possible. My thanks also go out to the staff and students at the Centre for Research in Modern European Philosophy (CRMEP) for many thought-provoking seminars and discussions, in particular Stella Sandford, whose seminar on psychoanalysis allowed me to view Freud's work with fresh eyes, and to Isabell Dahms, for her friendship.

I would also like to thank the staff of the Walter Benjamin Archive Berlin, in particular Nadine Werner, Michael Schwarz, and Ursula Marx, who provided invaluable assistance during the course of my visit to the archive and beyond.

For their helpful feedback on various aspects of my work, I would like to thank Sami Khatib, Steffan Wyn-Jones, Sam Dolbear, Iain Campbell, and Patrick Levy. Special thanks to those close to me—friends, housemates, loved ones—who supported me throughout, in particular my partner, Dan Hadley, Joana Perrone, Harry Akram, and Shirley and Frankie; Jacken Waters, Mo Budd, Izzi Valentine, Aidan Simpson, and Wail Qasim, for many dinners and for being there. Also to Alva Gotby and Peter Ely for PhD student solidarity, as well as Virgil Taylor for incisiveness and support during the writing and publication process.

Finally, I want to express my gratitude to my parents, Stefan and Dorothea Schulz, for their support of myself and of this project, to my brother Dominik Schulz for the encouragement, to my aunt, Ursula Sautter, for reading, and to my grandmother, Elisabeth Sautter, who was an inspiration always.

List of Abbreviations

AP – Benjamin's *Arcades Project*

BPP – Freud's *Beyond the Pleasure Principle*

CC–Adorno-Benjamin Correspondence

C – The Correspondence of Walter Benjamin

GSW I& II – Warburg's *Gesammelte Schriften I & II*

GS1-7 – Benjamin's *Gesammelte Schriften*

GW – Freud's *Gesammelte Werke*

SE–The Standard Edition of the Complete Psychological Works of Sigmund Freud

SW1-4–Benjamin's Selected Writings, vols. 1-4

OT–Benjamin's *The Origin of German Tragic Drama* (the Trauerspiel book)

WuN–Benjamin's *Werke und Nachlass. Kritische Gesamtausgabe*

Please see the bibliography for the editions referenced in this text.
Unless otherwise stated, all references to *Hamlet* are taken from the Arden Shakespeare, edited by Harold Jenkins.

Introduction

In 1935, Theodor Adorno wrote to Walter Benjamin that "Perhaps without being aware of the fact . . . you find yourself . . . in the most profound agreement with Freud; there is certainly much to be thought about in this connection" (CC, 93). Surprisingly, this dictum has not been met with the attention and scholarly investigation it warrants. The present text seeks to address this lack by investigating Benjamin's use of Freud's writing. Specifically, I have based my investigation of the Freudian impact on Benjamin on the concept of the fractured subject. In what follows, I will sketch the concepts of the subject Benjamin drew from, before delving into the relationship between Benjamin and Freud.

Elizabeth Stewart states in her book on the subject in Benjamin's work that "from his early statements regarding modernity's siege on meaningful experience, in his descriptions of the modern world of meaning and relationship as empty, to his preoccupations with perception in ordinary and extraordinary conditions, in particular in relation to modern technology, the topography of the subject is central to it all" (Stewart 2010, 67). Meanwhile Susan Buck-Morss observes that for Benjamin, "the cognitive experience of history, no less than that of the empirical world, required the active intervention of the thinking subject" (Buck-Morss 1993, 314). I suggest it is a more fruitful avenue of inquiry to focus on Benjamin's critique of the subject and subjectivism; his abiding interest in movements that overcome such a "thinking subject," and the attention he pays to its historical situatedness. All of these, I suggest, can be grouped together as the subject's *fracturing*. A problem in Stewart's reading is what we might term the "ethicisation" of Benjamin. Her book constitutes a quest for Benjamin's post-catastrophic, post-totalitarian subject, to be distilled chiefly from the

1

book on German tragic drama. However, these questions about the "good life" for the "good subject" seem to run counter to the more compelling issues raised by Benjamin's text. Its aim is not to provide guidance for the reconstruction of the psyche of an already-existing subject; rather, it performs a reading of the historical situation of the production of an art form and through this reading provides a commentary on the *inauguration* of a mode of being, namely, that of the fractured subject.

My investigation takes Benjamin's 1928 *Origin of the German Mourning Play* as its principal starting point. However, this is not the first text in which the question of subjectivity appears in Benjamin's work. In what follows, I will briefly discuss the precursors to the *Trauerspiel* study, in which Benjamin first touches on the question of the subject via a critique of the Kantian concept of experience. I will also consider Benjamin's dissertation on criticism in German Romanticism. These preliminary investigations will serve to set the scene for Benjamin's elaboration of the fractured subject in the book on German *Trauerspiel*.

THE SUBJECT BEFORE BENJAMIN

The subject is, at heart, a fraught concept, uniting several distinct yet overlapping conceptual lineages. In his genealogy of the concept of the subject in the history of Philosophy, Etienne Balibar attempts to disentangle some of these confluent and conflicting meanings, starting with the Greek *hupokeimenon*. This is often translated as "substrate" or the Latin *subiectum*. Balibar identifies three main overlapping but somewhat distinct aspects of the modern usage of the term "subject": subjectness (*subjectité* in French), subjectivity (*subjectivité*), and subjection (*sujétion*) (Balibar 2014, 1069), and states that "the psychological meaning of the term [subjectivity], which is dominant in ordinary usage, is the result of a series of transformations that began in the Middle Ages" (Balibar 2014, 1073), setting in motion a process in which these three aspects began to coalesce. Of particular importance is what Balibar calls a "pun" on two Latin etymologies at the heart of the modern usage of subject: "that of the neuter *subjectum* (which, like *suppositum*, has, ever since the Scholastics, been regarded by philosophers as a translation of the Greek *hupokeimenon*), and that of the masculine *subjectus* (equated with *subditus* in the Middle Ages)." The former "gives rise to a lineage of logico-grammatical and ontological-transcendental meanings, and the other to a lineage of juridical, political, and theological meanings." Of course, these different lineages intersect and blend—in Balibar's words, they "overdetermine" each other—"because, following Kant, the problematic articulation of 'subjectivity' and 'subjection' came to be defined as a theory of the constituent subject" (Balibar 2014, 1078). This tension constitutes for Balibar one of the central problems of modern philosophy.[1]

Oberprantacher and Siclodi, commenting on this distinction, suggest that the above pun "involves also the history of institutions insofar as the term 'subject' refers to all the variable *submissions* (aka 'subjection') to the authority of a power . . . besides referring to an invariable *substance* (aka 'subjectivity'), capable of transporting specific properties." (Oberprantacher and Siclodi 2016, 10–11). The authors also draw attention to the tension between "autonomous subjectivity" and "heteronomous *subjection*" mediated in the concept of subjectivation, which they identify as central to any discussion of the subject "given that it confronts us with an apparent contradiction in terms that concerns the emergence of the subject itself" (Oberprantacher and Siclodi 2016, 1–2). What we can discern from these brief preliminary remarks is that the concept of the subject is characterised by internal tensions—fractures—that encompass differing genealogies and lineages that philosophy has attempted to unite or conflate in different ways over the course of history. The question of the subject as agent or as passive vis a vis that which would subject it looms prominently. So do the differing lineages identified by Balibar: the juridico-political, the theological, the ontological or transcendental. The implication of Balibar's study of the concept of the subject is that it was always-already fractured, the result not of a direct transmission of Greek Philosophy into early modern accounts, but the unstable result of sometimes contesting, sometimes conflated genealogies. As we shall see, this is to play a central part in Benjamin's concept of the subject, which he explores both in terms of epistemological questions regarding possible forms of experience and knowledge and in terms of questions of power. I will begin with a discussion of Benjamin's engagement with the two most important sources of the modern concept of the subject: Descartes and Kant.

THE MODERNS: DESCARTES

Benjamin references both Cartesian dualism and Descartes' lesser-known work *Passions of the Soul* (1649) in his book on German *Trauerspiel*. The reference appears in a passage discussing the centrality of the body, that is, the *physis* capable of pain and suffering, in distinguishing *Trauerspiel* from tragedy, which is one of Benjamin's central aims in the book. Benjamin writes

> It is not only the Dualism of Descartes that is baroque; as a consequence of the doctrine of psycho-physical determination, the theory of the passions also deserves the closest consideration. Since, in fact, the spirit is in itself pure

reason, true to itself, and it is physical influences alone which bring it into contact with the world, the torture which it endures was a more immediate basis of violent emotions than so-called tragic conflicts. (OT, 217)

Benjamin thus identifies Cartesian dualism as a quintessentially baroque conception of the subject. As I discuss in more detail in my first chapter, the 1928 *Trauerspiel* book charts how the advent of modernity in the era of the wars of religion sets in motion a cataclysmic event for baroque humanity. Subjectivity is borne out of this, but, as also seen in Balibar's account, it is fractured from the start. To wit, the Cartesian subject is fractured, into thinking cogito and that which it is not—the body, the world, and so on—and, even though Descartes reintroduces the belief in a benevolent God as a foundational condition for his cogito,[2] the latter is radically divided from the divine.

Further, Benjamin reads Descartes' model of the mind-body connection as positing a mind completely detached from empirical reality. Only via embodiment is this link provided. Thus we arrive at the first, dual fracture of the subject in the baroque: mind from body, and from the divine. This model of the division of the body from the mind was only capable of emerging in the baroque due to the experience of theologico-political conflict specific to it. The suffering and melancholy mood reflected in the mourning plays is thus very different from tragic conflict such as that of Greek antiquity and instead grounded in physical suffering. Only in the context of such a baroque model of subjectivity—of a mind radically sundered from the body—is this melancholy experience possible. The body remains bereft: the *"entseelte . . . Koerper"* (GS1 393) by its very definition lacking a soul. Benjamin investigates how Cartesian dualism is experienced as painful fallout of this fracture, a *physis* devoid of *transcendent* meaning.[3] In the *Trauerspiel* book, Benjamin complicates Descartes' account of the subject by investigating the mourning that is provoked by its self-discovery in the split from nature and God. Benjamin's account thus implicitly brings to light what is repressed in the emergence of Descartes' subject: firstly, that this is not a universal, transhistorical subject, but that it could have emerged only at a certain time and in a certain historico-political configuration; and secondly, that the historical processes that made this new conceptualisation of subjectivity possible carried with them an experience of loss and lack. Benjamin investigates how this dual division—from the divine/cosmos, and from the body—remains operative in the modern, post-baroque subject as a fracture.

In an early fragment entitled "Über das Grauen I," Benjamin captures the kind of *Versunkenheit* (immersion) typical of the baroque, describing the experience of a profane immersion not into the divine, and "thus" not into the self, but into "something alien." To illustrate this, Benjamin describes a schema in which the "soul" functions as a maelstrom or eddy which absorbs the mind-body duality into itself in its movement into an other in this form of contemplation, leaving behind a body that is merely corporeal and thus robbed of the faculty capable of recognising its boundaries. This leads to an experience of porosity and diffusion: the body is bereft of its higher meaning and blurs into its surroundings. As Lea Barbisan observes, "What is left behind once the lived body (*Leib*) is taken away with the spirit it belongs to, is the *Körper*—a body the *ego* can neither recognize as a part of itself, nor dismiss as a mere thing" (Barbisan 2017, 3). As discussed in my first and second chapters, this aspect of the fracturing of the subject in modernity, intimately connected to its fracturing from the divine, is expressed as loss and suffering. Carolin Duettlinger also notes the ghostly presence of Freud's theory of the uncanny in this fragment, as for Benjamin, the appearance of the mother is cited as the paradigmatic source of this horror as her "familiar appearance becomes threateningly alien as the boundaries of self and other are dissolved" (Duettlinger 2007, 36). Additionally, we can perceive here echoes of Freud's writings on the actual neurotics, whose bodily symptoms are the result of a somatic tension that proves to be so overwhelming it "cannot enter the psychic field" (SE1, 195). Thus, "[t]he 'actual' neuroses point to a body that has lost its place in the continuum of time and memory" (Cohen 2015, 219) which, as Josh Cohen rightly observes, is a condition typical of modernity and was perceived as such by Benjamin. If we bear in mind Freud's suggestion in his 1926 *Inhibitions, Symptoms and Anxiety* that actual and psychoneuroses are more connected than their initial distinction suggests, that in fact "[t]he symbolic meanings of psychoneurosis may wrap themselves around a kernel of untranslatable, 'actual' bodily noise" (Cohen 2015, 227), we become aware of a dynamic in which the psyche repeatedly attempts to make sense of, and periodically fails, to account for the experience of the fracture between body and mind running through the modern subject. It is this dynamic that is at play in Benjamin's men of the crowd, the denizens of the nineteenth-century urban centre, Already in the early fragment on horror, Benjamin links the loss of boundaries of the fractured subject to the appearance of a sense of uncanny doubling:

That which is perceived . . . now breaks into him, from the alien body too the mind-body falls into the eddy, and what remains in the visual-facial perception [*Gesichtswahrnehmung*] of horror, apart from the feeling "this is you, in gazing upon the other" ("you" because there is no boundary), is the feeling: this is your double, directed at the "other" body, which is now without boundary or corporeality (GS6, 76, transl. mine).[4]

The absorption of the "Geist-Leib," the "mind-body" by the eddy created in the moment of contemplation of the alien leaves nothing behind but empty corporeal vessels which appear to be the same. Far from any intersubjectivity or mutual recognition, this process is a fundamentally uncanny and *grauenhaft*, a horrible one, dissolving the boundaries between self and other and indeed the very possibility of such boundaries. Benjamin concludes that the "originary phenomenon of the double" is at the root of similitude: it is not grounded in any pre-existing affinity, but expresses the emptiness left behind in the wake of the emptying-out, the fracturing of the subject, occurring under the "reign of the double" (GS6, 76). Benjamin points to the imitation of that which is the cause of the fright as an example.[5] This, in turn, brings the double close to Freud's hysteric emulation: "identification is not simple imitation but *assimilation* on the basis of a similar aetiological pretension; it expresses a resemblance and is derived from a common element which remains in the unconscious" (SE4, 150). The hysteric identifies with the other, or with all of humanity, based on a similarity of experienced suffering, of which the symptoms become an expression: "Identification is a highly important factor in the mechanism of hysterical symptoms. It enables patients to express in their symptoms not only their own experiences but those of a large number of other people; it enables them, as it were, to suffer on behalf of a whole crowd of people and to act all the parts in a play single-handed" (SE4, 149). Here, we see what enabled Freud to characterise Hamlet as a hysteric: to become a stand-in for all of humanity, and to enact this suffering as play. The proximity to Benjamin's baroque sovereign and the fractured post-baroque subject is also apparent here.

In his "Schemata for the Psychophysical Problem," most probably dating from 1922/1923, Benjamin restates the identity of *Geist* and *Leib*. What is new is the introduction of another concept of the corporeal: Benjamin now distinguishes between *Leib* and *Koerper*. In the *Leib*, humanity exists in space, and thus in relation to a present other, a not-I. In the *Koerper*, the individual human is referred back only to itself, and the infinity of its sensory experience (through overwhelming sensations of pain or pleasure). This boundlessness of the self paradoxically forecloses the possibility of an encounter with an other, a realisation of containedness in space (a distinction between I and not I, I and other subjects, I and objects). Thus, what happens in the *Koerper* is the projection of the individual subject onto the entire world.

However, in its plasticity and boundarilessness, the body also emerges as a site of potential. The *Leib* is contrasted with the body in terms of its relationship to others—in the *Koerper*, a single, solitary individual is referred to God. While the Leib allows for expansion, is characterised by plasticity, its elasticity, its ability to incorporate (an) Other/s. As Barbisan puts it, "The Leib is not to be confused with the personal body . . . It materializes at the intersection between individual life and historical process, thus determining the human being's experience in historical time and bearing witness to the entanglement of individual life with the collective process of history" (Barbisan 2017, 4). Benjamin thus modifies his position: In the earlier fragment on horror, his focus is on the horror experienced in the "depotentiating" of the mind-body, in the "Psychophysical Problem," he explores the political potential of a humanity depleted of the concept of transcendence. The choice, as Benjamin writes, is up to humanity: substitute the semblance of unity with the divine in the form of the *Koerper*, or focus on the political potential of the expansive *Leib*. Or, in the vernacular of the nineteenth century, to accept the semblance of the commodity or attempt to move beyond its reach.

That the concept of the body continues to play a role in this process in the nineteenth century and beyond becomes apparent in Benjamin's 1929 essay on surrealism. Weigel convincingly links Benjamin's use of the term "innervation" in this essay to Freud, for whom, in his early "Project for a Scientific Psychology" it "refers to recordings of excitations (Erregungsaufzeichnungen); its matrix is to be found in the genesis of his theory of the nerve tracts (Nervenbahnen); later it was then transferred to the facilitations (Bahnungen) or permanent traces (Dauerspuren) in the unconscious" (Weigel 1996, 247). As Weigel observes, Benjamin's early interest in the more neurophysiological origins of psychoanalysis is transformed in his later readings of Freud, where Benjamin's interest shifts to the unconscious, without doing away with the body.[6] This dimension of the somatic in Freud and Benjamin will be examined in more detail in the context of dreams in my fifth chapter.

KNOWLEDGE/EVIL:
THE DEMONIC QUALITY OF PURE COGITO

The question of forms of experience and the possibility of knowledge are central to Benjamin's fractured subject. Experience and the possibility of the attainment of knowledge/truth undergo a crisis with the advent of modernity. The loss of a spiritual teleology that has God as its centre and goal in the wake of the reformation and the wars of religion—what Howard Caygill terms the "decay of Christian experience following the Reformation" (Caygill 1998, xii)—results in a situation in which all reflection is doomed to godless infinity and baroque mourning. Read from the standpoint of Christian doctrine, to which for Benjamin the baroque remains mournfully faithful, the loss of the concept of the sacred, the desacralisation of life, is satanic. This evil then extends to reflection—the spiritual/*geistig*—and the material—as both are devoid of transcendence, eschatology, an ultimate end in the form of the divine. Benjamin here implicitly connects this to the fundamental tenet of Cartesian self-recognition of the subject: the semblance of autonomy, the "secession from the community of the faithful" (GS1, 404). The complement of this "soulless materiality" (*entseelte Stofflichkeit*) is "the purely material" (*absolute Geistigkeit*) (OT, 230/GS1, 404). Both are untruths in the sense that they state ontological difference where there is none[7]: "The purely material and this absolute spiritual are the poles of the satanic realm, and . . . consciousness is their illusory synthesis, in which the genuine synthesis, that of life, is imitated" (OT, 230). Consciousness is thus revealed as an effect of the profanation, the cosmological rupture constitutive of the baroque; nothing but a semblance of a synthesis between two forcefully sundered aspects of the subject.

This is linked to Benjamin's critique of philosophical subjectivism: "In the form of knowledge instinct leads down into the empty abyss of evil in order to make sure of infinity. But this is also the bottomless pit of contemplation. Its data are not capable of being incorporated into philosophical constellations." (OT, 231). This search for knowledge must remain without end as the ultimate end point—God—no longer serves to contain or absorb its dynamic. Benjamin again equates this infinite search for knowledge through the inward-looking reflection of *Tiefsinn* with evil—that is, the absence of the divine. The "data" thus gained cannot enter into philosophical constellations because it is missing the possibility of accessing truth, of transcendence. There is no end to its reflection, no possibility of verification, no guarantor of meaning outside the subject. This bad speculation of bottomless reflection gets lost in its own internal hall of mirrors; there is no object against which to measure itself and no divine telos in which it can find an end. Thus the "knowledge" it seemingly accesses in its brooding merely serves to drag it further *into* the infinite process of brooding. Evil itself, then, is a phenomenon of subjectivity for Benjamin, an "effect of the knowledge of evil" (Caygill 1998, 60). Objects, too, are affected by this development: baroque allegories signify "the triumph of subjectivity and the onset of an arbitrary rule over things" (OT 233). The meaning of the allegorical images is not "true" in the sense of an objective, or a revealed truth; rather, they are imposed by fiat by the allegorist.

Benjamin traces how bereft baroque humanity attempts to elevate itself from its reduced status through the intellectuality exemplified by the intriguer of the mourning plays. However, in the absence of a theological centre, this attempt at gaining knowledge is doomed: base matter flips over into its obverse, a *Geistigkeit* so extreme it exceeds language (and is no closer to true knowledge). This fantasy of an "absolute, that is, godless intellectuality" (GS1, 403) rather than the physis, is the root of evil. Its mental state, Benjamin writes, is mourning. Subjectivity, the subjective gaze on the objects of the world that turns them into allegories is mournful—for the symbol, which Benjamin identifies with the fulness that precedes the fractures of modernity.

The relationship between fractured subject and object-world will be further investigated in chapter 3, where I shift my focus to Benjamin's unfinished magnum opus on high modernity, the *Arcades Project*. For now, in the baroque, a subject emerges that is characterised by fracture—cogito sundered from the body, and from the possibility of divine truth and with it transcendence per se. This leads me to Benjamin's critique of Kant.

KANT

Benjamin changed his position vis a vis Kant over the course of his life. Late in 1917, he wrote to Gershom Scholem asserting the unshakeability of Kant's system, suggesting that "the question is much more one of the system's being set in granite and universally developed. The most profound typology of conceiving doctrine has thus far always become clear to me in Kant's words and ideas. And no matter how great the number of Kantian minutiae that may have to fade away, his system's typology must last forever" (CC, 97). Further, Benjamin asserts that whoever was not "looking on even the least letter as a *tradendum* to be transmitted (however much it is necessary to recast him afterwards), knows nothing of philosophy" (CC, 98). By the spring of 1918, however, Benjamin had changed his mind enough that he could write the following lines to Ernst Schoen:

> For me, certain—as it were, revolutionary—thoughts bear within themselves an urgent need to study their great adversaries very thoroughly so that it is possible to remain steadfastly objective when expounding them. The greatest adversary of these thoughts is always Kant. I have become engrossed in his ethics—it is unbelievable how necessary it is—to track down this *despot*, to track down his mercilessly philosophizing spirit which *has philosophized* certain insights that are among the reprehensible ones to be found in ethics in particular. (CC, 125)

This tension between venerating, preserving, and destroying the Kantian system comes to the fore in Benjamin's engagement with Kant's concept of experience in some of his early work, in particular "On the Program of the Coming Philosophy." This text was to provide an initial formulation of the problem of the subject by questioning its status as a basis for experience.

THE SUBJECT OF EXPERIENCE

In the fragment "On Perception," which serves as a preparatory note for "On the Program of the Coming Philosophy," Benjamin lays out his theory of the change of experience, locating it in the Enlightenment: "Previously the symbol of the unity of knowledge that we know of as 'experience' had been an exalted one; it had, even though to varying degrees, been close to God and divine. During the Enlightenment, however, it was increasingly stripped of its proximity to God" (SW1,   95). The profound changes in the nature of experience in modernity were the result of profanation. The unity of the pre-Enlightenment concept of experience with that of the divine was so strong that, following the loss of certainty about the latter, the former was also profoundly affected. Moreover, the Enlightenment is paradigmatic for modernity as a whole, in particular its "religious and historical blindness" (SW1, 101), its secularising, profaning character.

As in his brief engagement with Descartes in the *Trauerspiel* book, Benjamin's early writings on Kant are thus concerned with loss. Here, his focus is on what is lost in the process of admitting only certain types of experience; what must have already been lost in order for a flattened-out, impoverished model of experience to become not only possible, but para-digmatic, and thus what loss is expressed, negatively, in such a concept of experience. Just as Benjamin sees Cartesian dualism—the inauguration of modern subjectivity—as an expression of the loss of the baroque age, Kantian experience is—tentatively—revealed as a product of its time: "We may perhaps venture the supposition that in an age in which experience was characterized by an extraordinary superficiality and godlessness, philosophy, if it was honest, could have no interest in salvaging this experience for its concept of knowledge" (SW1, 95). Benjamin ultimately aims to enlarge the Kantian concept of experience, to detach it from the empirical sphere into which it is relentlessly being dragged, and thereby open it up to forms of experience deemed impermissible by Kant and the neo-Kantians in their conflation of scientific experience with experience per se. This would make it possible to overcome the subject-object split and open up a sphere of *Erkenntnis* beyond the empirical. As Peter Fenves points out, the concept of experience Benjamin's "Program for a Coming Philosophy" seeks to develop is unlike any previous one (Fenves 2006, 134). For Benjamin, at stake is not merely a return to a lost fulness of experience—as I discuss below, this is incompatible with Benjamin's conceptualisation of historical change. Rather, he is concerned with a "new and higher kind of experience yet to come," and it is the development of its "epistemological foundation" that is the challenge for Benjamin. Here, I focus on the ways in which the problems with Enlightenment—and thus modern—experience raised in this text foreshadow the fractured subject explored in more depth in the *Trauerspiel* book, which I discuss in my first chapter.

PURE VERSUS EMPIRICAL CONSCIOUSNESS

Benjamin starts the "Program" text off with a distinction, grounded in the second part of Kant's Prolegomena, where judgments of perception (*Wahrnehmungsurteile*) are derived from empirical consciousness, while judgments of experience (*Erfahrungsurteile*) are based in pure consciousness. Benjamin concludes that for Kant, at stake is never just the former, but always more characteristically the latter. Benjamin resolutely temporalises this experience, pointing to the historical contingency and specificity of Kant's own experience—its "unique and temporally limited" character; "naked, primitive, self-evident experience, which, for Kant, as a man who somehow shared the horizon of his times, seemed to be the only experience given—indeed, the only experience possible" (SW1, 101). Importantly, this experience expresses the character of its age—it is that of the Enlightenment, and in this is not too different from that of any other century "of the modern era" (SW1, 101). Thus it is linked to the profaned experience of the baroque, which for Benjamin gave rise to Cartesian dualism and the subject fractured from its body and from God. Benjamin describes this experience as "reduced to . . . a minimum of significance," and, thus emptied out, a "sad" experience (SW1, 101). This further links Kantian experience to the fractured Cartesian subject of the baroque with its attendant affect of mourning.

Where in the book on Trauerspiel, Benjamin's focus is on theorising baroque experience via the mourning plays, the critique of Kantian experience in the earlier text aims more explicitly at its overcoming. Central to this endeavour is an overcoming of the subject. At stake in the reworking of the Kantian project proposed by Benjamin is the recentring and reorganisation of a metaphysics, and, relatedly, of reconnecting the concepts of knowledge (Erkenntnis) and of experience (Erfahrung). Kant's mistake, which extends to modernity in toto, was not only to restrict his concept because of the conditions specific to his age, but also to then universalize this "religious and historical blindness" in his epistemology: "The notion of experience held in the Kantian age did not require metaphysics; the only thing historically possible in Kant's day was to deny [vernichten, destroy] its claims, because the demand of his contemporaries for metaphysics was weakness or hypocrisy" (SW1, 102). Kant's thought is insufficiently metaphysical for Benjamin in that it employs the wrong metaphysics, an "unproductive" one, which forecloses rather than opens up gateways between knowledge and experience: "In [this] epistemology every metaphysical element is the germ of a disease that expresses itself in the separation of knowledge from the realm of experience in its full freedom and depth" (SW1, 102). Likewise, the subject-object division on which Kantian epistemology is premised is read by Benjamin as mythical—a vestige of a bad metaphysics. Thus, "Even to the extent that Kant and the neo-Kantians have overcome the object nature of the thing-in-itself as the cause of sensations, there remains the subject nature of the cognizing consciousness to be eliminated" (SW1, 103). Benjamin seeks to investigate ways to overcome this subject-object split and arrive at a concept of experience that is not premised on it, and he concludes that the way to overcome this separation is to annihilate the elements of the bad metaphysics within epistemology, a process that "simultaneously refers it to a deeper, more metaphysically fulfilled experience" (SW1, 102). Benjamin locates the seed for this method in Kant's thought itself, whenever it draws close to "the exploration of experience on the basis of epistemologically secured principles" (SW1, 103). But Benjamin proceeds to go far beyond Kant in what follows, ultimately arguing for a concept of experience and of knowledge freed from the strictures of "human empirical consciousness" (SW1, 103). Because the Kantian concept of the cognizing consciousness is formed not independently from, but precisely out of, empirical matter; indeed, Kant's own empirical existence at a specific historico-political juncture—the Enlightenment—it displays the same aspects as the "empirical consciousness," which, in being confronted by objects in the material world, becomes a subject. Insofar as "This subject nature of this cognizing consciousness, however, stems from the fact that it is formed in analogy to the empirical consciousness, which of course has objects confronting it" (SW1, 103), this means that what is to be eliminated is the empirical. Fenves summarises this as Benjamin's quest for "a doctrine which completely detaches from the sphere of subjectivity and leaves behind it not just empirical consciousness, but consciousness in general" (Fenves   2006, 135, transl. mine). Here, then, we see Benjamin's early anti-subjectivist thought at its most explicit.

The connection between cognition and subjectivism becomes apparent at this point. Cognition is modelled on empirical experience. Thus the subject—object split is built into Kant's model, based on the experience of Kant and his contemporaries: emptied out of a fullness, a sense of oneness with the world (and God). In a secularising age where religious certainties are dissolving and no longer offer firm ground for knowledge, the subject becomes the only such pole of certainty, opening the floodgates to a withdrawal into the self and a radical severance between individual and world—and, as we see in Benjamin's comments on the Cartesian cogito, between body and mind. To assume this particular experience is universal is for Benjamin metaphysical in the bad sense, that is, mythical. Kant purports to have emptied his philosophy of such metaphysical residue, but it is inadvertently—unconsciously—smuggled in, precisely because he did not recognise his experience as contingent and specific to his time. Benjamin's aim is to transcend Kant's ontologisation of the subject-object split and make it possible for philosophy to attain concepts of knowledge and experience beyond the restrictions put in place by this split.

This foreshadows many of the themes taken up again in the *Trauerspiel* book: the tyranny of the concept of the subject, its radical division from the world, and its genesis from a loss of a mode of experience characterised by spiritual fulness, resulting in mournfulness. This subject is fractured from the moment of its inception, wrested from a now unnamable other mode of existing and experiencing; a differing relationship between humanity and cosmos.[8] What in the *Trauerspiel* book functions as a characteristic of baroque subjectivity—the subjectivist thrust of the futile search for knowledge in the absence of the possibility of transcendence—is formulated as a critique of a model of experience reliant on the subject-object split in Benjamin's early work on Kant. In his dissertation on Romantic Criticism, Benjamin further expanded his investigation into the overcoming of subjectivism.

ROMANTIC CRITICISM AS A COUNTER TO SUBJECTIVISM?

For Benjamin, "Criticism, which today is grasped as the most subjective of activities, was for the Romantics a regulative of subjectivity, contingency and arbitrariness in the emergence of works" (SW1, 160). Samuel Weber, commenting on this passage, observes that Benjamin is attempting to grasp "a notion or practice of 'reflexivity' that would not be rooted ultimately in a constitutive subject" (Weber 2008, 23) in his dissertation on Romantic Criticism. Benjamin turned to the Romantics because, as Beatrice Hanssen and Andrew Benjamin observe, their model of criticism "did not simply amount to a subject-centred, speculative appropriation of the object under analysis or to the passing of judgment in evaluation. Rather, Romantic criticism demanded an altogether different thinking, indeed 'activation,' of the object and hence a different construction of the artwork" (Hanssen and Benjamin 2002, 1).

While explicitly related to art criticism, Benjamin's dissertation "may be read as a programmatic statement of a philosophical criticism . . . The claim for the objectivity of the work of art and the related necessity of the practice of immanent critique formed the 'epistemo- theoretical presupposition' of Benjamin's own criticism, beginning with the essay on Goethe's *Wahlverwandschaften*" (Caygill 1998, 46). Thus Romantic Criticism provided Benjamin with a promising approach for thinking through alternatives to the subject-object split of the Kantian project, which he sought to contest. Following the Romantics, for Benjamin, the "truth of the object cannot be found in its appearance as an extension of subject but in the immanent content that fundamentally resists any attempt at such   a subordination" (Homburg 2018, 126). Homburg conceptualises this as a *"resistant objectivity"* in the work, which Benjamin seeks to preserve in the face of subjectivising tendencies of contemporary criticism.

However, as Homburg observes, Romantic Criticism did not ultimately take the truly novel thrust of its approach far enough: "Romanticism fails in its attempt to overcome its object by positing its immanent reconciliation in the form of a singular universal . . . Romantic criticism misses the mark when it idealises its object and, in this process, dissolves the object's particularity." Conversely, "Benjamin aims to maintain the integrity and particularity of the object and experience. At the same time, Benjamin also aims to account for the absence of the Absolute as an object of experience, that is, the fundamental condition of modernity" (Homburg 2018, 127). As Beatrice Hanssen and Andrew Benjamin argue, the shift in Benjamin's critical project from a focus on the Absolute in art to that on its disappearance in secularising modernity played out in his book on the German *Trauerspiel*, where Benjamin began "to cast doubt on the merits of a Romantic, reflective criticism that proceeded through 'potentiation' and a (melancholic) immersion in the object . . . Instead, Benjamin was to dedicate himself to modernity's physiognomy of ruins, to the allegorical narrative of death or the jagged line that separated nature and history from the plenitude of meaning" (Hanssen and Benjamin 2002, 4).[9] The work on *Trauerspiel* thus serves as a point of transition between Benjamin's earlier work, where he formulated critiques of the Kantian and the Romantic projects that were still steeped in the conceptual language of their object of critique, towards the more "materialist" analyses of his later work.

FROM THE SPHERE OF *ERKENNTNIS*
TO CHANGING *ERFAHRUNG*

In much the same way, Benjamin turned his attention in the *Trauerspiel* book not just to a possible overcoming of subjectivism in new forms of critique, but to an immersion in the experience of a depleted, fractured modern subject. As delineated above, in the *Programmschrift*, *Erkenntnis* no longer functions as the relationship between a subject and an object; rather, *Erkenntnis* becomes, over the course of Benjamin's text, something with its own sphere, quite separate from empirical experience, and within which the subject-object dichotomy can be overcome. What we see is a shift in Benjamin's interest in delimiting experience as detached from the empirical, towards delving *into* the empirical, in order to develop a critique of what is happening within it.

We can thus reconstruct in Benjamin's work a critique of this fractured subject, aimed at its overcoming, beginning in the period following the *Programmschrift*—the transition identified by Hanssen and Benjamin in the *Trauerspiel* book. It is this subject's impoverished form of experience which Benjamin also investigates in his later writing: its split from the divine and its split from the body. As I discuss below, this critique of subjectivity, taken as a function of historico-political processes, was to be deepened in Benjamin's later work on the modern city. As in the early work, the question of experience is central to this task, but it undergoes a shift: from the critique of a conceptualisation of experience that takes the subject/object split as its starting point, to critically examining the experience *of* this split in modernity in order to locate potential for its overcoming. Where in Benjamin's earlier texts, the focus is on the contrasting pair of empirical experience (*Erfahrung*) opposed to *Erkenntnis*, his later work increasingly investigates the change in modernity from *Erfahrung* as a particular, rapidly disappearing form of experience, to the individualised, disconnected *Erlebnis* characteristic of modernity. These changes, due in no small part to the changing technologies that form part of everyday life under capitalist modernity, have profound effects on the subject: As Esther Leslie notes, "When subjectivity becomes a matter of documents in the world and technological mediation it has become a social and a political issue rather than the preserve of the individual soul" (Leslie 2000, 70). Thus the very individualized nature of this subjective experience is revealed as an effect of the particular socio-political and, for the Benjamin of the late 1920s onward, economic constellation, just as its earlier iterations in the early modern period reflected the particularities of the "spirit of their age."

The two streams in Benjamin's thought on experience are not to be taken as totally separate: The considerations about experience as something to be had only at a specific time already form part of Benjamin's early writings on the topic. As we saw above, the point of departure of Benjamin's critique of the Kantian concept of experience is that it unwittingly reproduces certain assumptions because of Kant's own specific *empirical* experience. Crucially, this experience is not purely subjective in the sense of deriving from within the subject—rather, it is a product of the conditions under which the subject lives; in this case, the modern world around Kant. Thus, Benjamin's point of departure and way of reading Kant in the *Programmschrift* is consistent with his understanding of the philosophy of history in the *Arcades Project* and associated later writing. What, then, has changed? Where in his early text, Benjamin still aims at a transformation of epistemology from within itself, immanent to knowledge, and is in search of a metaphysics, even a theology, these insights are "materialized" in the later work, leading Benjamin to the conclusion that a critical project cannot happen purely within spirit (nor within religion). Rather, it is the transformation of the concrete material organisation of life in capitalist modernity that now forms the centre of Benjamin's interest: Both the ways in which historical change has transformed the conditions of possibility of epistemology and possible ways to enable continued transformation of the conditions of modernity themselves. Howard Caygill conceptualises this shift in Benjamin's position from the *Programmschrift* and the even earlier "Life of Students" to his 1933 "Experience and Poverty," where "he does not seek an idea or redemptive absolute which will integrate a shattered experience, but looks for the intimations of   new freedoms announced in the distorted, comical and even terrifying patterns of modern experience" (Caygill 1998, 32). What remains visible, however, in this "bereft experience" is the "removal of the absolute through . . . warps, distortions and exclusions" (Caygill 1998, 25). Thus, the depleted experience of the fractured subject becomes a focal point in Benjamin's later writing, starting with the melancholic experience of the baroque.

THE FRACTURE AS AN OPENING

The subject's fracture also functions as a site of potentiality: it is precisely in the constitutive fracture of the modern subject, the sense of loss and melancholia attendant on Cartesian mind-body dualism and Kantian foreclosure of metaphysical experience, that opens the way for something new. In the convolutes of the *Arcades Project* and associated texts, Benjamin charts the inauguration of a "more political" being in modern capitalism; a subject that is not one, fractured into types, capable of becoming a mass, a class, and thus going beyond both the limitations of the self-contained individual subject and its (limited) intersubjectivity. This focus on the potential of the fracture is foreshadowed in Benjamin's earlier work: Samuel Weber presents the link between the programmatic announcement in the *Programmschrift* and the *Arcades Project* as the refutation of a Hegelian dialectic, to include something beyond a perfect synthesis *as* a fracture that resists sublation or subsumption. Such breaking points (*Bruchstellen* in German) remain outside of the dialectical movement of a Hegelian concept, as a determinate place, who tend to "bring to a halt, at least temporarily, the progress of time by fixing it into, and as, a place (however 'broken'). The 'break' in the place—the break as a place—is what results when the destructive course of time is temporarily brought to a halt." In this, Weber notes, they resemble the baroque allegories "studied and construed by Benjamin" (Weber 2008, 167). A similar arrest of time, of the flow of events, is also present in Benjamin's reorientation of critique towards the "mortification" of works of art in the *Trauerspiel* book. Only in such an arrest can critique, and with it something new, occur. Thus, these interruptions and fractures "are for Benjamin not primarily negative or privative in character. They constitute privileged moments of what, in the following note, he describes as a 'constellation of awakening'" (Weber 2008, 167). The question of a true awakening will be investigated in my final chapter. As I discuss here, Freud's dream interpretation in particular influenced Benjamin's understanding of dreaming and awakening as sites where conscious and unconscious states merge, but can be analysed, and mutually illuminated in order to overcome the traumatic repetition of the same. Throughout his work, Benjamin is in search of such sites and critical methodologies that allow for overcoming the subject. In the 1915 fragment "Dialogue on the Rainbow," a dream becomes such a site of the dissolution of the subject where, as Caygill notes, "In place of the opposition between gazing subject and the gazed-upon surface, Benjamin elaborates a different relation" where "two components of Kant's account of experience—sensibility and the understanding—collapse into each other, and the experiencing subject which would contain them dissolves into its experience" (Caygill 1998, 11). Benjamin later identifies a similar process of the overcoming of the subject-object split and the experience of the fractured subject in surrealism (SW2, 208). However, in Benjamin's later work on dreams in the *Arcades Project*, what is accessed is not straightforward potentiality *within* the dream, or in altered states of consciousness such as the intoxication advocated by surrealism. Rather, along more Freudian lines, the dream reveals a distorted or displaced unconscious desire, which must be accessed in analysis and, for Benjamin, critique. Benjamin expands the analysis of individual dreams to an analysis of the nineteenth century as a "dreaming collective" (AP, 546). Psychoanalysis thus aids Benjamin in understanding the fractured subject as well as pointing beyond it: already in the *Trauerspiel* study, it is the age that expresses something of the character of the subjectivity typical of it, while in the *Arcades Project*, the methods and concepts of psychoanalysis furnish some of the tools necessary to analyse the nineteenth century.

READING BENJAMIN'S FREUD

Benjamin's register of works read, the *Verzeichnis der gelesenen Schriften*, which he kept from about 1916/1917 to around mid-June 1940 (GS7.1, 437f), contains a number of Freud's works: *Jokes and Their Relation to the Unconscious* (1905), "Psycho-analytic Notes   on an Autobiographical Account of a Case of Paranoia (Dementia Paranoides)," including Freud's postscript,[10] "On Narcissism: An Introduction" (1914), "Five Lectures on Psycho-Analysis" (1909), and *Beyond the Pleasure Principle* (1920). As Nadine Werner (2015, 85) and Sigrid Weigel (2016) point out, this list is incomplete. To wit, in "The Work of Art in the Age of Mechanical Reproduction" (1935), Benjamin refers to Freud's *Psychopathology of Everyday Life* (1904), and the *Interpretation of Dreams* appears in the 1937 Fuchs essay. Benjamin also knew Freud's "Über den Gegensinn der Urworte" (1910), printed in "Kleine Schriften zur Neurosenlehre" (1913), both mentioned in "Books by the Mentally Ill." Gershom Scholem also states that Benjamin wrote a "detailed" paper about Freud's theory of drives in 1918 (Scholem 1981, 71), thus we can assume he was familiar with "Triebe und Triebschicksale" (1915). In a letter to Gretel Adorno in 1935, Benjamin also mentions Freud's text on telepathy from the *Psychoanalytic Almanach*.

As Werner notes, "Frequently, Benjamin does not explicitly reference Freud when referring to him,"[11] speculating that this is due to Benjamin's method of appropriating Freudian thoughts and concepts "by detaching them from their original context in order to enrich his own thought" (Werner 2015, 84). Additionally, given the frequent reprisals of and detailed references to previous writing in the corpus of Freud's work, Benjamin would have had at least a passing familiarity with the core presuppositions of more works than the ones he read in full. For instance, according to the *Verzeichnis*, Benjamin read Freud's book on jokes in 1918. Here, he would also have encountered, in summary form, the themes of the *Interpretation of Dreams*, as Freud provides a synopsis and stresses the links between dreamwork and jokes throughout, in particular on condensation and displacement. Similarly, the "Five Lectures on Psycho-Analysis" cover much of Freud's earlier work in summary fashion. Central touchstones for Benjamin's reading of Freud discussed in this book are *Beyond the Pleasure Principle*, which Benjamin had read by 1928; memory theory from *The Interpretation of Dreams* in the *Arcades Project* and Benjamin's other dream-theoretical work, and 'Mourning and Melancholia', as well as the two case studies of Haitzmann and Schreber discussed in chapter 2.

Where Susan Buck-Morss asserted that "It is wrong to emphasize the significance for Benjamin of psychonanalytic theory. In the 1930s, his reception of Freud was still largely mediated, coming from two distinctly unorthodox sources, Surrealism and the Frankfurt Institute" (Buck-Morss 1993, 464), this list should go some way towards dispelling this notion. Contrary to Buck-Morss, whose verdict on the Benjamin-Freud connection is heavily influenced by Scholem, this text aims to show that Freud was an important and direct influence for Benjamin, in particular in relation to Benjamin's investigation of the fractured subject. Benjamin's reception was by no means mainly mediated by others—as evinced, among other evidence, by the *Verzeichnis*. Where Benjamin's engagement with Freud *is* mediated, such as in Convolute K of the *Arcades Project*, it is mainly via Freudians such as Theodor Reik as well as Erich Fromm—a more "orthodox" Freudian intellectual lineage than the one posited by Buck-Morss.

Freud's importance for Benjamin is increasingly being recognised, in particular in the German literature, which I engage with in what follows, alongside the steady trickle of literature published in the anglophone world dealing with various aspects of Benjamin's relation to Freud. Benjamin's early verdict on Freud as part of the priesthood of the bourgeoisie (SW1, 289) is by no means to be taken as a dismissal of the latter's work. Rather, we can identify at least two uses of Freud by Benjamin: As a theorist of the nineteenth century, the sage of the bourgeois psyche, and as a source of theoretical insight, concepts, and methodology. These two uses are interrelated, insofar as Benjamin makes similar claims about their rootedness in the age that produced them about every other thinker he draws from, including Marx.[12]

There is much that connects the method of psychoanalysis to Benjamin's theoretical endeavour. However, I am by no means proposing to read Benjamin "as" a Freudian, or to collapse their theoretical lineages and projects. Going beyond the relationship of a "constellation" between the two thinkers proposed by Nägele (1991, 57), and with Lindner and Werner, I see Benjamin's reception of Freud as driven by the principle of *Entwendung*, a creative appropriation of Freudian concepts and methodology that bears in it the notion of intellectual theft. As Werner points out, Benjamin is not concerned with proving Freud's hypotheses, but with putting them to work in his own theoretical (and historical) context.[13] Throughout, I note the ways in which Benjamin modifies and radicalises Freud's concepts and methodological insights. As Margaret Cohen notes in *Profane Illumination: Walter Benjamin and the Paris of Surrealist Revolution*, Benjamin "is particularly interested in the therapeutic treatment of irrational and symptomatic phenomena, the fact that psychoanalysis values such phenomena as rich forms of expression and seeks their significance with a battery of tactics that are not encompassed by the activity of rational critical construction" (Cohen 1993, 37). Of course, Freud was himself attuned to the pathological dimension of "normal" modern subjects in phenomena such as dreams and slips of the tongue. The "healthy" suffer from the same complexes as the ill; they are merely expressed differently in the former, and Freud conceptualises the difference as largely a question of degree. These slippages between what is pathological or neurotic and what is normal are common to both Freud and Benjamin: in the *Programmschrift*, Benjamin describes the Kantian subject of experience as "mythology, on a par with any other 'epistemological mythology' such as those of the mad, or 'primitive' peoples" (SW1, 103). In a radical step, Benjamin associates the empirical subject of consciousness itself with madness:

> Experience, as it is conceived in reference to the individual living human and his consciousness, instead of as a systematic specification of knowledge, is again in all of its types the mere *object* of this real knowledge, specifically of its psychological branch. The latter divides empirical consciousness systematically into types of madness. Cognizing man, the cognizing empirical consciousness, is a type of insane consciousness. (SW1, 103–4)

Benjamin's linking of Kantian epistemology to the experience of "primitive" peoples and the mad serves to destabilise its claim to universal truth, showing instead its comparability to other forms of "myth" that organise experience differently. Where in the *Programmschrift*, the concept of madness serves in part as a polemical formulation distancing Benjamin's position from that of Kant, we already see in this early text a link between madness and the will to a taxonomy of the empirical mind. In the *Trauerspiel* book, Benjamin further expands this link, investigating the potential of psychologically "deranged" states such as madness and melancholic affective states to express a truth in distorted form. What is revealed is its fracture: melancholia and madness are reactions of the modern subject to its fractured state.

FREUD AND THE FRACTURED SUBJECT

In *The Future of an Illusion* (1927), Freud conceptualises the compulsion to work and the denial of impulses (*Triebverzicht*) as the starting points of culture. Over the course of history, Freud writes, the psyche has undergone a change: it internalises the external constraint imposed on it by society, forming the super-ego. This process is repeated in every child's development, allowing it to become "moral and social." Thus, "Such a strengthening of the super-ego is a most precious cultural asset in the psychological field" (SE21, 10), as it is what makes society possible. At the intra-psychic level, the demand to be a coherent subject is superimposed on the psyche of the individual, fractured as it is between different agencies, variously conceptualised by Freud as unconscious and conscious; ego, id, and super-ego, who each have their own agenda and pull in different directions. Psychoanalysis makes visible this fracturing of the subject into different agencies and drives running counter to one another. For Freud, it is only in thus exposing, and ultimately accepting, these fractures that suffering can be eased.

I will discuss how Benjamin radicalises this insight in pointing to the historical specificity of this process. In examining the specific circumstances that lead to the formation of symptoms at the social level, as well as their historical transmission, Benjamin extends Freud's understanding of the fractured subject in showing that the demand of being a subject is itself untenable from the moment of its inception—thus it is expressed in melancholia and other forms of psychopathology. I will discuss how Benjamin draws on the methodology and concepts of Freudian psychoanalysis in order to conceptualise these affective states of the fractured subject and in order to point the way to the ultimate overcoming of this subjectivity. A reading of Freud via Benjamin thus heightens the visibility of the latent political charge of Freud's work and psychoanalysis more generally, while a reading of Benjamin via Freud can make apparent the Freudian legacy in Benjamin's thinking on such concepts as the dream, the unconscious, and, ultimately, the subject. It is such a reading this text attempts to provide. I will argue that what Benjamin draws from Freud, then, is not a cohesive model of the human psyche, but an experimental approach to the application of the psychoanalytic method and its concepts.

THE TEXT

In my first chapter, I perform a close reading of Benjamin's book on the German *Trauerspiel*, translated as tragic drama or mourning play, tracing how it paints a picture of the baroque as a fragmented, deeply riven era scarred by the European wars of religion and the Reformation. These signified a rift in the fabric of Christianity's symbolic order: in their wake, its explanations, its theological truths were no longer universally valid. Christian religious doctrine as such was destabilised, shattering the cosmological horizon of European society. This historical and spiritual experience, Benjamin argues, finds expression in the mournfulness of the artistic production of the baroque. Benjamin charts how religious forms, concerns, and questions persist in a profaning age where the possibility of their being adequately answered has vanished. The discrepancy between the claims of a worldview that continues to be shaped by religion and the simultaneous inaccessibility of spiritual certainty are expressed as suffering and mournfulness in the *Trauerspiel*. Benjamin is interested in these plays because their mournfulness goes beyond artistic style; they express the essential character of their age. This mood is crystallised in the baroque sovereign, torn between the poles of martyr and tyrant. Shakespeare's Hamlet emerges as the quintessential baroque sovereign on Benjamin's reading, which I contrast with that of Carl Schmitt. I will show that their different readings of the play are grounded in their different understandings of sovereignty, which has implications for the status of myth. Through my reading, I reconstruct Benjamin's necessarily unwritten rejoinder to Schmitt's argument about Hamlet in his 1956 *Hamlet or Hecuba*. This allows me to trace how the fractured sovereign becomes the model for subjectivity, inaugurated as a result of the loss of the cosmology of the Middle Ages, the fracturing of the ethical community exemplified in the yearning for the historically no longer possible tragic mode, resulting in the lapse into myth and melancholia.

In my second chapter, I confront Benjamin's *Trauerspiel* book with Freud's "Mourning and Melancholia" (1917) and to two of his case studies. What I aim to show in this discussion is that the emergence of melancholia and possession in the wake of the cosmological loss of the baroque form two poles of the response to the impossible demand of subjectivity. I discuss the relationship of this formation of subjectivity in the baroque and beyond in Benjamin's work in relation to Freud's work on paranoia and psychopathological world-building. While the previous chapter established melancholia and "madness" more broadly conceived as a locus of the emergence of a truth—however wrong the subjective beliefs of the mad and the melancholic may be—in this chapter I critically examine the role of psychopathology in Benjamin's work beyond the *Trauerspiel*. I will show that Benjamin ultimately conceived of these derangements as a moment in a dynamic process—one might call it a dialectic—of moving beyond, towards a non-pathological mode of relating to the world and the self. In this context, I read Benjamin's figure of the critic against Freud's psychoanalyst.

In my third chapter, I investigate the changes the fractured modern subject undergoes in the aftermath of the baroque. I will argue that post-baroque society, examined in work produced by Benjamin after the *Trauerspiel* book, still reflects its splitting of the world from truth, and thus the uneasy position of the fractured subject. What follows the baroque forms the post-history of its shock to European self-understanding and trust in theological certainties; thus its structures of power become a reiteration of that initial, failed, iteration of sovereignty and the attempt at creating a new truth in a profaned, post-sacral world. In Benjamin's *Arcades Project*, the processes of mourning and melancholia are transposed into nineteenth-century capitalism. Like Pausanias, who "produced his topography of Greece around A.D. 200 at a time when the cult sites and many other monuments had begun to fall into ruin" (AP, 82), Benjamin writes the history of the arcades after their heyday has passed. In ruin, their bones become visible, they are reduced to their essential characteristics. Similar to the translucent vessels of truth in the *Trauerspiel* study, it is this rumination that allows their truth content to shine through. The commodity form comes to dominate in this era with a more totalising reach than previously, mediating the experience of life in what Benjamin calls the "dream-world" of nineteenth-century Paris. Thus, it becomes apparent here that Benjamin fuses Freudian and Marxian categories in his analysis of nineteenth-century capitalism. I argue that Freud's account of the death drive and repetition-compulsion in *Beyond the Pleasure Principle* (1920) furnishes Benjamin with the tools to make sense of the mechanism of the resurfacing of the mythic in capitalist modernity. The life-world of the nineteenth century metropolis thus becomes a web of symptoms for Benjamin, a way of approaching the social that draws from Freud's *Psychopathology of Everyday Life* (1904). One of the most prominent theoretical points of connection between them is methodological: As I discuss in my third chapter, Benjamin uses Freud's approach in the *Psychopathology of Everyday Life* in reading symptoms, recognizing pathology from its signs in the organism of the nineteenth century. With the aid of Freud, Benjamin is undertaking an aetiology of capitalist modernity, investigating the expression of its pathology in its cultural forms.

Simultaneously, as I investigate in my fourth chapter, nineteenth-century capitalist society also brings forth several types which form some of the central axes of Benjamin's investigation in the *Arcades Project*. These fractured post-baroque subjects embody the expressions of the pathology typical of their age: their futile search for novelty and "experience" expressive of their melancholia, structured by loss and lack. I then turn to Benjamin's discussion of the interrelated changes in memory and experience in modernity, highlighting the centrality of Freud to these reflections. The fractured subject's experience has changed in modernity: *Erfahrung*, communal experience, is no longer possible; *Erlebnis*, isolated experience, comes to replace it. At the same time, this means that life in the modern metropolis happens as in a dream.

This leads to an examination of Freud's influence on Benjamin's dream theory in my fifth and sixth chapters. I will show that Benjamin follows Freud's theory of the dream and the unconscious but expands it to the collective. For Benjamin, as for Freud, a "false dawn," an analysis from within the dream, is a threat to true awakening. I examine surrealism and art nouveau as two such moments, whose potential Benjamin recognises as much as their limitations. In the sixth and final chapter, I discuss Benjamin's emphasis on true awakening. I further pursue Benjamin's fusion of Freud and Marx in his dream analysis, demonstrating that dream analysis has a pivotal historico-political function for Benjamin: He draws from Freud in formulating it as a therapeutic manoeuvre, and from Marx in conceptualising it as a move beyond class society. I trace how the "arrest of thinking" in the dialectical image is akin to the renarration and examination of memories in psychoanalysis. For both Freud and Benjamin, the possibility of going beyond memory narratives, the possibility rewriting the narrative is located precisely at the point where it breaks off, opening the possibility of using the fracture of the subject as a means for its overcoming. The importance of the historical materialist and a collective movement beyond the reiteration of trauma in history come to the fore here. This leads me to the question of what Benjamin pits against the fractured post-baroque subject and the bourgeois subject of nineteenth-century capitalism. While stressing that while Benjamin eschews formulating a new positive, I look to Benjamin's "Destructive Character" and an autobiographical dream for Benjamin's gesturing beyond the fractured subject.

NOTES

1. Balibar takes issue with the conventional account that he identifies as Heidegger's genealogy of the subject: from hypokeimenon straight to Descartes' supposed subjectum, complicating it with the introduction (or intrusion) of medieval Augustine philosophy. He contests Heidegger's attribution of this cogito—subject to Descartes, calling it instead a "Kantian invention" (Balibar 2014,1081).

2. Benjamin does not discuss this aspect of Descartes' *Meditations*. Also worth noting is the fact that Balibar, as mentioned above, contests this reading of Descartes as foundational for the modern concept of the subject. However, even if this ascription to Descartes is a mistake first by Kant and then repeated by Heidegger, as Balibar himself points out, "we cannot undo what Kant has done" (Balibar 2014, 1081). He also acknowledges that Descartes' cogito "anticipates" (ibid) its nominalization.

3. Despite Descartes' own insistence on the existence of God, this is not a God in the pre-baroque, pre-Reformation, pre-modern sense that is precisely shattered in the loss of the fullness of experience characteristic of previous culture.

4. "Das Wahrgenommene, vor allem das im Gesicht Wahrgenommene bricht nun in ihn hinein(,) auch aus dem fremden Körper fällt der Geist-Leib in den Strudel und es bleibt in der Gesichtswahrnehmung des Grauens neben dem Gefühl: das bist Du beim Anblick des andern ('du' weil keine Grenze da ist) andererseits das Gefühl: das ist dein Doppel(,) auf den 'andern' nun aber entgrenzten und entleiblichten Körper bezogen" (GS6, 76).

5. While this occurs in the encounter with an other, we may here also detect echoes of the psychologisation of the body in the dream, discussed in the fifth chapter.

6. Weigel also notes that "The character of allegory as a form of writing in the Trauerspiel book was evidently not arrived at either without excitation (Erregung), as Benjamin writes there that the allegorical gaze transforms 'things and works into excitatory writing [erregende Schrift]' (GS I, 352)" (Weigel 1996, 247).

7. In Benjamin's *Schemata zum psychophysischen Problem*, they are identified as different perspectives, as opposed to ontologically distinct objects (GS6, 78).

8. This constellation of criticism of the impoverished Enlightenment concept of experience is taken up again in *To the Planetarium* (SW1, 486f), where Benjamin contrasts the modern, post-Enlightenment mode with that of "the ancients," characterised by richness and a feeling of oneness with the universe, where the subject-object boundaries between observer of the cosmos and the cosmos itself, introduced by modern ways of looking at the stars by means of telescopes, blur.

9. The authors also note that Benjamin's work on Goethe forms an intermediary step to his position in the *Trauerspiel* book: "Taking the concept of *Kritik* even further, Benjamin now distinguished between the *Sach-* and *Wahrheitsgehalt* (material and truth contents) of Goethe's novel, between commentary and criticism" (Hanssen and Benjamin 2002, 4).

10. Scholem (1981, 71) recalls Benjamin's participation in a seminar on Freud during his years in Bern, for which Benjamin read both Schreber's memoirs and Freud's analysis (noting that he was more taken by the former).

11. All translations of this text mine.

12. On this point, see also Cohen (1993, 37).

13. In a similar vein, Sarah Ley Roff suggests in her article "Benjamin and Psychoanalysis" that "examining the relationship between Benjamin and psychoanalysis may serve to highlight modernist transformations in concepts of authorship and work to which both Benjamin and Freud contributed" (Ley Roff 2004, 115).

Chapter One

Baroque Sovereignty and the Fractured Subject

Ursprung des Deutschen Trauerspiels,[1] published in 1928, forms the culmination of Benjamin's early thought on history and epistemology, focusing on the connection between truth, madness, and sovereignty. Benjamin here undertakes a critique of conventional theories of drama and calls for the revaluation of the *Trauerspiele,* baroque German mourning plays, as important cultural artefacts in the face of their dismissal by conventional scholarship. In examining these plays in their historico-political context, it becomes clear that Benjamin is providing more than a contribution to literary theory: The study of these sidelined texts not only serves as a challenge to the habitual classification of genres and epochs, but allows the connection between aesthetics, politics, and history to be addressed in new ways. Crucially, the themes of baroque melancholia, sovereignty, and truth emerge as an interconnected triad, a thematic constellation considered in this chapter. As I will show, this leads to a conceptualisation of the subject as a fractured figure in the aftermath of the baroque.

THE "EPISTEMO-CRITICAL PROLOGUE"

What emerges forcefully from the "Epistemo-Critical Prologue" to the *Trauerspiel* book is the question of the relationship between truth and history. Benjamin writes, "Again and again the statement that the object of knowledge is not identical with the truth will prove itself to be one of the profoundest intentions of philosophy in its original form, the Platonic theory of ideas. Knowledge is open to question, but truth is not" (OT, 30). Truth, while linked to cognition, is not synonymous with it. Having focused on the "certainty of knowledge that is lasting" in his earlier philosophical sketches,

27

in the "Epistemo-Critical Prologue," Benjamin returns to the question of empirical experience and restores some of its importance. Following this, in a dense exposition to the book on *Trauerspiel*, Benjamin explains how *Erkenntnis* functions as a mediating process, operating on empirically observable phenomena. Through the concept, the phenomena are "dissolved" into their elements, the various parts of which form the ideas. These ideas must be assumed to be existing in a separate sphere, that of truth; however, they need the empirical to find expression. As Weber describes this process, the ideas

> can only be presented or staged—*dargestellt*—by taking leave of the realm of pure ideas and descending to that of empirical, phenomenal experience, and this in turn can be accomplished only through a reordering or reorganization, a dismantling and dispersion effectuated by the concept on the "thing-like elements" *(dinglicher Elemente)* that constitute the phenomena. (Weber 2008, 7)

Thus there is a dialectical motion at work between empirical reality and the realm of ideas. Benjamin charts how the ideas enter empirical reality in the form of phenomena, which in turn can attain salvation only in the realm of ideas, as truth. Empirical reality thus contains a "latent" reference "to those objects of theology without which truth is inconceivable" (OT, 29).[2] Crucially, truth, then, is not *bildhaft*, imagistic, nor an object of *Anschauung*; intuition or contemplation; it is rather an "intentionless state of being" (OT, 36). It follows that the most the object of empirical enquiry—historical objects—can hope to attain in terms of an epistemological function is to be as transparent as possible, in order to let their "truth content" shine through. This distinction between factual and truth content is clarified in the first version of the prologue (GS1, 927).[3] Immersion into the minutiae of the *Sachgehalt* is thus crucial for making visible the *Wahrheitsgehalt* contained therein. This, of course, is a methodological injunction and brings Benjamin to his examination of the baroque *Trauerspiel*.

THE *TRAUERSPIEL* STUDY

Benjamin differentiates the *Trauerspiel* from tragedy, and their differential relation to history and myth forms the backbone of this distinction: "Historical life, as it was conceived at that time, is its content, its true object. In this it is different from tragedy. For the object of the latter is not history, but myth" (OT, 62). As Max Pensky notes, "Tragedy arises from myth; Trauerspiel, however, is embedded thoroughly within historical time, and this embeddedness, so complete that it rarely need be expressed manifestly by the baroque dramatists themselves, underlies and generates the catastrophic violence and lamentation so characteristic of the genre" (Pensky 1993, 113). For Benjamin, the *Trauerspiel* forms an interruption within the genre of the tragic and can no longer be assessed according to the same criteria, as it is of an utterly different historical era, one that no longer allows the play to be external to its historical moment. It is thus, in a sense, itself a form of *Ursprung*—as Benjamin understands origin not as a specific point in time or an initial form, but a dynamic of interruption, intended to "describe that which emerges from the process of becoming and disappearance" rather than being a point of genesis. Thus, "[o]rigin is an eddy in the stream of becoming, and in its current it swallows the material involved in the process of genesis (OT, 45)." History, then, is a central dimension of philosophy for Benjamin. The latter never arrives at its final form—the doctrine—through mere thinking, disconnected from an engagement with historical reality: "Philosophical doctrine is based on historical codification. It cannot therefore be evoked *more geometrico*" (OT, 27). The philosophical-critical method, for Benjamin, must consider the historical object, remain close to it in the manner of contemplation and, in its choice of objects, be broad in scope as well as inclusive of what is commonly considered lowly or unworthy of serious study. This informs Benjamin's examination of the *Trauerspiel*—his, as he observes himself, seemingly overly extensive study. His reflections, he suggests, are informed by the consciousness that thinking is most fruitful when it dwells with the *"Geringste"* the least, or lowliest, as Benjamin suggests in the first version of his "Epistemo-Critical Prologue." Thus his focus will be on this when considering works and forms of art in order to gauge their content.[4] In this, Benjamin refers to his method and aim in the *Trauerspiel* book as the salvation of the phenomena through the philosopher who can deliver them into the realm of ideas—making visible their truth content which, as discussed in the "Epistemo-Critical Prologue," will be all the more visible for the wretchedness and ruination of the form of the *Trauerspiel*. Caygill observes of *The Life of Students* that

> The thought of an immanent perfection present in the most derided aspects of experience moves from an absolute idealism which rejects the present in the name of an absolute idea to a materialism which discerns the absolute in what is rejected by the present order. The expulsion of the absolute from the present may be discerned precisely in those things that the present regards as insignificant, absurd and unwanted. (Caygill 1998, 8)

Benjamin retains this interest in the detritus of history, the possibility of gaining insights—accessing truth content—precisely in that which is sidelined. But his focus is slightly reframed: In the *Trauerspiel* book, he is on his way to developing his later materialist critique "dedicated to exploring the power of the rejected and outmoded, and to finding a form of critique which would 'point out the crisis lying in the essence of things' without having to translate the immanent absolute into a redemptive idea" (Caygill 1998, 9). What is at stake here is the temporal nature of such truth, the breakdown of the semblance of totality in the symbol, and the melancholy that accompanies any attempt to reconstruct totality in a profaned world.

In contrast to critics who would apply the standards of tragedy or stylistic unity derived from later romantic artworks to the baroque *Trauerspiel* and find it wanting, Benjamin considers the historico-political context within which this art form arose as central to an appreciation of its value. The baroque is here understood as a fragmented, deeply riven era characterised by the European wars of religion. That the art of this era should reflect these bloody conflicts is hardly surprising and goes some way to explaining the pervasive mood of melancholia that Benjamin discerns in the mourning plays. However, the specificity of the mood of this era goes beyond a mere reflection of the strife of its age. Rather, this strife itself can be understood only as a war about truth, provoked by the Reformation and the European wars of religion. These wars signified a rift in the fabric of Christianity's symbolic order: its explanations, its theological truths were no longer universally valid. Therefore the validity of religious doctrine *as such* was destabilised—and the former claim to universal truth of church doctrine called into question, shattering the cosmological horizon of European society. As Stewart puts it: "Everything within creation seems to have suffered an indelible catastrophic rupture" (Stewart 2010, 9). This historical and spiritual experience finds expression in the mournfulness of the artistic production of the baroque. Benjamin charts how religious forms, concerns, and questions persist in a profaning age where the possibility of their being adequately answered has vanished: all of the energy of this profaning age is "concentrated on a complete revolution of the content of life, while orthodox ecclesiastical forms were preserved" (OT, 79). Benjamin notes that crucially, the baroque was still operating within a Christian religious context: "For all that the increasing worldliness of the Counter-Reformation prevailed in both confessions, religious aspirations did not lose their importance: it was just that this century denied them a religious fulfilment, demanding of them, or imposing upon them, a secular solution instead" (OT, 79). The discrepancy between the claims of a worldview that continued to be shaped by religion and the inaccessibility of spiritual certainty are expressed as suffering and mournfulness in the *Trauerspiele*, whose worldly, profane solutions to the loss of transcendence proved to be less than satisfactory. Hence the mournfulness of the baroque, an epoch torn between religious concerns and the loss of meaning of religious answers.

THE BAROQUE SOVEREIGN

As Samuel Weber writes, "the relationship between the Trauerspiel and history is far from a one-way street: if baroque theater is concerned primarily with history, this history is in turn construed as a kind of Trauerspiel." At stake in the mourning plays is "not just 'historical life' as such, but rather 'historical life as represented by its age'" (Weber 1992, 6). Likewise, the sovereign "represents" rather than "is" the epoch—a distinction Benjamin insists is derived from the juridico-political sphere, not art: "He holds the course of history in his hand like a sceptre. This view is by no means peculiar to the dramatists. It is based on certain constitutional notions. A new concept of sovereignty emerged in the seventeenth century from a final discussion of the juridical doctrines of the middle ages" (OT, 65). The madness and melancholia of the baroque are crystallised in its sovereign, who, due to the new political formation of this period, is emblematic of its spirit. Benjamin details the nature of this new form of political power, charting the progressive defeat of the church in the seventeenth century, a development that establishes authority as thoroughly worldly: in the move from a theocratic conception of the state to absolute power centred in the figure of the sovereign. Benjamin continues "Whereas the modern concept of sovereignty amounts to a supreme executive power on the part of the prince, the baroque concept emerges from a discussion of the state of emergency, and makes it the most important function of the prince to avert this" (OT, 65). Baroque, unlike modern sovereignty, is a response to an age riven with religious strife and derives its justification from the promise of stability. Crucially, the "state of exception" this baroque sovereign is meant to avert is not initiated by the regents themselves, but by "war, revolt or other catastrophes"—events outside of the control of the sovereign. Benjamin sees this new order as "counter-reformatory," which, as "an antithesis to the historical ideal of restoration it is haunted by the idea of catastrophe. And it is in response to this antithesis that the theory of the state of emergency is devised" (OT, 66). This is an important point: from within the triumphantly humanistic Renaissance tradition emerges an absolutist political framework, an intensification of its "worldly-despotic" aspect become autonomous. Benjamin here draws attention to the tyranny and centralised power undergirding the idea of stability and a flourishing community in the Renaissance, premised on the ever-present threat of a crisis, a state of exception. The frenetic fixation on the *Diesseits* in the baroque is haunted by this sense of being under threat, made worse by the suspicion that the immanent is really all there is: "The religious man of the baroque era clings so tightly to the world because of the feeling that he is being driven along to a cataract with it. The baroque knows no eschatology; and for that very reason it possesses no mechanism by which all earthly things are gathered in together and exalted before being consigned to their end" (OT, 66). There is nothing left beyond sovereign power in the baroque; no higher authority, just the promise of averting the worst excesses of the state of exception.[5] Thus this sovereignty takes centre stage and becomes a stand-in for the previous holder of the position of ultimate truth-giver: religion. This explains the occasional exaltation of the sovereign in baroque art; however, in this, it remains "pagan": "In the Trauerspiel monarch and martyr do not shake off their immanence" (OT, 67). Both are utterly of *this* world. The doctrine of the divine right of kings most forcefully revives the divine as an attempt to compensate for the loss of both political and religious authority.

The sovereign is thus wretched and mortal, unable to stand the weight of his office. This is grounded in his "creaturely" nature—it renders him unfit as a stand-in for ecclesiastical power, and thus unable to even meet the demands of his political office. As Beatrice Hanssen notes, the word *Kreatur* functioned as a Latinate equivalent of the German *Geschöpf*—that which is created, in its totality (Hanssen 1998, 103–4). She notes its use in the *Trauerspiel* book in relation to the sovereign, who is "the lord of creatures," ambiguously embodying both his exalted position and at the same time his lowly nature, via the identification of the creaturely with the physical, and sometimes "animality."[6] Andrew Benjamin conceptualises the dual character of the term as follows: "*Kreatur* embraces animals and human beings as creatures (of god, theologically) and as bodies and flesh subjugated and exposed to the sufferings of the body and the flesh, and ultimately exposed to death" (Benjamin 2005, 109). However, voided of the theological dimension in the wake of the baroque crisis of religion, only the emptied-out *physis* remains in the creaturely.[7] As Rainer Nägele puts it: "In the baroque Trauerspiel, the subject appears not as creator, but as *Kreatur* . . . In psychoanalytic terms we would have to speak of the status castration, that is, its symbolic representation as circumcision in the constitution of the subject and of the social community" (Nägele 1988, 13).

Here, then, we perceive for the first time the proximity of Benjamin's conceptualisation of the subject to psychoanalysis. This reduced subjectivity of the baroque sovereign is experienced as suffering and expressed as different forms of derangement, or, in a more anachronistically psychoanalytical register, mental illness. In this text, Benjamin opts to remain close to the categories of the age he is studying, referring to madness and melancholia. Thus, Benjamin comments baroque playwright Andreas Gryphius' lines "You who have lost sight of the image of the Highest: behold the image that has been born unto you! Ask not why it enters into a stable! He is seeking us, who are more like all the animals than the animals themselves" with the words "This latter is demonstrated by despots in their madness" (OT, 86). It is precisely the loss, the fact of once having not been a mere animal that is at stake in the creatureliness of humanity: a dimension of suffering is opened up in the reduction of humanity to animality through the voiding of its transcendental aspect in the process of the loss of religious certainty. Thus Benjamin writes of "the punitive mark of creatureliness, the human visage" (SW2.1, 156). In this analogy, it is precisely the human side of the creaturely, in the loss of its aspect which could formerly be identified with the divine, that is turned into a punishment. The fractured subject is thus branded,[8] its dual loss in the Cartesian split—from transcendence, and from a holistic conception of the body/mind—rendered painfully visible.

Here, the links between sovereignty and subjectivity begin to become apparent: Sovereignty emerges as the blueprint for the subject qua sovereign individual as such: in command of history, simultaneously representative of humanity as such as history-making, and of history itself. The sovereign functions as the only true subject in this account, the one imbued with the power, through his political position, to execute his will—but he fails to use this power successfully. He becomes the paradigmatic case of the modern subject, but the demand to be a subject is not limited to him. It is important to note that unlike Carl Schmitt in *Hamlet or Hecuba* (1956), Benjamin is not referencing actually existing, historical baroque monarchs, but the figure of the baroque monarch as he functions in the *Trauerspiele*. As such, any claim about the political formation of the baroque era is mediated via its representations in its cultural production: We are dealing not merely with a historical account of the relation between sovereignty and subjectivity, but with the role given to these sovereigns by baroque playwrights reflecting on their age. This allows Benjamin to make the link between the community as a whole, as reflected by the mourning plays/playwrights, and the sovereign even clearer. Rather than representing an origin in the non-Benjaminian sense—as a source from which sovereignty flows—the sovereign of the *Trauerspiel* is a Benjaminian origin, an "eddy in the stream of becoming," a momentary conflux of historical contingencies which allows the constitutive factors of the fractured subject to become visible in a representation. The *Trauerspiel* thus serves as a study of the inauguration of the modern concept of the subject out of the destruction of what came before, and the crisis of meaning and authority thus provoked: a subject capable of willing, decisiveness, action. Subject and agency are bound up with each other; a subject is a subject qua being an agent, an actor. However, Benjamin demonstrates that this command to decisiveness and the exertion of will on the external world is doomed to failure from the start. He first posits the emergence of the modern subject and then shows the unattainability, the impossibility of any such state of subjecthood. Thus, the subject is revealed as fractured from the beginning, torn between the demand placed on it and its inability to meet it. This is expressed in its internal rivenness between the two affective poles manifesting in the sovereign: the melancholic inability to act and a manic, tyrannical hyperactive side.

The sovereign functions in the *Trauerspiel* as the paradigmatic embodiment of the fracture of the modern subject. His split between creature and political authority results in his refracting into two distinct genres and characters: the tyrant and the martyr. "This juxtaposition," Benjamin notes, "appears strange only as long as one neglects to consider the legal aspect of baroque princedom. Seen in ideological terms they are strictly complementary. In the baroque the tyrant and the martyr are but the two faces of the monarch. They are the necessarily extreme incarnations of the princely essence" (OT, 68). Once we consider the juridico-political aspect, that is, the political power enshrined in the office of the sovereign, these seemingly separate characters indeed reveal themselves as a Janus-faced tyrant/martyr, eliciting both pity and fear. However, unlike in Greek tragedy, these don't result in catharsis but remain as verdicts on the historical reality of baroque sovereign power, which, in the figure of the sovereign, becomes both pitiable and fearful. Eventually, the latter aspect takes over, and the sovereign becomes synonymous with the tyrant: tyrannical power is latent in his role. The real or potential state of exception, with its attendant emergence of dictatorial power, comes to be the defining feature of sovereignty. Meanwhile, the fractured ruler remains drawn into his creaturely dimension, wretched and inadequate to the tasks that fall to him—unable to maintain order and make decisions that avoid the state of exception. It follows that, paradoxically, anyone called upon to rule, placed in the position of the ultimate, singular decision- maker, is unable to do so:

> The antithesis between the power of the ruler and his capacity to rule led to a feature peculiar to the *Trauerspiel* which is, however, only apparently a generic feature and which can be illuminated only against the background of the theory of sovereignty. This is the indecisiveness of the tyrant. The prince, who is responsible for making the decision to proclaim the state of emergency, reveals, at the first opportunity, that he is almost incapable of making a decision. (OT, 70–71)

Melancholia takes hold, paralysing the ruler, who is meant to be holder of the sovereign power to *act*. Thus, the initial promise and *raison d'être* of sovereignty—averting the state of exception—fails, is indeed doomed to failure, as the sovereign, himself nothing but a creature, cannot make good on the promise and threat of stability through the sword with which the power of his office endows him. It is not surprising that the sovereign, fractured between his creaturely human and his exalted-political aspects, *"entkleidet"* of his creaturely instincts, robed instead in the mantle of absolute power, is riven between melancholia and the ultimate lapse into tyrannical madness. Rather, it expresses the untenable strain of subjectivity in the wake of the dissolution of transcendence. As Weber notes, "it is clear that the dilemma of the sovereign in baroque drama is also and above all that of the subject as such: it is no longer determined by its head— that is, by its consciousness, its intentions—but by forces that act independently of conscious volition, that buffet and drive it from one extreme to another" (Weber 2008, 190). This is where the aspect of the martyr becomes visible again, in one of the dialectical reversals Benjamin deploys throughout the text—at the precise moment of the sovereign's display of his tyrannical power, "he falls victim to the dispro-portion between the unlimited hierarchical dignity, with which he is divinely invested and the humble estate of his humanity" (OT, 70). In the baroque, the certainty of divine appointment has vanished; all that remains is a dialectic of power and the creaturely, the wretched humanity, played out in the figure of the sovereign. The disproportion of his power to his being, the deranged relationship between the two, thus comes to be mirrored in the sovereign's own derangement, his *"Machtrausch,"* intoxication with power. However, this only forms the obverse of the *Handlungshemmung* of the melancholic; the tyrant's *Machtrausch*, wild and irrational action, is just as different from decisive action to stabilise the realm as the inactivity of the martyr.

Benjamin specifies the form of stability meant to avert the state of exception: "a dictatorship whose utopian goal will always be to replace the unpredictability of historical accident with the iron constitution of the laws of nature. But the stoic technique [of the martyr] also aims to establish a corresponding fortification against a state of emergency of the soul, the rule of the emotion" (OT, 74). This, then, is the repressive function of the tyrant transposed to the psychic level: asceticism, "chastity," and specifically the regulation of female sexuality. For the first time, we here see Benjamin himself drawing the links betweenpolitical authority, psychic repression, and the pathology of male rule which will become apparent throughout the *Trauerspiel* book and beyond: it will resurface in the nineteenth century in figures such as Baudelaire. This, then, is the moment where sovereign power becomes dictatorial, and where for Benjamin the question of nature and history come into play again: In the attempt to restore order precisely within the state of exception, establishing the person of the sovereign as the sole guarantor of this order, with no recourse to a legal framework or any division of power. The attempt to replace human history, its changing political and legal formations, with one transcendental, "iron" one, is equal to a fall back into the natural order and thus into myth.

The baroque age thus ushers in and simultaneously undermines the absolute sovereign—neither as tyrant nor as martyr can he act successfully, *politically*. Sovereignty must assert meaning and "truth" and thus avoid the state of exception, but, in the context of the historical circumstances of the baroque era, fails to do so; cannot *but* fail to do so, as its sovereign is torn between creaturely powerlessness and subjection to mortality, nature, and the simultaneous task of precisely instantiating these very same iron laws of nature to which he is himself subject. Baroque sovereignty, as a response to the downfall of the pinnacle of certainty in the form of transcendental religious truths, thus suffers from its status as "post-history": anything that follows the downfall of such truths will always be haunted by the suspicion that it, too, is transient. This is the melancholy of its immanence. In this profaned and profaning age, Benjamin writes, the exercise of dictatorial power comes to be the touchstone of spirit (*Geist*); but this exercise of power places an unbearable strain on the sovereign:

> This capacity requires both strict inner discipline and unscrupulous external action. Its practice brought to the course of the world an icy disillusion which is matched in intensity only by the fierce aspiration of the will to power. Such a conception of perfect conduct on the part of the man of the world awakens a mood of mourning [*Trauer*] in the creature stripped of all naïve impulses. (OT, 98)

It is thus precisely at the point where the sovereign attains the pinnacle of worldliness that his creaturely side begins to mourn—for the loss of something *beyond* this worldly immanence. However, what the *Trauerspiel* book demonstrates is that what is at stake for Benjamin is not the "no longer," the loss of a supposed previous rationality of the subject. Rather, the "dilemma" of the subject—its fracture—is, as Benjamin notes in his comments on Descartes, inaugurated in the moment that *physis* and the mind are split, and that, as in Benjamin's critique of Kant, metaphysics is sundered from cognition. These form the constitutive fracture of the modern subject. Melancholy, madness, and other impediments to the rational volition of the sovereign-subject emerge as symptoms of this constitutive split in early modernity, and they present an opening of Benjamin's thought to psychoanalysis. Before pursuing this in my next chapter, I will further investigate the link between sovereign and fractured subject in the figure of Hamlet.

THE CASE OF HAMLET:
WALTER BENJAMIN CONTRA CARL SCHMITT

The melancholic mood so characteristic of the *Trauerspiele* interrupts the flow of (dramatic) action or "happening" (*Geschehen*) within the play, making visible a truth value through their disruptive function. *Wahnsinn* thus becomes a kind of *Wahr-sinn*, a sense for the truth emerging in madness: The gaze of the melancholic is not simply deranged, it is also deranging, focusing on the cracks within the social fabric and the truths presented by the age. These derangements are a function of a social disorder, making it visible by mirroring the dislocation and displacement, the *Ver-rücktheit*, of formerly fixed theologico-political arrangements and institutions that declared themselves as eternal truths. On this reading, perhaps we can think of madness itself as an origin—in its function as an interruption, an "eddy in the stream of becoming" (OT, 45), changing the course of what would otherwise appear as the smooth flow of history. It is an injunction to understand its emergence, its (patho)genesis.

This is at play in *Hamlet*, where the characters at court are concerned with understanding the cause of Prince Hamlet's madness, as if isolating and then rectifying the single cause they are convinced must be at the root of his derangement would make him—and thus the realm—whole again. Benjamin's reading of the play as the most illuminating embodiment of the idea of *Trauerspiel* is thus consistent with his characterization of the baroque sovereign. The centrality of interruption and the break with a given form which the *Ursprung* reshapes through its own force is one of the factors that allows Benjamin to let Shakespeare's *Hamlet* emerge as the most emblematic mourning play of all. This is grounded in the centrality of stylistic rule-breaking for the genre of the *Trauerspiel*, leading Benjamin to claim that "The finest exemplifications of the *Trauerspiel* are . . . those in which there are playful modulations of the *Lustspiel*. For this reason Calderon and Shakespeare created more important *Trauerspiele* than the German writers of the seventeenth century, who never progressed beyond the rigidly orthodox type" (OT, 127). Benjamin refers to Novalis, who writes that in the work of the "genius" Shakespeare "there is indeed an alternation between the poetic and the anti-poetic, harmony and disharmony, the common, the base, the ugly and the romantic, the lofty, the beautiful, the real and the imagined: in Greek tragedy the opposite is true" (OT, 128). This disruption of the conventions of classical Greek theatre through a muddying of its demarcations regarding what is and is not appropriate matter and form for a tragedy demonstrate the exemplary status of *Hamlet* as a *Trauerspiel*. As Benjamin goes on to discuss, the comparative "gravity" of German *Trauerspiele* is part of their nostalgia for precisely those Greek tragedies they can no longer be, but still attempt to imitate.[9] It is hard to overlook the parallels to Shakespeare's Prince Hamlet in Benjamin's observations on the sovereign martyr-tyrant. In particular, Hamlet's second soliloquy in 2.2, in which he raves about the contrast between the exalted nature of man and his own disillusionment with humanity springs to mind, and indeed the ending of the play. The crucial passage that relates Hamlet's madness to the doubling/rendering apart of baroque sovereignty occurs in 5.2, where Hamlet, prior to his duel with Laertes, declares his madness as not only separate from himself, but his enemy.

The two faces of the sovereign as martyr/tyrant are thus emblematised in Hamlet, who is always at the mercy of his changing moods and cannot command them, nor marshal his rage when a decision is called for regarding Claudius. Hamlet is aware of this but unable to change. This is one of the many features that lead Benjamin to read Hamlet as the sovereign of a *Trauerspiel* rather than a tragic hero: for Greek tragedy, "It is not the intensity but the duration of high feeling which makes the high man" (OT, 115); this is a stable mode of being that has become entirely impossible in the baroque, characterised instead by the instability of the "sheer arbitrariness of a constantly shifting emotional storm" (OT, 71). This rivenness and the mental anguish it causes thus expresses a thoroughly *historical* truth. Hamlet's madness, which seems to fluctuate throughout the text, destabilises the very idea of rationality / irrationality as stable, easily identifiable states of mind. Hamlet's contemporaries appear irritated and unsettled at least as much by the *inconsistency* of his madness as by its appearing in the first place. Hamlet's friend Horatio functions as the voice of "reason" or at least scepticism within the text—but he is destabilised from the outset. The vexing question of whether Hamlet is mad or not; feigns madness, and if so, whether that would not in fact imply rationality; whether he is mad some of the time or all of the time; and so on, is not so much about an inner truth pertaining to Hamlet himself. In Benjamin's reading, there *is* no inner truth of the character Hamlet contained within the play. Rather, in his vacillations he is representative of an age characterised by strife and disintegration.

Hamlet's much-lamented powerlessness stands in striking contrast to his political role as a prince. What sets Shakespeare's play apart from the German *Trauerspiele*—even as it makes it the most "successful" of its kind in Benjamin's eyes—is the self-awareness of the play, its playing with politics *as* play, the central role given to the play within the play. It thus embodies the performativity of the *role* of the baroque sovereign, placing the question of truth, play, and representation at the heart of the political.[10] It is a feature of Hamlet's melancholic derangement that he fails to see himself as a sovereign, and thus fails to act as one. Hamlet relates everything back to himself in his *private* capacity as grieving son and scholar; all events he encounters in the play act as fuel for his melancholy musings on humanity and later, death. His failure as a sovereign is thus grounded in an excess of subjectivity. Hamlet's madness not only drags the court down into ruination with him; it also affects the people of Denmark, cryptically hinted at throughout the play as a faceless multitude. This, for Benjamin, is a typical feature of baroque sovereignty: "For if the tyrant falls, not simply in his own name, as an individual, but as a ruler and in the name of mankind and history, then his fall has the quality of a judgment, in which the subject [*Untertan*] too is implicated" (OT, 72). His fate is a judgment on the state of the realm, and his madness no mere private affair; indeed, acting merely as a private person rather than a political one bound by the task of sovereignty—to assert dictatorial power—is what characterises his failure. Thus one of the sources of the dramatic tension of the play is the tension typical of the baroque between the mere creaturely life of the sovereign and his exalted position of power. Hamlet's mental breakdown, whether (partly) feigned or not, highlights the precariousness not just of the human mind, but that of the whole political community. Hamlet is "th'observed of all observed" as Ophelia comments in 3.1.156; his every move intensely watched over by his adversaries at court. His body itself is a stage on which the health of the country—or lack thereof—plays out, and should Hamlet's mind be rotting, or *appear* to be rotting, then something is indeed "rotten in the state of Denmark" (1.4.90). This is the crux of Hamlet's role: If he is seen to be acting mad, then it does not matter if Hamlet the private person "is" mad, since as sovereign, he functions purely as a representative of his realm.

However, Hamlet's rivenness exceeds this tension. Hamlet's central conflict, in Benjamin's reading, is that he feels bound by the moral code of a bygone age, that is, compelled to act like a tragic hero, even as that mode of acting has fallen out of favour, indeed has become senseless in his own age. He thus embodies the melancholy of the baroque, doubly so in that he tries to be both mythic hero and act within a Christian context. On this reading, Hamlet emerges as a *Trauerspiel* rather than a revenge tragedy. Naturally, Hamlet fails in his attempt to exact revenge in the manner of a tragic hero—rather than rushing to avenge his father, uncaring of the possible consequences, he wants to find out the truth of the ghost's words: whether his father truly was poisoned. Hamlet is thus torn between the injunction from the supernatural figure and the urge to verify his words via empirical proof. This paradigmatic ambivalence is exactly where Carl Schmitt locates Hamlet's failure.

HAMLET OR HECUBA

In an infamous letter of 1930, Benjamin thanked German jurist and political theorist Carl Schmitt for his contribution to Benjamin's book on German tragic drama:

> You will very quickly recognize how much my book is indebted to you for its presentation of the doctrine of sovereignty in the seventeenth century. Perhaps I may also say, in addition, that I have also derived from your later works, especially the *Diktatur*, a confirmation of my modes of research in the philosophy of art from yours in the philosophy of the state. (GS1, 887)[11]

In response to this seeming endorsement of Schmitt, Scholem later observed that Benjamin

> had an extraordinarily precise and delicate feel for the subversive elements in the oeuvre of great scholars. He was able to perceive the subterranean rumbling of revolution even in the case of authors whose worldview bore reactionary traits; generally he was keenly aware of what he called "the strange interplay between reactionary theory and revolutionary practice." (Scholem 1976, 195)

There has been a resurgence of interest in Benjamin's controversial endorsement of Schmitt.[12] Where Weber (1992) stresses the methodological focus on extremes as the main point of connection between the two thinkers, recent scholarship mostly focuses on the legacy of Schmitt's concept of sovereignty, in particular with reference to Hobbes.[13] While in 1973, Schmitt himself retrospectively positioned his 1938 book on Hobbes as a response to Benjamin,[14] I propose instead to read his 1956 *Hamlet or Hecuba* as the more salient point of connection between the two thinkers, allowing their different conceptualisations of sovereignty and myth to come to the fore, illuminating the specificity of Benjamin's account.

In the appendix to *Hamlet or Hecuba*, Schmitt contests Benjamin's central claim about *Hamlet* as a *Trauerspiel*. He states that, although Benjamin takes recourse to Schmitt's definition of sovereignty, he underestimates the differences between the English and the German social and political situation and therefore their cultural and artistic products, such as plays, which for Schmitt "is equally essential for the interpretation of *Hamlet* because the core of *this* play cannot be grasped by means of the categories of art and cultural history, such as Renaissance and Baroque" (Schmitt 2006, 53). Schmitt locates this difference in the "antithesis between barbaric and political" (Schmitt 2006, 54). For Schmitt, the early seventeenth century in England remained a "barbaric" age; one where the differentiation and detachment of the political as a distinct sphere had not yet occurred. The same holds true for art; both art and the political, Schmitt states, were still embedded in "life." Thus, he claims that no pre-modern state can meaningfully be termed a "state" as the political power of the sovereign had not yet been established. The separation of worldly rule from the church had not yet been accomplished; something, Schmitt asserts, that only occurred in the emerging state system of continental Europe, which was formed following the religious wars and put an end to them by detaching church and state, declaring the latter a political sphere above interreligious quarrels. The ensuing public order and ostensible stability serves, in turn, to legitimate this new political construct.

Schmitt describes Tudor England as "on its way" towards statehood in this sense in the period between 1588 and 1688 (the century spanning the destruction of the Spanish Armada and the expulsion of the Stuarts), but developing along a different path to that taken by continental Europe. Schmitt places Shakespeare's play at the start of this development; it signifies an "*Aufbruch*," a departure. Schmitt is as enthusiastic about this historical moment of England's ascendancy as he is morose about what he perceives as the (momentary) downfall of European civilisation in the era of religious wars. This sharply contrasts with the period from which *Hamlet* emerges—the build-up to the civil war in England, itself concerned with the question of truth, reaching a bloody impasse. On Schmitt's understanding, this could be solved only by the invention of sovereignty, which inaugurates an order above sectarian religious strife.

The issues of sovereignty and stability discussed with regards to the later developments in the seventeenth century—dealt with in Schmitt's other writings—are foreshadowed in the cusp-of-the-century timeframe of *Hamlet or Hecuba*. Schmitt was well aware of the political and religious tensions in England at this time, and a discussion of these forms the backdrop of much of his thinking in *Hamlet or Hecuba*. Ostensibly, no open civil war occurred around the coronation of James I and VI[15] (and he indeed acceded to the throne due, in no small part, to secret machinations, a point reflected in the courtly intrigue of Hamlet). However, as Schmitt discusses, the invasion of the Spanish Armada in 1588 signified a formative event for the political consciousness of the era and inaugurated a century of strife. Schmitt paints the picture of a society characterised by an unstable, "negative" peace; central to its landscape were certain political taboos surrounding James' ascendancy to the throne. This, for Schmitt, is the root of their "incursion" into the play. The existence of this latent conflict was, of course, demonstrated by the eruption of the English civil war and the Thirty Years' War within a few decades. Schmitt thus identifies a partial resolution—more of a temporary cessation—of the ongoing religious strife of the Elizabethan era, but while it may last for a while, a model of governance that ensures a more lasting peace must be found.

On Schmitt's reading, what is absolutely pivotal to the overcoming of religious and political strife and attendant instability is a new myth to tie together the political community—and only a sovereign can provide this. Motivated by this quest, Schmitt undertakes a brief overview of the literature pertaining to the question of the origin of tragedy, dismissing Nietzsche's views on music and the notion of *particular* myths, as the latter is a merely literary source. However, Schmitt states, "the definition is correct to the extent it considers the myth a piece of the heroic legend, not only the poet's literary source, but a living common knowledge, embracing poet and audience, a piece of historical reality in which all the participants are brought together by their historical existence" (Schmitt 2006, 40). Schmitt's aim to establish the primacy of myth is further demonstrated in his question whether the *"Bildungswissen"* of Schiller and his contemporaries "is capable of creating a common presence and public space," the answer indicating whether history here serves as an origin of tragedy or a mere literary source for a *Trauerspiel* (which Schmitt, contra Benjamin, regards as the inferior variety of what is essentially the same genre). He bluntly states: "I do not think that knowledge of history may replace the myth" (Schmitt 2006, 40).[16] Where Benjamin is at pains to distinguish myth from history, and indeed, this relation to the historical is what sets *Trauerspiel* apart from tragedy for him, Schmitt strives to collapse myth back into history, and thus to re-mythologise historical events. The tragic, for Schmitt, must remain a transhistorical category; *Trauerspiele* must retain the potential to become elevated to myth if post-Classical society is to enjoy any measure of stability, as the existence of a myth that ties together the community (be it national or, as in *Hamlet or Hecuba*, European) is so crucial to this. Thus, Schmitt suggests, even to him and his contemporaries, "Mary Stuart is something more and something else than Hecuba. Neither is the fate of the Atrids so close to us as that of the unfortunate Stuarts. His royal lineage has been shattered by the fateful religious divisions of Europe. It was in the history of that lineage that the tragic myth of Hamlet germinated" (Schmitt 2006, 45). Schmitt, like Benjamin, recognizes that Greek myth is not nearly as close to the mind of the baroque theatregoer, or indeed his own contemporaries, as the Stuarts, who are historical figures. However, for Schmitt, the possibility of the emergence, or rather, creation of a new myth out of this historical matter must be retained. What is so deeply tragic about the fate of the Stuarts, to Schmitt, is their embodiment of the fractured "European spirit." This would, at first glance, appear not to be too far removed from Benjamin's centring of the historical context of religious strife on the baroque mourning play. However, the difference in emphasis is a crucial, and political, one: Where Benjamin is interested in the possibilities opened up by the experience of the loss of meaning, the melancholic mood resulting from the disappearance of religious certainties, for its ability to destabilise the conventional narrative of historical events, Schmitt laments the downfall of "Europe's fate." His text is haunted by a sense of "greatness" lost and not yet regained, perhaps that very same flourishing of Renaissance art which, in Benjamin's reading, was the *Vorgeschichte*, the prehistory, to the ensuing religious strife and instability of the baroque. For Benjamin, the baroque ushers in a sovereignty that is always under suspicion, undermining political authority into his own day, and thus destabilising the model of subjectivity that is modelled on this form of authority. Schmitt, on the other hand, regards the period that gave rise to Shakespeare's dramas as a historical aberration. The tragedy of the Stuarts, for Schmitt, is that they did not read the sign of the times correctly, "incapable of freeing themselves from the ecclesiastical and feudal middle ages" (CS, 56). Read through the lens of the historical figure of James the I and VI, Hamlet thus becomes a tragic myth because he stands as a warning against the dangers of sectarianism.

In his closing praise for Shakespeare, Schmitt attests the playwright the status of "genius" based on his scrupulous political sentiments. Schmitt ascribes Shakespeare the *political* foresight to know what figure, in a context of bewildering, frenetic *Aktualität*, would be capable of being elated, intensified into a myth. He does so guided by respect for the violence and political taboos of his age; these allow him, on Schmitt's reading, to also obtain an inkling of a possible solution to the succession squabble and religious wars over truth: a new myth. For Benjamin, of course, the "Gestalt" that Shakespeare pulled out of his *Aktualität* in the form of Hamlet is not capable of mythologization in this Schmittian sense; it *cannot* be, because this has become a historical impossibility. Benjamin traces how the inaugural step of sovereignty, enacted in baroque history and in the *Trauerspiel*, is thus *itself* a failure from the start—as if, like some baroque artworks, it is conceptualised as ruin from its inception. What follows can be nothing but the reiteration of that same failure throughout its post-history.

Benjamin and Schmitt thus work from similar postulates—both understand the idea of sovereignty as premised on the promise of stability in an unstable age. Where they differ is in their response to and their perceived reason for its inauguration: For Benjamin, the sovereign's task is to provide continuity, averting the state of exception. He is supposed to reinforce the existing order rather than break with it. Schmitt, in contrast, proposes a radical break in the political order as the foundational act of the sovereign—the creation of a new regime, ushering in a new truth, and ultimately ensuring peace through a foundation myth. For Benjamin, this attempt is doomed to failure—all the sovereign can aim to do is to stave off disintegration, and even in that he is ultimately doomed to ill-success. Hamlet is emblematic of this. Thus Schmitt and Benjamin disagree on what constitutes Hamlet's failure: Schmitt reads the end of the play as an instance of an admittedly ineffective ruler, who, perhaps recognising this truth about himself in his final moments, gives his dying voice to Fortinbras, thus averting the state of emergency—Fortinbras, arriving with an invading army, seeming like a much more likely candidate for successful sovereignty on Schmitt's reading. At the same time, Hamlet's failure to himself act as a sovereign in his lifetime allows him to be turned into a myth, expressing the real historical failure of the Stuarts and the need for sovereignty beyond internecine religious conflicts. Schmitt crucially does not read Hamlet as synonymous with the Stuarts or any other particular historical figure; rather, he manages to represent and, *as play*, insofar as he embodies these political tensions of his age, transcend their fate, thus becoming tragic. Schmitt is not primarily concerned with the figure of Hamlet himself, so much as he is with demonstrating that the play is precisely not a "pure" play: it is the historical context which "irrupts" into the play that allows it—and its creator—to be judged adequately. Hamlet's failure thus designates Shakespeare's success as a political playwright and mythmaker on Schmitt's reading.

The disagreement is partially grounded in Benjamin's and Schmitt's differing periodisation of Hamlet. On Benjamin's reading, the play is baroque, while Schmitt classes it as premodern and thus "barbaric." The implication is that this unstable form of sovereignty needs to be superseded by a more fully dictatorial—and thus successful— model.[17] Published in 1956, and thus divided from Schmitt's other works on sovereignty by the events of World War II and Schmitt's post-war fall from grace in academic and political circles, it may thus be read as an attempt to revindicate his call for sovereign dictatorship through the (ostensibly) politically far less sensitive matter of literary criticism.[18] Benjamin, meanwhile, reads Hamlet as an unsuccessful sovereign incapable of avoiding the state of exception; his melancholia and madness serving to make visible the rivenness of his age and the inherent instability of its concept of sovereignty. The play can thus be said to be successful precisely in its failure, but in a different way to Schmitt's reading: Hamlet's fractured consciousness is emblematic of the age and demonstrates the instability of any system of sovereignty and mythmaking, rather than constituting a call for *more effective* myths. Hamlet's relationship to myth cannot but be one of citation and ineffectual *"nachspielen."* This is to do with the historical boundedness of the tragic: as the product of a historically rooted age—antiquity, and place—Greece, the tragic form of the mythic age was the site of a split: fate is fractured, and the tragic hero breaks out of its continuum. Benjamin conceptualises Greek tragedy itself as the locus of this rupture. Thus, Benjamin highlights the specificity of the sacrifice of the hero in tragedy as

> being at once a first and a final sacrifice. A final sacrifice in the sense of the atoning sacrifice to gods who are upholding an ancient right; a first sacrifice in the sense of the representative action, in which new aspects of the life of the nation become manifest . . . The tragic death has a dual significance: it invalidates the ancient rights of the Olympians, and it offers up the hero to the unknown god as the first fruits of a new harvest of humanity. (OT, 107)

The temporal dislocation of the sacrificial hero in Greek tragedy is thus grounded in its specific historical context and concerns a movement away from myth. Benjamin quotes his own text "Fate and Character" (1919) here, stressing that it is not in law that this process take place, but in tragedy. Here, "demonic fate is broken"—"Not, however, in the replacement of the inscrutable pagan concatenation of guilt and atonement by the purity of man, absolved and reconciled with the pure god. It is rather that in tragedy pagan man realizes that he is better than his gods" (OT, 109–10). For Benjamin, this is what sets pagan myth apart from the truly theological. Scholem comments that

> In those years—between 1915 and at least 1927—the religious sphere assumed a central importance for Benjamin that was utterly removed from fundamental doubt. At its center was the concept of *Lehre* (teaching), which for him included the philosophical realm but definitely transcended it. In his early writings he reverted repeatedly to this concept, which he interpreted in the sense of the original meaning of the Hebrew *torah* as "instruction," instruction not only about the true condition and way of man in the world but also about the transcausal connection of things and their rootedness in God. (Scholem 1981, 69)

As Georg Dörr observes, "The fact that myth is negatively connotated in this context is almost self-evident. Myth, like the Law, and the symbol, belong to natural or creaturely—and thus pagan life" (Dörr 2007, 115, transl. mine). This distinction is crucial—the lapse back into the mythic at the moment of the failure of Christian doctrine is precisely why the baroque produces *Trauerspiele* rather than tragedies. [19] Hamlet is no tragic hero; he *cannot* be, because his struggle is thoroughly immanent to his age. He dithers and fails to carry out the revenge demanded by the ghost of his father. Hamlet fails to act; fails to elevate himself above ambivalence. Thus, Hamlet settles on mournfully acting out the command of the lost object (fate, certainty)—but it is just that, acting, in the sense of putting on a show, a performance—both in his own conduct and literally, in the play within the play—which becomes a substitute for the decisive, political action of a sovereign.

The specific madness and melancholia of Hamlet, his *Handlungshem-mung*, finally turns into its obverse—rash action at the end of the play. On Benjamin's reading, this signals not so much a decisive assertion as a final gesture of defiance and insanity. Hamlet has given up on finding the truth; he is mad at the world, and finally he succumbs to "this drossy age" (5.2). His revenge is not enacted as a measured or heroic act, but a wild scuffle involving the entire court and scores of accidental deaths. The attempt to be a tragic hero, which is sustained throughout the play, finally dissolves in an almost farcical slaughter scene, the point at which Hamlet is most obviously distanced from the tragic hero. Benjamin writes that "He wants to die by some accident, and as the fateful stage properties gather around him, as around their lord and master, the drama of fate [*Schicksalsdrama*] flares up in the conclusion of this *Trauerspiel*, as something that is contained, but of course overcome, in it" (OT, 137). Hamlet's conduct thus makes visible the mythic residue, the persistence of older forms of play and associated tropes in the *Trauerspiel* and, by extension, in the baroque mind. Fortinbras' arrival on stage, for its part, completes the picture by illustrating the impossibility of a Schmittian Hamlet myth in the baroque: after the end of history, the death of the king, there is always already a new king in waiting. This, ultimately, is the truth of sovereignty for Benjamin—far from performing ultimate closure and guaranteeing stability, it does precisely the opposite. The *Trauerspiel* is the form that expresses this most clearly.

THE RETURN OF RELIGIOUS SOLUTIONS?

Benjamin does not conclude his reading of Hamlet at this point. Hamlet's melancholia and madness, his failed attempt to act in accordance with both the model of the mythic hero and Christian doctrine finally point beyond the meaninglessness of baroque experience. However, they do not become mythic—rather, their resolution is to be found within religion. After noting the Christian origin of the allegorical gaze of the baroque, Benjamin explores the connection between antiquity and medieval Christianity, as the latter functions as a mediator between the other two. He highlights that European society as a hegemonically Christian culture was presented with a paradox: antique myths and gods were pagan demons, yet still provided the foundation for artistic production. The baroque solved this problem by subsuming ancient Greece; assimilating antiquity and its Gods into Christianity. The *Bildgedaechtnis* (image memory) of ancient Greece, revived in the baroque, brought into existence a *Bilderspekulation* (image speculation) which brought these images of the mythic past into the present via the intervening ages. This was, as Benjamin explains, only possible *allegorically*, once Greek culture had been killed off; as a dismembered corpse offering up its parts for reassembly by a later, melancholy gaze. Torn from their context, they become fragments the baroque artist can work with. This is the same principle underlying the "pious mortification of the flesh" which together with the Christian view of ancient gods as demonic formed the goal of "allegorical exegesis" (OT, 222). In being killed off, these cultural fragments attain an afterlife, are made sacred by the baroque allegorist.

Crucially, the mediation of medieval Christianity remains partial, unsuccessful, incomplete. Pagan antiquity is never fully subsumed by the European Middle Ages. The *Trauerspiele* highlight the fragmentary nature of this form of mediation, showing the cracks in the opulent façade, the artifice, the stagedness. They attest to the existence of a remainder and simultaneously constitute an attempt to banish the mythic residue of the previous civilisation and its cosmological horizon. The baroque attempts this in allegory, an exercise in re-signifying the fragments of a broken world: "If the church had not been able quite simply to banish the gods from the memory of the faithful, allegorical language would never have come into being. For it is not an epigonal victory monument; but rather the word which is intended to exorcise a surviving remnant of antique life" (OT, 223). The relationship to Antiquity is ambivalent—for Benjamin, there is no triumphal march of history from ancient Greece through medieval Europe to the Renaissance and modernity. Instead, in the aftermath of the cosmological rupture of the baroque, Europe turns to pagan Antiquity in its attempt to restore an ethical community in a founding myth. Benjamin states that "Ancient tragedy is the fettered slave on the triumphal car of the baroque *Trauerspiel*" (OT, 100). This process of the subsumption of Greek myth is a violent one and constitutes an attempt to restore order that is itself premised on violence. It merely replaces the ideal type of the philosophy of history of the counter-reformation, "the acme: a golden age of peace and culture, free of any apocalyptic features, constituted and guaranteed *in aeternum* by the authority of the Church" (OT, 80), with a political order equally stabilised not by ecclesiastical, but profane rule.[20] These tendencies become visible in the period of the desolate, worldly, absolutist rule of the baroque. Before any legitimacy can truly take hold, before the space left empty when religious certainty was toppled is filled by a new authority, in mourning for the lost and unsuccessful attempts to revive it, another space is opened up where sovereignty itself appears as unstable. It is precisely this interval between two myths, the—momentary—disenchantment of the world that in its arrest of effective (sovereign) action, its melancholy, reveals the play of sovereignty *as play*—and thus destabilises it.[21] As we shall see in the following chapters, Benjamin is to retain this focus on interruption and arrest throughout his work.[22] We also see here, for the first time, that the fracturing of the subject in the early modern era constitutes an opening towards something else, a condition of its own overcoming.

For Benjamin, this is where religion, seemingly paradoxically, once again resurfaces as a possibility. The space that melancholia and mad, ineffective sovereignty thus opens up also allows for a miracle, the intrusion of truth from "outside." Crucially, it is the lack of a successful politician, in the Shakespearean sense—an intriguer—that leaves open these gaps—fractures—within the baroque political community as well as in some of its artworks. The tension between ancient forms and post-reformatory Christianity, between the brief spell of Renaissance humanism and the melancholy of the baroque is not only apparent in its sovereign, but also in the figure of the courtier, most notably Polonius. Like Hamlet, he teeters on the brink of his age, but where the former refracts into the martyr-tyrant, Polonius is torn between the earlier humanist vision of an advisor as a sage truth-sayer to the sovereign and the emerging Machiavellian concept of the courtier as intriguer.[23] For Benjamin, the presence of a successful intriguer within the *Trauerspiel* would bring it the closure that would stabilise sovereignty—transmuting the baroque into a Machiavellian Utopia, where its martyr/tyrant is completed through the political acumen of the intriguer. Were that to be the case, the *Trauerspiel* would attain allegorical completion, its mournfulness evaporating. Thus, it is precisely the absence of such a figure that lets the *Trauerspiel* remain open to the entrance of theological truth.

In the final passage of the book, Benjamin again stresses the Christian character of the baroque, which he finds present in Hamlet. Schmitt disagrees on this point and asserts that Hamlet is not Christian "in any specific sense" (OT, 52). This formulation inadvertently draws close to its own refutation; what is at stake in *Hamlet* is precisely an "unspecific" Christian-ness—as discussed earlier, its theological forms still provide the backdrop; only its answers can no longer suffice. We are dealing with a profaned, but not secular world—hence its mournfulness. Benjamin's study of the baroque traces its move from wretched godlessness to a final implicit reaffirmation of the theology whose downfall forms the backdrop of its existence. Precisely because it "knows no eschatology," the *Trauerspiel* becomes eschatological. This is the meaning of Benjamin's cryptic last sentence: "In the spirit of allegory," the *Trauerspiel* "is conceived from the outset as a ruin, a fragment.

Others may shine resplendently as on the first day; this form preserves the image of beauty to the very last" (OT, 235). It opens up a negative space for beauty-as-truth to enter, via philosophical criticism. This links back to the concept of origin, discussed at the beginning of the text—Benjamin writes that it will only be accessible to the dual insight that understands it as the "restoration of revelation" [*Restauration der Offenbarung*, transl. mine] (GS1, 935) which must necessarily remain unfinished at the same time.

With this in mind, it becomes possible to understand more clearly why Benjamin takes Hamlet's declaration that "There's special providence in the fall of a sparrow" (5.2.215 –16) as an indication of the Christian ethos of the play. On this reading, Hamlet's life, in all its wretchedness, points to the inversion of its sadness into blissful existence in Christian providence: "Only in a princely life such as this is melancholy redeemed, by being confronted with itself" (OT, 158). In passing through the stages of baroque melancholia, madness, and finally a turn towards those very same religious truths whose downfall initiated the melancholia and indeed the baroque itself, Hamlet mirrors Benjamin's reading of the baroque age *in toto*. In this, and in recognising his transience and demise as a *historical* fact, something to be narrated (as Hamlet instructs Horatio to do in his last words), Shakespeare allows Hamlet that very self-reflexivity about his age which is missing in the German *Trauerspiele*. It is this self-recognition that, for Benjamin, evens the ground for the inversion of melancholy into its opposite, the potential arrival of truth, as alterity, and it is this that makes *Hamlet* the "perfect" baroque mourning play as it both inaugurates and abolishes the genre, providing a study in the riven consciousness of the baroque sovereign, only to then cancel it out at last within the context of potential redemption.

It is also here that the problem of subjectivity comes to the fore again. At the end of his study, Benjamin resolves the figures of the baroque mourning plays back into allegories, revealing that it was the subjective gaze of melancholy of the baroque, crystallising in its playwright, that created them in the first place. In a theoretically and stylistically dense passage, Benjamin traces the passing of the allegorical dialectic from the recognition of the corpse as the "only fitting allegory of death, the moment of intersection of guilt and transience" (Pensky 1993, 127) to the introduction of the problem of evil into the text, to its final dialectical inversion, in the recognition that evil belongs to the sphere of myth and thus signifies, in a theological register, nothing but the absence of God. As Pensky notes,

> Melancholia, at the bottom of its descent, transforms itself from absolute subjectivity to the selflessness of absolute faith. Once again, subjectivity stands for the whole breadth of experience of the world as godforsaken and meaningless; the end of melancholia in faith is the self-extinction of the mournful subject, and this means that the allegories, creations of the subject, deconstruct themselves into ciphers of God's presence. (Pensky 1993, 134–35)

Pensky concludes that this surprising ending of Benjamin's study cannot be read straightforwardly as either embracing what he calls the "dialectics of mourning" as moving towards an "actual" encounter with God *or* as rejecting this particular type of baroque theology as an ultimate relapse into myth as a result of the dissolution of any materialist content in the dialectic. The main problem for Benjamin, on Pensky's reading, becomes the formulation of a critical methodology that avoids the pitfalls of the melancholy hypersubjectivity that marks the end of his *Trauerspiel* study, including its political petrification, while preserving the dialectical relationship between potentially messianic insights and the objects of the world contained in baroque allegory. Stewart links the moment of illusory, absolute subjectivity, to psychopathology:

> This inflation of the subjective, though it presents itself as leaving subjectivity behind as "evil," suffers from the same flawed and faithless Christian reversal. A subjectivity that lets go of itself only when it believes to be mirrored by the fullness of God, has been faithless and mythical all along. Such belief is typical of a psychology of omnipotence. (Stewart 2010, 69)

She also notes that Benjamin's introduction of the miracle of the visions of Saint Theresa at this point in the text link back to Schmitt's analogy of the miracle to the state of exception, as does the baroque's narcissistic self-representation in the balcony:

> An empty space. Subjectively, one is to imagine—hallucinate—the Sovereign-God standing there. On the other hand, objectively, there is no one there, and this fact turns the baroque symbolism of power into ostentatious spectacle, just as it turns that baroque "upswing" of allegory that loses itself—empties itself, in fact—into miraculous delusion and phantasmagoria. (Stewart 2010, 70)

Thus, Benjamin's conclusion leaves the baroque suspended between its religious concerns and its inadequate religious solutions, freezing its allegorical dialectic in place. With this gesture, subjectivity is likewise suspended between absolute emptiness and creaturely dejection—melancholia—and grandiose self-inflatory identification with the divine—narcissism.

Schmitt refutes Benjamin's point about providence, citing variation between the different versions of the play. He concludes that to pay attention to these variations would be to open up the theological controversies at the heart of the religious wars once again. This, of course, is what Schmitt wants to avoid at all costs. He *needs Hamlet* not to be Christian, as otherwise it would not point the way towards a suprareligious sovereign capable of containing the antinomies of Protestant and Catholic doctrine that led to the religious wars. His reading of Benjamin's interpretation of Hamlet is thus dismissive of Benjamin's aporetic take on the play, performing discursive closure in strongly rejecting the claim about its Christian character.

For Benjamin, Fortinbras' takeover signals the restitution of "business as usual" of early modern sovereignty—the arrival of a monarch fit to govern, ensuring the ongoing stability of the realm. Everyone in Hamlet's family is somehow implicated in the crisis initiated with Claudius' murder of Old Hamlet. While Fortinbras is external to it, he is external to it, he is still part of the historical moment that gave rise to the plot of the play—implying that the same scenario could repeat itself. What Hamlet's assertion and the continuation of sovereignty-as-usual offstage thus mean for Benjamin, in opposition to Schmitt, is the continuation of the instability of sovereignty. In not paying attention to the wretchedness of the baroque and the melancholy suffering and madness of its ruler, Schmitt elides the questions these pose to the very foundation of sovereignty. Schmitt performs the same movement on *Hamlet* the play as the characters within the play attempt to perform on Hamlet—to find the root of the instability and excise it; to suture the tear, to perform closure, discursive or otherwise. For Schmitt, the question of the madness of the sovereign simply never poses itself—after all, the sovereign *decides* what is true and sane, thus he cannot be mad. Of course, such a conception of truth is far removed from any normative or logical category, purely immanent to power, and thus either loses its intelligibility completely or else must be seen as itself "deranged."[24]

HISTORICAL RUPTURE VERSUS MYTHMAKING

For Schmitt, post-classical society must retain the potential to produce more than *Trauerspiel*, that is, a capacity for the tragic, as post-reformatory stability in Europe depends on the creation of a new myth. The sovereign must be decisive and declare the state of exception, providing such a new myth for the foundation of the body politic. For Benjamin, as we have seen, the resurgence of myth is bound up with violence[25]—in his reading, the continuum of natural-mythic history of sovereignty is in need of interruption. The melancholy *Trauerspiel* and its deranged sovereign go some way towards accomplishing this: they present the gap between *Heilsgeschichte* and profane historical events as they are experienced in the baroque and, in making visible this gap, open up a space for the alterity of truth to become discernible. If we take seriously the dialectical movement Benjamin delineates in the "Epistemo-Critical Prologue," history is the matter, the *Sachgehalt*, within which the *Wahrheitsgehalt*, the truth content, is hidden. In the midst of bloody historical happening, melancholia and other forms of "derangement"—mania, "madness"—emerge as a chance to capture the "real" truth beyond empirical reality as it presents itself.

European historical consciousness is revealed as doubly riven—in its unsuccessful attempt to return to Christian doctrine, repressing the Reformation and the Thirty Years' War, *and* in its attempt to take recourse to the ancient Greeks in its search for a way to ground both the community and the fractured modern subject. Where the Greek tragic hero has an inkling of his superiority over his gods, the baroque lives in the wretched aftermath of the downfall of its divinity. The *Trauerspiel* is left turning back on itself and spinning incessantly, suspended between the religious solutions and their devaluation, the appeal to the ethos of classical antiquity and its historical impossibility. The sovereign, its paradigmatic figure, is torn between creatureliness and the echo of the absolute validity of divine truth that no longer holds. Thus the subject, too, is fractured—there is no longer any eternal, transcendental truth to be found in religion, and at the same time, the baroque subject is not able to be an ancient Greek hero, elevating himself from out of mythic fate.

NOTES

1. On the problem of translating "Trauerspiel" as "tragic drama," Ilit Ferber notes: "Taking into account Benjamin's commitment to the distinction between Trauerspiel and tragedy and, moreover, its vital importance in justifying his claims, it is worth noting one grave error in the English translation of the text's title. Osborne's translation of Trauerspiel as 'tragic drama' ignores the efforts Benjamin makes to precisely distinguish the Trauerspiel from tragedy. 'Mourning Play' or simply Trauerspiel, rather than 'German Tragic Drama,' would have been much more appropriate, and it does give the impression that the translator is at some odds with his own decision" (Ferber 2013, 177).

Weber (2008, 143) also points to the problematic status of this translation: "The unstated position that presides over the English translation, in the form of its title, is that however significant the distinctions may be, they nevertheless take place within the continuity of a self-identical genre— tragedy," which as we shall see is precisely what Benjamin contests throughout.

2. Benjamin uses the term "latent" in the German original (GS1, 926), which Osborne's translation renders as "implicit," obscuring the linguistic proximity to Freud.

3. This version was not included in Benjamin's *Habilitationsschrift* and does not appear in Osborne's English translation of the book.

4. See GSI, 939.

5. See Agamben (SE, 56) for an alternative reading of this passage. Agamben asserts that Benjamin in fact wrote "eine" (a) rather than "keine" (no) eschatology. However, given Benjamin's argument about the loss of transcendence in the baroque, the more established version of "no eschatology" fits far better.

6. In this work, Hanssen reads the concept of *Kreatur* as also carrying a more positive aspect: that of an attention to the non-human, exceeding the constraints of anthropocentric subjectivity, which she explores in relation to Benjamin's work on Kafka.

7. It is worth noting that Benjamin's interest in the figure of the *Kreatur* went beyond his *Trauerspiel* book and resulted in his collaboration with Buber's eponymous journal, aiming to explore anthropology beyond either theology or the "profane."

8. The German reads "das Sträflingsbrandmal der Kreatur" (GS3, 152), the "branded mark of the creature."

9. Perhaps anticipating the obvious objection that Hamlet cannot be taken as emblematic of the German *Trauerspiel*, Benjamin also cautions against the overemphasis of the role of the nation for the assessment of the *idea* of the genre, suggesting that the conflation of "German" and "*Trauerspiel*" may function as a "*Hemmung*," an inhibition, of the actual idea—its truth. While acknowledging that the artworks of specific linguistic groups and "*Volksbezirke*," the areas of distinct peoples, often form ideas in themselves, Benjamin suggests that the *Trauerspiel* may be better understood as European in character—which would imply the "*Wesenheit*" of German *Trauerspiele* cannot be understood through themselves alone and are affected by the works of Calderon and Shakespeare.

10. Notably, even the ghost of Old Hamlet is not identical with his person—a sundering between the ghost and the deceased is performed throughout his appearances in the play; he is referred to variously as "this thing; fantasy, dreaded sight, apparition, 'it,' a portentous figure *so like* the king, his 'image,' an illusion" etc. (1.1–1.2.).

11. transl. Samuel Weber (1992, 5).

12. See for instance Samuel Weber, "Taking Exception to Decision: Walter Benjamin and Carl Schmitt," *Diacritics* vol. 22, no. 3/4, "Commemorating Walter Benjamin" (Autumn–Winter 1992), 5–18; Marc de Wilde, "Meeting Opposites: The Political Theologies of Walter Benjamin and Carl Schmitt," *Philosophy & Rhetoric* vol. 44, no. 4 (2011), 363–81; Horst Bredekamp, "From Walter Benjamin to Carl Schmitt, via Thomas Hobbes," *Critical Inquiry* vol. 25, no. 2 (Winter 1999), 247–66; Susanne Heil, *Gefährliche Beziehungen: Walter Benjamin und Carl Schmitt* (Stuttgart: Metzler, 1996); Victoria Kahn, "Hamlet or Hecuba: Carl Schmitt's Decision," *Representations* vol. 83, no. 1 (Summer 2003), 67–96; Massimiliano Tomba, "Another Kind of *Gewalt*: Beyond Law Re-Reading Walter Benjamin," *Historical Materialism*, vol. 17, no.1 (2009), 126–44.

13. See Kahn (2003), Heil (1996), and Bredekamp (1999). Where Bredekamp reaffirms Benjamin's "esteem" for Schmitt as reflected in his art theoretical approach and "relentless politicisation of time," positioning Hobbes as the missing link between the two thinkers, Kahn contests the claim about Schmitt's positive view of Hobbes, suggesting instead that *Hamlet or Hecuba* is to be read as a rebuttal of the detrimental effects of Hobbes' concept of sovereignty.

14. See Schmitt's letter to Viesel, 4 April 1973, in: Viesel, *Jawohl, der Schmitt*, 14. However, as Bredekamp observes, "At first glance, it may seem questionable whether Schmitt really had Benjamin in mind when he wrote his critique of Hobbes. It is possible that he, looking back in 1973, was seeking some share in Benjamin's fame. He may have viewed this as a welcome opportunity to disguise the book's open anti-Semitism by describing it as a veiled answer to a Jewish emigrant, in this way appearing to take him seriously and even honor him" (Bredekamp 1999, 261).

15. See Roger Lockyer, *James VI and I* (London: Longman, 1998) on the secret correspondence between James I and VI and ministers of the court of Elisabeth I.

16. One might, of course, contrast this with Hamlet's own tortured and laborious attempt to find out the historical truth of the death of his father instead of replacing it with his, or the ghost's "myth."

17. See Carl Schmitt, *Die Diktatur: Von den Anfängen des modernen Souveränitätsgedankens bis zum proletarischen Klassenkampf* (Berlin: Duncker & Humblot, 1994, originally published 1921).

18. See also V. Kahn, "Hamlet or Hecuba: Carl Schmitt's Decision." In *Representations*, vol. 83, no. 1 (Summer 2003), 67–96, for a discussion of the role of *Hamlet or Hecuba* in Schmitt's post-war attempts at rehabilitation.

19. The opposition of Christianity and the mythic-pagan is destabilised throughout Benjamin's work. See for example his remark in "Robert Walser" (1929), where Benjamin, discussing the transition out of the "madness of myth," states "It is commonly thought that this process of awakening took place in the positive religions. If that is the case, it did not do so in any very straightforward or unambiguous way. The latter has to be sought in that great profane debate with myth that the fairy tale represents" (SW2, 260). On Benjamin's relegation of Christianity to the mythic, see also the discussion of Benjamin's "Capitalism as Religion" in the next chapter.

20. The German has "*durchs Schwert der Kirche*" (GS1, 259)—"by the sword of the Church," rendering the violent aspect of ecclesiastical authority more apparent.

21. Weber (1991, 493) also locates the potential of *Trauerspiel* to resist mythical law at this moment of the "dislocation" of tragedy.

22. This, of course, provides a bridge to Benjamin's earlier "Critique of Violence" (1921), where he draws from Sorel's model of the general strike as a way to conceptualise a "real" state of exception. See Butler (2012, 73). Agamben (2005, 52–56) suggests Schmitt's concept of sovereignty in *Political Theology* is formulated as a response to Benjamin's "Critique of Violence."

23. On this point, see Joanne Paul, "The Best Counsellors Are the Dead: Counsel and Shakespeare's Hamlet," *Renaissance Studies* vol. 29, no. 3 (June 2015), 1–20.

24. It is noteworthy that all three mythological figures of European literature quoted by Schmitt—Don Quijote, Hamlet, and Faust—are not only scholars: They are also similar in their madness. In the case of Don Quijote and Hamlet, this madness is intimately bound up with their "untimeliness" and inability to detach from previous social formations, be it the spectre of feudalism or that of ancient Greece. In the case of Faust, meanwhile, it is driven by the desire to strike a bargain with the devil that is caused by his unquenchable thirst for knowledge. The crucial role of madness in complementing the image of truth and sovereignty thus becomes visible even in—or perhaps because of—Schmitt's silencing of it.

25. On this point, see also Siegfried Menninghaus (1986).

Chapter Two

Melancholia, Possession, Critique

In this chapter, I discuss the interrelationship of melancholia, possession, and the fractured subject in Benjamin and Freud. Building on the preceding discussion of the inauguration of the fractured subject in Benjamin's book on German tragic drama, I examine the relationship of the formation of subjectivity and melancholia in the baroque in connection to Freud.

In her discussion of Benjamin's early work on theatre, Ilit Ferber states that the "division between mourning and melancholy is absent from Benjamin's book on *Trauerspiel*, in which he uses the terms *Trauer* and *Melancholie* interchangeably, not surrendering to the distinction between normality and pathology which psychoanalysis has made commonplace" (Ferber 2006, 66). However, I maintain that reading Benjamin's *Trauerspiel* book and Freud's 1917 *Mourning and Melancholia* together not only reveals the influence of the latter on the former, but calls into question the distinction between the two concepts in Freud as "overly secure" (Ferber 2006, 66).[1] As this re-reading of Freud with Benjamin will show, there are slippages in Freud's texts which contest the notion that psychoanalysis posits a rigid distinction between mourning and melancholia, normality and psychopathology.

In the second part of my chapter, I examine the issue of possession in relation to Freud's case studies of Schreber and Haitzmann. Known to both Freud and Benjamin, Schreber serves as an example from high modernity of the ongoing crisis of sovereignty in the post-baroque era, while Freud's Haitzmann case study helps elucidate Freud's account of psychopathology in the early modern era. What I aim to show is that melancholia and possession form two poles of the fractured subject's response to a loss, as well as an impossible demand, the demand of subjectivity itself. The subject is thus revealed as fractured between this demand and its inability to meet it.

MELANCHOLIA AND THE FRACTURED SUBJECT

As discussed in the previous chapter, the fractured subject arises as the religious person of the baroque, formerly bounded by a cosmological horizon and understood as primarily a member of the religious community of Christian humanity with God, is robbed of their former certainties about their standing in the order of the world in modernity. Bereft of these bonds, the former community fractures into subjects, who are interpellated as individually responsible for their own spiritual salvation in the context of the rise of Protestantism. Bound up with this is the constitutive fracture of the subject in the form of the Cartesian split, which results in the overvaluation of *"Geistigkeit"* over and above the *physis*, which Benjamin sees as the root cause of the problem of subjectivism. Sundered from its unity with the divine, and its body, the subject's search for knowledge remains fruitless, and the impossible demand to put the self in God's stead as the ultimate guarantor of truth and meaning is experienced as mournful suffering.

There is a further dimension to the inactivity to which the melancholia of the baroque gives rise. Robbed of all transcendence,[2] the martyr is closely linked to the figure of the brooder, who pores over the fragments of the past. Torn from their original context of meaning, they have become torso; ruins, and are repurposed for allegorical construction in the Baroque. In the absence of a stable context of signification, the meaning imposed on them by the brooding allegorist remains entirely subjective, and thus unstable. The brooder is the quintessential melancholic subject insofar as he is haunted by the sense that there is lost meaning to the fragments, which he tries to rearrange but can never recapture. Subjectivity is linked to melancholia, then, for its prolonged state of mourning for an unknown object.

Baroque melancholia is thus a state of inaction in the face of an overwhelming demand premised on the loss of stable, divine power, and the response of the brooder to the loss of the possibility of attaining stable meaning and truth. Understood through the book on German tragic drama, baroque and post-baroque subjects can be read as frustrated tragic heroes, enjoined to act *as if* they had a clearly defined ethical framework to uphold, but finding only themselves as guarantors of meaning. This constitutes a doomed attempt by the fractured subject to regain a lost fulness, as the social configuration that gave rise to tragedy cannot be recaptured by fiat.

The baroque projects this lost wholeness and ethical community of classical antiquity onto ancient societies, which Benjamin alludes to throughout the book. There is thus a double process of mourning for two interconnected objects at play: for the loss of the tragic mode, the possibility of the ethical community of antiquity, and for the cosmological wholeness of pre-Reformation Christianity. In the downfall of the latter, the former is appealed to as an alternative source of meaning and stability. Benjamin thus performs a radical re-reading of the Enlightenment and Renaissance appeal to antiquity as a founding moment of European identity: it emerges not as a straightforward origin at the root of later developments, but as an *Urgeschichte*, a mythic and mythologized origin-story that is quoted as a compensatory fantasy arising at a point of crisis. For Benjamin, at stake is the fractured subject's attempted compensation for a loss. In what follows, I examine Freud's account of the response to such a loss in "Mourning and Melancholia" before relating it back to Benjamin.

MOURNING AND MELANCHOLIA

Freud begins his 1917 text *Mourning and Melancholia* by commenting on some homologies in the functioning of dreams and pathologies and mourning and melancholia. If dreams are to "narcissistic mental disorders" as mourning is to melancholia—a process that is the "prototype" of the aberrant one in normal life (SE14, 243)—then we might surmise from the start that the two are more interconnected than their analysis (in the sense of "splitting apart") might suggest. The relationship of the affect to temporality—its duration—serves as the primary marker of difference between the two states in the text. In *Mourning and Melancholia*, Freud posits an ego that withdraws into itself as a result of the shock of the loss of a loved object. Both mourning and melancholia are a response to this object loss, but, in Freud's formulation, "in mourning it is the world which has become poor and empty. In melancholia it is the ego itself" (SE14, 246). Freud goes on to describe this process, the turning inward of the ego: Libido is removed from the lost object and, rather than being displaced onto another object, withdrawn into the ego. Here, it provokes an identification with the lost object. Thus, the self-reproaches of the melancholic are actually directed against the loved object, but in internalised form. Ambivalence towards the lost object is expressed as self-hatred (SE14, 252).

What notion of a self, then, are we dealing with here? A self that has absorbed the lost object through its identification with it. The return of object cathexis in melancholia thus allows, or even forces, the ego to treat *itself* as an object. It entails the redirection against itself of the destructive will which is its original response to objects in the world—an ultimately auto-cannibalising narcissism. Freud speculates about this correlation between narcissistic object-choice and proneness to melancholia and concludes that melancholia is a sort of hybrid pathology between mourning and narcissism:

"Melancholia, therefore, borrows some of its features from mourning, and the others from the process of regression from narcissistic object-choice to narcissism" (SE14, 250). Thus, the split that occurs at the level of the subject in the process of melancholia indicates both a fracture that is a doubling— where a part of the ego becomes the judging conscience and another the judged ego-object—and a reduction, a lessening—in terms of its own self-regard; in its emptying out. Much like the baroque sovereign is split between the martyr and the tyrant, melancholia for Freud has a tendency towards inversion into its opposite: "mania" (SE14, 253). Freud reaches the preliminary conclusion that even more than melancholy, mania is characterised by narcissism:

> The accumulation of cathexis which is at first bound and then, after the work of melancholia is finished, becomes free and makes mania possible must be linked with regression of the libido to narcissism. The conflict within the ego, which melancholia substitutes for the struggle over the object, must act like a painful wound which calls for an extraordinarily high anti-cathexis. (SE 14, 257)[3]

Freud's starting point was the assumption, which "several psycho-analytic investigators have already put into words . . . that the content of mania is no different from that of melancholia, that both disorders are wrestling with the same "complex," but that probably in melancholia the ego has succumbed to the complex whereas in mania it has mastered it or pushed it aside" (SE14, 253). However far from "mastering" the complex that gave rise to both melancholia and mania, the ego is shown to fall under the sway of its primary affect of narcissism.[4]

As outlined above, Benjamin's baroque sovereign fractures into the tyrant and the martyr. Benjamin sees Gryphius' first play as best representing the confusing interplay of these "antitheses": "The sublime status of the Emperor on the one hand, and the infamous futility of his conduct on the other, create a fundamental uncertainty as to whether this is a drama of tyranny or a history of martyrdom" (OT, 73). The tyrant, prone to rashness, governed by the id, and ultimately subject to mania; the martyr incapable of acting at all, inhibited by the superego demand to live up to his political role. We can see the closeness of the inner split of Benjamin's baroque sovereign, caught between melancholia and mania, and the struggle of post-baroque humanity between the creaturely and the demands of subjectivity, to Freud's account of the struggle between ideal-I/ superego and the primary narcissism of the id.

The relevance of Benjamin's *Trauerspiel* book to a broadly conceived psychoanalytic tradition was not lost on *Imago*, the journal edited by Freud, whose remit was the connection of psychoanalysis to the humanities and later the natural sciences. In his 1931 review of Benjamin's book for *Imago*, Alexander Mette reads it against Freudian theory, in particular schizophrenia. He concludes that "the peculiar juxtaposition of melancholy and mania [in the baroque drama] and the strange way in which they coincide with the phenomena of schizophrenia point to a difficult struggle for the validation of the Super-Ego and the maintenance of object cathexes" (Mette 1931, 538).[5] Moreover, Freud's account of the ego's becoming "poor and empty" in melancholia is mirrored in the ultimate flatness and lack of interiority of the sovereign of the mourning plays as described by Benjamin. Notably, a relation to power is at stake in both processes—in Freud's account, the ego's power to rein in the id and withstand and filter superego commands is called into question; in Benjamin's, the sovereign subject's power to act on the self and the world, always-already impossible to exercise. Benjamin identifies the melancholic mood that permeates culture as a whole in the baroque as a consequence of the lost religious certainties, a mood which is crystallised in the figure of the sovereign in the mourning plays. Mourning as a cultural *Lebensgefühl* and mode of subjectivity in the baroque is thus consistent with Freud's account of melancholic loss, insofar as the creators of *Trauerspiele* are not necessarily fully conscious of the loss that has been sustained and that is expressed in their production.

This unconscious nature of the loss is precisely what for Freud characterises melancholia: a sense of the loss of an unknown object. Indeed, as Freud outlines in his 1920 essay *Beyond the Pleasure Principle*, it is precisely the repression of a trauma that gives it its strength.[6] Thus, it lingers; and it lingers *as* melancholia, precisely in that the original loss is obscured, experienced instead as a nonspecific lack, a pervasive mood of sadness and emptiness. The mourning plays serve as a repository of this mood, an index of the melancholia of their age, and catalogue its specific manifestation or symptoms.

For Freud, melancholia is a temporary state, to be overcome by the ego once it has emerged victorious from an ambivalent struggle in the unconscious, finally knowing itself to be better than the lost object (SE14, 257–58). On Freud's account, melancholia will naturally come to an end, once its work has been accomplished. In this, it follows closely the accomplishment of the work of mourning—except that here, too, its end is often a swing into narcissism, an excessive self-love rather than the one that is "just right" to overcome the pull of the loss. The stability of the subject is thus revealed as a delicate balancing act, the boundaries between normal and pathological as not only thin, but constantly shifting. Indeed, if we follow the account outlined above, reading *Mourning and Melancholia* with the *Trauerspiel* book, the subject is the object that is always-already lost and simultaneously making an impossible demand on the individual—thus this struggle can never truly come to an end. The condition of mourning persists, its work never accomplished, for as long as humanity tries—and fails—to live up to subjecthood.

The baroque never attains the state, characteristic of Greek tragedy: the moment where the hero emerges as superior to the gods. Melancholia thus functions as a disavowal of the finite work of mourning, a steadfast refusal to give up the lost object. This is the attitude displayed in the mourning plays where, as Benjamin notes, while the religious answers may have lost their validity, the questions themselves had lost none of their power. Benjamin writes of mourning as "the state of mind in which feeling revives the emptied world in the form of a mask, and derives an enigmatic satisfaction in contemplating it . . . the theory of mourning, which emerged unmistakably as a *pendant* to the theory of tragedy, can only be developed in the description of that world which is revealed under the gaze of melancholy man" (OT, 139). What the melancholy gaze makes visible, then, is the impossibility of overcoming mourning in a world that is bound to the refusal of giving up the tragic mode even as the sociohistorical conditions of its existence have ceased to be. Tragedy and mourning function in the same realm, they have an end, a resolution, an ultimate return to an ethical community.

This social aspect is present in psychoanalysis, especially its early phase, as noted by Jutta Wiegmann. She states that during, in particular, the "cathartic" period of his early writings (1880–1895), Freud located present suffering exclusively in repressed traumatic events in the past, and later returns to the notion of catharsis (Wiegmann 1989, 36). At stake is the lessening of suffering, and ultimately the ability of the individual to function once more in a society of others.[7] Conversely, the mourning plays are precisely what their name indicates—a theatrical re-enactment of mourning, an attempt at tragedy that is bound to fail. They function in the realm of melancholy, where the revival and contemplation of the emptied world is endlessly drawn out.

The "revival" or "reanimation" of the emptied-out world in the form of a mask, then, is what plays out in the subjectivity of the fractured subject, much as for the later Freud in *Beyond the Pleasure Principle*, the ego serves as a shell, buffering from the shocks of the experience of modernity. The subject's supposed sovereignty functions as a mask for the emptiness of the baroque world and the fracture running through the early modern subject. It can thus be seen as on a par with other excessive ornamentation that is compulsively accumulated and heaped skywards, another feature of the mourning plays noted by Benjamin. This "enigmatic satisfaction" of which Benjamin writes can be made sense of with Freud's account of melancholia: in this state, the subject remains attached to the lost object in the reiteration of the feeling of loss, thus perversely prolonging its suffering in the attempt to ease it.[8] Stewart likewise notes that mourning, for Benjamin, serves as a "coping mechanism. It begins an idiosyncratically baroque attempt to re-master and re-intend the world. In it the subject confronts loss by recollecting 'reality' in bits and pieces and by re-building itself in constant dialogue with the objects that it must ultimately relinquish" (Stewart 2010, 37). However, this attempt is doomed to failure. As Monagle and Vardoulakis suggest in pointing to "the nothing at the core of sovereignty," the subject is ultimately hollow: "sovereign claims to authority are always grasping towards an illusory universality. They claim an always deferred higher power as a source of legitimacy" (Monagle and Vardoulakis 2003, 1). At the same time, the modern subject is fractured between the demand to act *as* a subject, that is, to be a coherent subject exerting its will on the world, and the impossibility of occupying such a position.

Thus the subject itself is a symptom—a representation of the loss of the concept of God as a guarantor of stable meaning, an uneasy representation that mimics and simultaneously marks the loss of an imagined fullness of experience. It indicates, too, the imaginary quality of that fullness itself: as Rebecca Comay (2005, 89–90) posits, "Melancholia would thus be a way of staging a dispossession of that which was never one's own to lose in the first place—and thus, precisely by *occluding structural lack as determinate loss*, would exemplify the strictly perverse effort to assert a *relation with the non-relational*" and asks "[c]ould perversion be the mark of the subject's impossible relationship to a loss which is ultimately not its own to acknowledge in the first place—but so too, equally, the index of a certain promise?" The latter part of Comay's question, the potential of melancholia to make visible in its perversion that there may be a "promise" or a possibility for a changed gaze that does away with the mask of subjectivity, will be explored in my final chapter. Of note is the process by which the theory of mourning is to be developed here: by working through the symptoms, the representations of the feeling of melancholy, from the standpoint of melancholia. This again draws the *Trauerspiel* book into proximity to Freud.

Benjamin continues his reflections on the enigmatic satisfaction of the contemplation of the masklike façade, the appearance of the empty world. As Judith Butler comments, "The world is revived in a masked form, in a masked way, not as a mask, but through a form of masking and as its result. The masking does not precisely conceal, since what is lost cannot be recovered, but it marks the simultaneous condition of an irrecoverable loss that gives way to a reanimation of an evacuated world" (Butler 2003, 471). This "marking" of an irrecoverable, ultimately unknowable loss is expressed as a symptom. It does not conceal; there is no "underneath" the mask, no recoverable content

that remains unchanged in the process of masking. Rather, it is an unconscious registering of a trauma, pointing to a caesura in whose aftermath the
world and the self are reconstituted, "reanimated" yet fractured, emptied out,
"evacuated" of the former fullness of meaning.

It is important to note that the perversion of subjectivity extends further
than melancholia—or, rather, that melancholia is not its only aspect. The
mask is revealed as that of the "Janus-faced sovereign" of the *Trauerspiel*,
displaying both the aspect of mourning and of acting out in rage. I will
develop the second of these twin aspects in relation to possession. As we shall
see, in possession, too, the "empty world" is revived in masked form, which
hints at an underlying pathology.

POSSESSION AND
THE LINGERING OF THE FRACTURED SUBJECT

In the book on German tragic drama, Benjamin radically historicises the
concept of the subject. As objects of history, concepts are passed on and
persist after the moment of their inauguration has passed. The fractured
subject of the baroque world, suspended perilously between the two poles of
the demand for decisive action and stable meaning and their impossibility,
nevertheless endures, but endures changes over the course of its development in modernity. Likewise, the attempt to construct meaning, an utterly
subjective endeavour in baroque allegoresis, is transformed with the development of capitalism, as I discuss in my next chapter.

What emerges forcefully in both Freud's *Mourning and Melancholia* and
Benjamin's book on German tragic drama is the porosity of the subject to
contents that are other to it. Its generation out of loss, its fracture, its emptiness, demand a constant attempt to be filled anew, through being possessed
or taking possession. In the baroque, this demand manifests in the form of
stylistic hyperornamentalisation in visual art, music, and drama. In the commodity world of nineteenth-century capitalism, Benjamin turns to in the
Arcades Project, a proliferation of material objects fulfils much the same
purpose. The baroque serves not only as prehistory for Benjamin's own day,
it does so by lingering into the nineteenth century. The accumulative drive
to fill the world with objects and to possess them is a way to attempt to
compensate for the haunting of capitalism at the moment of high modernity
by early modernity's loss of the fullness of life.

The change from the early modern period of the baroque to the high
modern one of the nineteenth-century and ultimately Benjamin's own day is
captured in Benjamin's first review from 1926 of Hugo von Hofmannsthal's

play "Der Turm," where Benjamin praises the play as a contemporary *Trauerspiel*. Benjamin sketches an image of a parabola, with creature and Christ as the two poles on either side and the prince at its apex, as characteristic of the "old," that is, baroque, *Trauerspiel*. In contrast, the new, contemporary *Trauerspiel* reserves no triumph for its hero: "Sigismund perishes. The demonic forces of the tower become his master. Dreams rise up from out of the earth, and the Christian heaven is long since vanished from them." (GS3, 33, transl. mine).[9] This stands in stark contrast to the possibility of divine intervention present in the works of baroque playwrights such as Calderon, identifying the baroque *Trauerspiel* as an ultimately Christian form, expressing how much the culture that produced it remained faithful to Christian cosmological horizons even as these were torn apart. In the nineteenth and twentieth century, even the ultimately unsuccessful appeal to this cosmology is overcome.

These themes are explored in Benjamin's 1921 "Capitalism as Religion." Here, he explores how the function of religion as emptied-out ritual is transposed to the economic sphere in capitalism, so that it comes to function as religion: "A religion may be discerned in capitalism—that is to say, capitalism serves essentially to allay the same anxieties, torments, and disturbances to which the so-called religions offered answers" (SW1, 288). The religious questions whose answers the baroque book reveals as insufficient are here answered by capitalism.[10] The text also establishes the opposition between the theological and the cultic, which is to remain throughout Benjamin's work and is manifest in later writings such as the *Arcades Project*: "In capitalism, things have meaning only in their relationship to the cult; capitalism has no specific body of dogma, no theology" (SW1, 288). It is thoroughly immanent, a religion emptied out of any reference to the transcendental, and thus the actually theological. Formerly a "parasite" of Christianity in Western culture, the economic formation of capitalism developed and grew "until it reached the point where Christianity's history is essentially that of its parasite—that is to say, of capitalism" (SW1, 289). Thus, the later development takes over the former in the transition from the baroque to high modernity in the universalisation of the commodity form, a development which was only beginning to emerge in early modernity.

Benjamin here also follows Nietzsche, the third figure he connects to the cult of capitalism. Moral guilt lays the groundwork for people capable of having debts—thus the "demonic ambiguity" of the concept itself hints at the entanglement of the cultic religious (Christianity) and the economic (capitalism) (SW1, 289). In the originary unfolding of capitalism, that out of which it developed, upon which it was parasitic, becomes a moment in its history.[11] Before moving on to a closer reading of this development, traced by Benjamin in the *Arcades*

Project, in the next section I will examine how the twin issues of melancholic loss and possession play out in Freud's 1923 case study "A Seventeenth-Century Demonological Neurosis" and his 1911 study of the Schreber case, "Psycho- analytic Notes on an Autobiographical Account of a Case of Paranoia (Dementia Paranoides)," from which Benjamin drew.

TWO CASE STUDIES: "A SEVENTEENTH-CENTURY DEMONOLOGICAL NEUROSIS"AND THE SCHREBER CASE

At stake in possession is a process similar to that at play in melancholia. Far from the strong delimitation of manic from melancholic states that is sometimes supposed, Eric Santner suggests in his book on the Schreber case that "Freud admits that his analysis of paranoid mechanisms do not sufficiently delimit them from other psychic disturbances in which libido is withdrawn from the world, such as occurs, for example, in mourning" (Santner 1996, 58). Santner observes that Freud uses similar language to define both paranoia and mourning: "In paranoia, thanks to a fixation point at the stage of narcissism, the free-floating libido withdrawn from the world becomes the source of a pathologically heightened secondary narcissism" (Santner 1996, 58). However, Freud remarks *a propos* of the Schreber case that "The mechanism of symptom- formation in paranoia requires that internal perceptions—feelings— shall be replaced by external perceptions" (SE12, 63). In this, we see a relationship of inside and outside, world and self in paranoia that is the inverse of that which occurs in melancholia—where the self absorbs everything in the latter, it is experienced as porous, penetrated by the world, in the symptomatology of the former. There is, then, good reason to consider melancholia and possession as two closely related responses to a similar trauma, while remaining attentive to the ways in which they differ.

"A SEVENTEENTH-CENTURY DEMONOLOGICAL NEUROSIS" (1923)

That possession and melancholia both function as responses to a loss becomes apparent in Freud's "A Seventeenth-Century Demonological Neurosis." The specific neurosis of possession Freud examines in the text is premised on the loss of the father of the painter Haitzmann, who in the aftermath of his bereavement falls into a deep depression, becoming unable to work. Haitzmann strikes a bargain with the devil, who pledges to replace his father for nine years, after which time the painter will entirely belong to him. Akin to melancholia, which on Freud's account can prolong and intensify mourning unduly, Haitzmann's fantasy of possession emerges from his mourning for his father. This may give rise to the conclusion "that the man had been attached to his father with an especially strong love, and we remember how often a severe melancholia appears as a neurotic form of mourning." This, Freud states, is correct. However, "we are not right if we conclude further that this relation has been merely one of love. On the contrary, his mourning over the loss of his father is the more likely to turn into melancholia, the more his attitude to him bore the stamp of ambivalence" (SE19, 87). As also posited in "Mourning and Melancholia," ambivalence towards the lost object is a key feature in the emergence of melancholia. Of note, too, is the fact that Haitzmann's case occurs in the same temporal context as the mourning plays and, as we shall see, exhibits the baroque condition.

This also links Haitzmann to Hamlet: In *The Interpretation of Dreams* (1900), Freud refers to Shakespeare's play in connection to Oedipus Rex. Freud is attentive to the historical difference between the two figures, suggesting that the repression operative in *Hamlet* was not present in antiquity. Freud thus draws a chronology not too dissimilar to that of Benjamin: a break occurs with the advent of the early modern era, that is, in the baroque. Hamlet's wish fantasy is visible only in its symptoms, that is, its "inhibiting consequences" (SE4, 264). Freud locates the source of this *Handlungshemmung* in what he later was to term the "Oedipus complex": the ambivalent relationship to his father grounded in his desire for his mother.[12] This is the reason "Hamlet is able to do anything—except take vengeance on the man who did away with his father and took that father's place with his mother, the man who shows him the repressed wishes of his own childhood realized" (SE4, 265). The conclusion to be drawn from his analysis is thus that Hamlet is a "hysteric" (SE4, 265). At the same time, Hamlet allows Freud to stress once again his theory that "though this be madness, yet there is method in't" (2.2.205)—Hamlet "had to disguise himself as a madman," in the sense that all psychopathology (among which Freud here numbers dreams) is ultimately a disfigured expression of "true circumstances" (SE5, 444).[13]

The text of the Haitzmann case study performs a curious double movement with regards to the question of the source of neuroses of possession, and thus of the relationship between psyche and world. Freud implicitly recognizes but suppresses their interconnectedness, as the point of the text is the translatability of earlier forms of accounting for what psychoanalysis sees as psychopathologies into its own register. At the same time, Freud states that what sets seventeenth-century notions of possession apart from neuroses as diagnosed by modern psychoanalysis is that the latter are contained within the psyche of the individual. The demons not only dwell in, but *emanate from*, the mind of the "ill," in the form of unconscious, repressed wishes and drives. What modern psychoanalysis rejects, Freud writes, is the projection of these "mental beings" into the outside world. In trying to account fully for early modern neuroses through the concepts of psychoanalysis, Freud thus goes one step further and denies a reciprocal relationship between the psyche and the world, positing instead a unidirectional move from the psyche of an individual outwards. We are confronted here with the issue of borders and boundaries and the porosity of the subject—both between the object-world it encounters and the historical other. These issues resurface later on in Freud's text in the form of the interlinking of historical and psychological processes, destabilising the notion that there is one easily identifiable source of neuroses.

Nevertheless, possession is experienced as an attack from without, a fantasy of being taken over by an other. More forcefully than melancholia, possession in the early modern era was seen as coming from outside, so much so that "The official liturgy of the Catholic Church itself insisted that exorcists must know the symptoms that distinguish a possessed person from other individuals who suffer from melancholia or any other illness" (Clark 1999, 394). With Benjamin's account of the baroque, we can read it as a response to a loss of original fulness—the loss of the unity of God and the world—a pathological way the shadow of primary narcissism resurfaces in a psychoanalytic register. It fills the gap between how the self and the world are experienced (as not full, lacking) and the demands of subjectivity, *itself* a response to a loss.

Like the baroque sovereign/subject, Haitzmann's melancholia manifests as the inability to carry out the task he is called upon to perform—to work, and thus ensure his ongoing survival. Freud posits the fantasy of demonic possession as Haitzmann's attempt to solve this inability to work—if the loss of his father, the original cause for his catatonia, is cancelled out by being filled with a new father figure, perhaps his ability to act will return. Freud then turns to the most puzzling aspect revealed by his analysis: How is it that the devil can become a possible object of transference for filial love? Freud offers up the ambivalence experienced towards the father, and any father figure, as an answer. He proceeds to discuss that the feminisation of the devil in Haitzmann's neurosis can be explained by the repressed desires to both bear his father a child and be nurtured by him.

THE SCHREBER CASE

This links the Haitzmann case to that of Daniel Paul Schreber, a prominent jurist whose delusions sexualized his relationship to God.[14] Bearing, as Freud notes, strong resemblance to Schreber's father, this God was to procreate with Schreber in order to raise a new, superior species of humans. Freud describes the process of transference in which the lost relationship with the father or brother—the latter himself being a "surrogate"—is recreated in that with Schreber's doctor, and ultimately projected onto God. As in Haitzmann's case, the ambivalence of the relationship to the father figure, be it Schreber's biological father or God, comes to the fore here, this time in the doubling and splitting Schreber performs with regards to both God and his stand- in, his doctor Flechsig. Where Haitzmann veils his identification of God and the father further by disfiguring or displacing it onto the devil, Schreber's delusion takes the form of a more straightforward identification, but via the intermediary of his doctor, and the attribution of quasi-demonic traits to this God-figure.

Schreber attributed his paranoid episodes to the stress associated with his appointment to posts of increasing responsibility. As Santner (1996, xiii) notes: "Schreber made his discoveries at the very moment he entered, by way of a symbolic investiture, one of the key centres of power and authority in Wilhelmine Germany, the Saxon Supreme Court." Unable to deal with the demands of his office, he lapses into delusion. This links Schreber's case to that of the baroque sovereign, who, faced with the tension between his creaturely, finite existence and the exalted demands of his political position, becomes unable to make a decision and refracts into the martyr/tyrant. The sovereign, robbed of the originary father figure, God, becomes inactive and despondent.[15] Just as the sovereign expresses the suffering and melancholy of his age, Schreber's "discoveries were grounded in an intuition that his symptoms were, so to speak, symptomatic, that they were a form of knowledge concerning profound malfunctions in those politico-theological procedures that otherwise sustain the very ontological consistency of what we call the 'world'" (Santner 1996, xiii). It is also in this way Freud's case studies of Haitzmann's seventeenth-century demonological neurosis and of nineteenth-century judge Schreber relate to Benjamin's sovereign/subject of the baroque: Encapsulated in possession is an aspiration to, as Freud was to write of the hysteric, become the representative not just of a self, but of all of humanity. As Stuart Clark (1999, 393) observes in his study of witchcraft and possession, in the early modern era,

Possession was interpreted as an eschatological sign and exorcism (in the Catholic rite) as an enactment of the promises of Revelation. The stages through which the history of a case passed—from the loosing of devils to possess, to their binding to pronounce and depart—were seen as analogous to those which regulated the course of history in its entirety. Conversely, the experience of demoniacs was seen as a kind of allegory for the condition of human society as it moved into its final phase; in this state, the whole world was (as Pierre Viret put it) "possessed by devils."

Possession thus functioned as a kind of spectacle; an enactment, a dramatisa-
tion, a staging of the course of human history and its hope for redemption.
Thus, possession signifies also an attempt to become like the sovereign in
this respect: the representative of humanity. Such, too, is Schreber's quasi-
messianic delusion—he is to save humanity via his suffering. Like the baroque
sovereign, Schreber embodies and expresses the suffering of his age. Schreber links himself and his condition explicitly to Hamlet—as Santner points
out, he quotes his lines that "'*there is something rotten in Denmark*' . . . to
indicate the extent of the corruption of the normal relationship between God
and himself as well as the physical states of decomposition that were among the
byproducts of that disordered relation" (Santner 1996, 6). Schreber's delusions
of being dead and decaying fit into this pattern too: "The metaphors Schreber
uses to evoke this literal and figurative rottenness strongly resonate with the
terms with which a general sense of decay, degeneration, and enervation were
registered in fin-de-siècle social and cultural criticism" (Santner 1996, 6).
Thus, the demonic possessions outlined in "Schreber's *Memoirs* [1903] attempt to bring into a narrative and theological system the crisis of authority—
the *rottenness* in the state of Denmark, the breach in the Order of the World"
(Santner 1996, 37). The malaise of the baroque sovereign-subject persists into
modernity, transposed into the world of professionalism.

In his "Books by the Mentally Ill" (1928), Benjamin notes the modernity
of Schreber's text, where knowledge of technology, specifically railways,
is projected onto the divine. The modernity of Schreber's psychopathology
is also apparent in Freud's reference to the testimony of one of Schreber's
doctors: Schreber comes to terms with his heightened sensitivity to light and
sound, his perception of being already dead, his feeling of being submitted
to manipulations at the hand of something alien, by compensating for it with
the delusion that all of this serves a higher, sacred purpose. As Benjamin
notes, Schreber's perception of other people is consistent with this: "The
idea of the end of the world, not uncommon among paranoids, obsesses
him to such a degree that he can conceive of other people's existence only
as a frivolous delusion. To enable him to come to terms with it, his writings abound in references to 'casually improvised men,' 'miracle dolls,'
people who have been 'magicked away'" (SW4, 124). Scholem (1981, 71)
notes the impression Schreber's formulation of the "*flüchtig hingemachten
Männer*," here translated as "fleeting-improvised-men," made on Benjamin.
No longer proof of the existence of a world exterior to the subject, these rushed,
artificial creations are met with distrust; but so is Schreber's own subjectivity.
At stake is the condition of post-baroque suffering of the fractured subject in
high modernity: As Santner writes, "Schreber experienced what threatened
his rights/rites of institution under a number of different 'ideological' signs:

as a feminization not always reducible to homosexualization; as the threat of contamination by machine-like, depersonalized linguistic operations; as the prospect of 'Jewification' (metamorphosis into the Wandering Jew)" (Santner 1996, 55). Schreber's "own private Germany," Santner's term for Schreber's response to these threats, "consists of his attempts, using the available repertoire of cultural values and valences, to interpret and to assign meaning to a maddening blockage in meaning that prevented him from assuming his place as a master of juridical hermeneutics and judgment" (Santner 1996, 55). In other words, Schreber's paranoid delusions function as a response to the fracture of the subject in the aftermath of the loss of universally valid theological truth.

A CRISIS OF THE MASCULINE SUBJECT

The fixation on emasculation and an experience of sexual fluidity, experienced as threatening by both Haitzmann and Schreber, is no coincidence. As Santner puts it, "In a certain sense, Schreber's *Memoirs* could be seen as an attempt to answer the question implicit in this list of pathologies: *What remains of virility* at the end of the nineteenth and beginning of the twentieth century?" (Santner 1996, 9).[16] In the Haitzmann case study, Freud also points to the prevalence of this particular form of neurosis in his own age, grounded in a simultaneous fear of and fascination with the loss of masculinity. Such "masculine protest" expresses an unresolved conflict between "masculine and feminine attitudes (fear of castration and a desire for castration)" (SE19, 92), torn, then between the fear of the loss of male power and the wish to be relieved of its burden. In both Schreber's and Haitzmann's delusions, femininity is equated with (sexual) passivity. Masculinity *itself* remains intact, is impenetrable, thus both Schreber and Haitzmann have to become women if they are to be used by God/the father. What Freud terms the "feminine attitude to the father" (SE19, 91) common to both can be read, in its passivity, as a reaction against the demands of—male—subjectivity.

As I discuss in the following chapters, Benjamin was alert to the way this anxiety about masculinity played out in high modernity in the figure of Baudelaire and in fears over femininity linked to death. Of particular interest in this context is Benjamin's pronouncement in "Central Park" (1939) that "It belongs to the Via Dolorosa of male sexuality that Baudelaire regarded pregnancy as a kind of unfair competition" (SW4, 173). Like Schreber, who solved the problem of remaining heirless in imagining himself as the incubator of a future humanity engendered by God, and like Haitzmann, who imagined himself impregnated by the devil-father, Baudelaire's is a specifically masculine psychopathology centred on reproductive/estational capacity, or the lack thereof. Schreber ties the ability to reproduce to a yearning for death, and redemption, exemplified in his feeling that "enormous numbers of 'female nerves' have already passed over into his body, and out of them a new race of men will proceed, through a process of direct impregnation by God. Not until then, it seems, will he be able to die a natural death, and, along with the rest of mankind, will he regain a state of bliss" (SE12, 17). We see here the inauguration of the death drive of the subject expressed in the desire to be redeemed in the moment of creaturely, biological reproduction. At the same time, a way to make the thoroughgoing immanence of life—its creatureliness, lacking in all transcendence—sacred once more is thus opened up precisely in the profane reproductive act.[17]

THE AFTERMATH OF THE DIVINE

Common to the sovereign, to Haitzmann, and to Schreber is an ambivalence characteristic of the relationship to God. Given Benjamin's diagnosis in the book on German tragic drama, we might reformulate the complexes of all three as responding to the question "What happens after God dies?" Melancholia, protracted mourning, is thus recast as a *"nachträglicher Gehorsam,"*[18] retrospective obedience, and its obverse, a continuation of the ambivalent relationship with the father figure, culminating in the denigration of God as punishment for his abandonment of modern man—bearing all the features of the relationship to, and mourning for, the father as described by Freud.

Indeed, Schreber casts his paranoid delusions in the grandiose terms of a struggle with God, from which he emerges triumphantly: "From this apparently unequal struggle between one weak man and God Himself, I have emerged as the victor—though not without undergoing much bitter suffering and privation—because the Order of Things [*Weltordnung*] stands upon my side" (SE12, 19).[19] This is then a further compensatory dimension to Schreber's paranoia: the suffering of the post-baroque condition is recast as a victorious, triumphant affect. Freud and Benjamin both note that Schreber's peculiar theological system, where God can approach humanity only in the form of corpses, gives us a glimpse into the destiny of the divine in the aftermath of the devaluation of religious answers: far from elevating humanity in a redemptive gesture, God is no longer adequate to living humans and can deal only with the dead. However, the victorious emergence of the subject from this struggle is not to last long. As Freud notes, Schreber was "'the only real man left alive,' and the few human shapes that he still saw— the doctor, the attendants, the other patients—he explained as being 'miracled up, cursorily improvised men'" (SE12, 68). Elias Canetti (1978, 448) links this survivorship to a sadistic, and indeed narcissistic drive in Schreber that speaks of a pathological "will to power":

> Schreber is left as the sole survivor because this is what he himself wants. He wants to be the only man left alive, standing in an immense field of corpses; and he wants this field of corpses to contain all men but himself. It is not only as a paranoiac that he reveals himself here. To be the last man to remain alive is the deepest urge of every seeker after power.

On this reading, Schreber's delusion "in which the ego was retained and the world sacrificed" (SE12, 69) again points to the narcissistic tendency inherent in the demand of subjectivity: its reach always pointing beyond the self, striving to either annihilate the world outright or annihilate it in absorbing it into the self. In this apocalyptic fantasy, Schreber expresses the characteristic mood of the nineteenth century, just as the baroque sovereign is emblematic of the suffering of his own age. As we shall see in the following chapters, many of the elements of his delusions appear in Benjamin's study of nineteenth-century Paris in the *Arcades Project*, where melancholia is transformed into spleen, with an attendant sense of history as an ongoing catastrophe, and individuality is a semblance erected in the face of the increasing massification in cities. The fleeting nature of experience in modernity is mirrored in Schreber's sense of hasty, provisional human beings who are not "real" in the sense of being full subjects.

Despite his victory over God and the rest of humanity, the sense of not being an autonomous subject with intact boundaries is painfully experienced by Schreber himself. He describes his life as an ongoing survival of torturous physical maiming and dismemberment, his organs subject to destruction and miraculous reconstruction at the hands of God. This constant process of divine restitution following mortification of his body results in his immortality—as long as he remains a man, Schreber cannot die. All his bodily processes have become directed by miracles. He is directly animated by the divine, taken out of the context of the world and its laws and subject to direct, unmediated intervention by God in every aspect of his biological life. His most creaturely, bodily processes are themselves guided by constant divine intervention, while Schreber is under a "thinking compulsion" in order to prove to God at every moment his mental or psychic activity.[20] Thus, Schreber solves the dilemma of the baroque sovereign-subject by elevating the creaturely *itself* to the sacred by way of his psychopathology, aiming to restore its theological dimension. Here, the fractured, empty post-baroque subject is literally filled anew—with God himself.[21]

This conceptualisation of the relationship between self and God bears striking resemblance to Benjamin's account of the sovereign in the *Trauerspiele*, who "in conformity to the occasionalist image of God, is constantly intervening directly in the workings of the state so as to arrange the data of the historical process in a regular and harmonious sequence" (OT, 97). Not only is Schreber subject to divine intervention at his most creaturely, this also happens as a way to reaffirm the order of the world.

Schreber, incapable of carrying out his task as a judge adequately—that is, to come to decisions—resolves his inner tension by succumbing to God's commands. The religious, the absolute will of God, is appealed to precisely at the moment where personal will fails political office, and both are revealed as inadequate. What these case studies make visible, if read in conjunction with Benjamin's book on German tragic drama, is the condition of the post-baroque subject and the untenability of sovereignty and ultimately subjectivity itself, also intimated in the work of Freud. Subjectivity itself is revealed to be a fantasy of possession, an attempt to gain a fulness of being in the absence of God. The nineteenth-century subject fails to provide a stable signifier around which to construct itself; there is, in fact, nothing transcendental about it, it is, like the baroque age, fully immanent.

Meanwhile, Freud diagnoses that what is ultimately at stake in Haitzmann's psychopathology is the wish to secure his material existence. The creaturely aspect, his material need and dependence on society for his ongoing survival are heightened in his delusions and transposed into a theological register, manifesting as struggles over his soul between the devil and God. In the end, the latter wins: Haitzmann enters a religious order, which, as Freud notes, lays both his inner turmoil and his material struggles to rest. Religion as something that, at its etymological root, is a binding together (*religare*) was to offer Haitzmann the means to remain bound to a community, and to life. Freud concludes with an acknowledgment that at the heart of this demonological neurosis was a battle for individual survival, culminating in the struggle to accept the renunciation of his desires, his libidinal lust for life, and the acceptance of the ascetic lifestyle to which the monastic order would compel him. However, this renunciation remained perilous—as Freud notes, Haitzmann was repeatedly subject to temptation by the devil, especially when drunk—able to avert him each time only "by the grace of God" (SE19, 78). This formulation is to be taken literally in Haitzmann's case—again and again, he restaged the battle for his soul, in a way that reassured him of God's ongoing presence. Thus the religious answers, which for Benjamin lost their validity after the reformation and the religious wars of the early modern era, were to provide only an uneasy answer for Haitzmann. Schreber, hallucinating at a later point in time, creates a highly subjective system of psychopathology that nevertheless expresses something essential about his age. Where Haitzmann still had a common religious symbolism at his disposal, Schreber has to resort to a novel and convoluted expression. Nevertheless, he also draws on ancient symbolisms, as in the case of the sun-god—his pathology, encompassing both modern technologies and mythic *Urgeschichte*, is thus typical of the nineteenth century.

TAKING POSSESSION OF THE OTHER

The complement of this compensation for a loss in the form of possession by an other is the taking possession *of* an other in a narcissistic gesture of subsumption. For Freud, the ambivalence displayed to the devil-father by Haitzmann is characteristic of the relationship to the ultimate father figure, God, and unearths the source of this ambivalent tension: The gods of antiquity contained a good/evil dualism within themselves, which was subsequently split into God and his obverse in Christianity. In his analysis of Schreber, Freud recognizes this process of splitting as a psychological, but also a historical one. He links the Manichean worldview of good and evil in Christianity to historical processes of conquest and ensuing cultural change. For Freud, the gods of the conquered attain demonic traits over time and become reviled. Benjamin shares Freud's awareness of this process, and his writings show clear traces of Freud's "Notes on a Case of Paranoia." Referring to the "gnostic-manichean doctrine" according to which the world is destined to take the demonic into itself, he writes in the *Trauerspiel* book how "scorning all emblematic disguise, the undisguised visage of the devil can raise itself up from out of the depths of the earth into the view of the allegorist, in triumphant vitality and nakedness," and notes that "[i]t was only in the middle ages that these sharp, angular features were etched in the originally greater demonic head of antiquity" (OT, 227). The process of the demonisation of pagan Antiquity in the Middle Ages is mirrored in the valorisation of Classical culture in the Renaissance and baroque. Crucially, for Freud this historical process of ambivalent splitting is mirrored in the psychological one. Freud thus alerts us to the presence of the other at the heart of European Christianity, as well as to the homology between psyche and world. Freud often alludes to the relationship of cultural-historical development (phylogenesis) and individual development (ontogenesis) as analogous. "Primitive society" appears in his texts to illustrate points about the development of the psyche towards greater complexity of social organization, and thus greater repression. For Freud, there is thus a remainder, a remnant of the past and traumatic experience in particular that lingers and informs later moments of history as well as individuals.[22]

For Benjamin, of course, these remainders are also present: as ruin, distorted in their form, necessarily incomplete and fragmented. As allegories are to thoughts, material ruins are to the "realm of things." In the book on German tragic drama, Benjamin states that in ruins, human history is physically merged into the natural setting (OT 177–78)—the ruin functions as a nexus between human history and nature which points to the limits of autonomous, willed action, and thus of the sovereign subject. Just as for Freud the atavistic past, personal and world-historical, appears time and again at the level of the individual, calling its power over itself into question just as surely as the id does within Freud's second topography of 1923, Benjamin's ruins destabilise the present and the subject within it. Ruins, too, point to an other that came before, an other that must be dealt with somehow—accounted for, absorbed, destroyed. Benjamin was to write in his last text, "On the Concept of History" (1940), that "[t]here is no document of culture which is not at the same time a document of barbarism. And just as such a document is never free of barbarism, so barbarism taints the manner in which it was transmitted from one hand to another" (SW4, 392).

This insight is already at play in his book on the German mourning plays, where the subsumption of Greek culture in the baroque is described as a most violent act. Here, baroque interpretation "penetrates" antiquity in what Benjamin terms a "gesture of submission," a gesture which functions as a guarantor of the authority of the new era, confirming the "power of the present" is the medium of the past. Hence, it "regarded its own forms as 'natural,' not so much the antithesis, as the conquest and elevation of its rival" (OT, 100). A teleology is presupposed by the baroque's self-understanding as the heir of Antiquity. Benjamin here reveals this historiographical notion of an unbroken line running from Ancient Greece into Renaissance Europe as a fantasy, covering up a real act of historical violence—an act which, if we read it with the statement from "On the Concept of History," commits further violence itself in passing on this tradition.[23] This allows us to relate the supposedly high regard in which Renaissance and baroque culture hold "the Classics" to the process of the over-valorisation of the murdered father by his descendants that Freud was to outline in *Moses and Monotheism* (1939). Benjamin's account, however, goes one step further than Freud's: for him, antiquity is only *imagined* to be a murdered father, and a further gesture of violence is enacted in this imagining: The baroque may not recognise this, repurposing it as an "origin," but it has subsumed its "rival," antiquity, in a violent fashion. Far from a mimetic naturalism, its forms, such as the *Trauerspiele*, are the result of the process of historical change, an ultimately unsuccessful incorporation of the past other into the present. Following this account, we can read Benjamin's writings on his own time as a commentary on the catastrophic results of the attempt to make everything subject to the self; to subject every other to the subject. Benjamin's writing thus traces the precursors of twentieth-century fascism to the nineteenth century and the baroque, connecting it through the Renaissance of European culture with its "shackling" of Greece to the triumphal procession of early European modernity. What we see in Freud and Benjamin is the subsumption and ostensible valorisation of cultural and historic others as two sides of the same coin: the killing of the other, which is then readmitted and venerated as an "ancestor." This opens up an additional perspective on baroque melancholia. It finds its ground not just in the wretchedness of its own age, with the loss of the certainty of the undivided truth of Christianity. Hidden beneath that lies a deeper, more obscured history of the killing and cannibalisation of the pagan other that preceded it. The totalising reach of subjectivity in its ultimate form—narcissism—can thus be linked in both Freud and Benjamin to historical processes of conquest and ensuing cultural change, notably the absorption of pagan gods into Christianity. For Benjamin, as we have seen, allegory emerges in the baroque as a new form of accounting for the tension between the image of heroic antiquity of the Renaissance and the demonic side revived in the Middle Ages. The baroque embodies the tension not just between the Christian and the pagan, but between their tradition and revival in the Middle Ages, the Renaissance, and the Counter-Reformation. What is at stake for Benjamin, conversely, is a kind of grasping for a materialist understanding of history—unsurprisingly perhaps; it is often forgotten that *One-Way Street* (1928), usually counted amongst Benjamin's "materialist" writings, was written at the same time as the book on German tragic drama. As Benjamin writes *a propos* the *Trauerspiel* book in a 1931 letter to Max Rychner: "This book, of course, was certainly not materialistic, even if it was dialectical. But what I did not know at the time I wrote it, soon thereafter became increasingly clear to me: namely, there is a bridge to the way dialectical materialism looks at things . . . But there is no bridge to the complacency of bourgeois scholarship" (C, 372). Crucially, Benjamin moves the focus away from individual creative genius, which as Pensky points out, "the genuine theological impulse that underlies the emergence of melancholia as a mode of creativity is not the schema of the individual at all, but rather consists of the development of a relationship between subjectivity as such and the physiognomy of its object realm" (Pensky 1993, 104).[24] Concretely, it is in the cultural form most emblematic of the baroque, the mourning plays as a genre, that "*Trauer*, intense mournfulness, penetrates through the model of the autonomous contemplative genius, and in this depersonalization points toward the image of the thinker too as merely one form of earthly mass" (Pensky 1993, 104–5). Indeed, as Benjamin notes in the fragment "Das Heidentum ist eine dämonische Gemeinschaft" (Paganism is a demonic community): "Paganism arises when the sphere of the genius-like human quality . . . is elevated to the sphere of spirituality itself, to demoniccommunity"[25] (GS6, 90, transl. mine)—for Benjamin, the genius cannot rid himself of the demonic, and insofar as the subject is enjoined to act as a genius, it, too, must fall back into the mythic. Left unchecked—unanalysed—these primitive contents will, for Benjamin following Freud, continue to resurface in distorted form. I will now investigate the question of psychopathology as an attempt to resolve this traumatic resurfacing of past forms in its appeal to theology and transcendence.

POWER, MADNESS—TRUTH?

In his short text "Books by the Mentally Ill," Benjamin sees the link between the items in his "little library of pathology" in "the elaboration of a theological cosmology, which encompasses an enormous range of perverse and imaginative permutations of the relations between the human, the cosmos, and the divine," as Caygill (2016, 150) puts it. We can add Freud's Haitzmann case to this list: In both the Schreber and the Haitzmann cases, what is at stake is not merely psychology, but also theology. Both neuroses revolve around religious symbols and the interplay of divine forces, too great a burden to bear for the fledgling subject, invaded by both God and the devil. At stake too is the question of political authority in the wake of the baroque downfall of divine authority and its aftermath. Given the failure of God, and of the sovereign, to provide a stable centre of meaning and authority, who can posit the law, inaugurate or end the state of exception?

These issues lead Santner to connect the Schreber case to Benjamin's early text "Critique of Violence" (1921) via Benjamin's review of Schreber in "Books by the Mentally Ill," "as a displaced meditation on Schreber's encounter with the force or violence immanent to law, with the 'state of exception' internal to the regulation of bodies and identities in society" (Santner 2001, 56). Benjamin's "Critique" unveils the rule of law as existing "without ultimate justification or legitimation . . . the very space of juridical reason within which the rule of law obtains is established and sustained by a dimension of force and violence that, as it were, holds the place of those missing foundations" (Santner 2001, 57). This is consistent with Benjamin's position in the *Trauerspiel* book, where he notes that the bipolarity of the sovereign, fractured into two distinct characters in the form of the tyrant and the martyr in most of the plays, is untenable once the juridical aspect of baroque sovereignty is taken into account: "The theory of sovereignty which takes as its example the special case in which dictatorial powers are unfolded, positively demands the completion of the image of the sovereign, as tyrant" (OT, 69). Juridical power has a tendency towards the tyrannical extreme, just as, we might add, the subject has a tendency towards a return to narcissism. Benjamin's "Books by the Mentally Ill" not only provides a link between the texts of his collection, but also connects them to Benjamin's own writing. He opens his brief study with a taxonomical conundrum of his own: how to classify these books, while then pointing to the pathology of *Gruppier-ungswahn*, the compulsion to classify. The detailed taxonomies drawn up in these books, for Benjamin, points to a similarity of nineteenth-century epistemologies to the mode of knowing of mental illness. The fact of the publication of these texts, Benjamin says, has something "disconcerting" about it—destabilising the notion of writing as "part of a higher, safer realm" (SW2.1, 130). Benjamin concludes the text with the words "If this brief essay should arouse interest in it, and if these all too brief excerpts could stimulate the reader to turn his attention to the posters and leaflets of the insane, then these lines would have fulfilled a twofold purpose" (SW2.1, 130). Benjamin ranges himself among the mad, hinging on the impossibility of finding a publisher for his book on German tragic drama—the very text in which he discusses the mad sovereign of the baroque, melancholia, and the pathology of subjectivity. Thus, Benjamin positions his text alongside the production of the mentally ill writers of his collection and indeed calls into question the divide between writing, judging, and knowing on the one hand, and the constructions of the "mad" on the other.[26]

This, then, is also the locus of the re-emergence of the question of truth. Freudian psychoanalysis provides reality-testing and the psychoanalytic relationship between analyst and analysand as tools to relate psychopathology to truth. However, Santner complicates this picture by adding the figure of the analyst into the chronology of post-baroque sovereign-subjects: "the analyst, like the classical monarch, has two bodies; the analyst's second, call it 'sublime' body, is produced—and produces, in turn, analytical and therapeutic effects—to the extent that the analysand posits the analyst as a subject with special knowledge of one's deepest desires and secrets" (Santner 1996, 25). Thus, he concludes that "Freud's attraction to and passion for the Schreber material was above all a function of his own deep involvement with the 'rites of institution' at a moment of significant crisis—one might even say at a moment of 'signification crisis'—within the institution of psychoanalysis" (Santner 1996, 26). Not only does the analyst draw close to the analysand, the reverse process occurs, too—and it, too, is historically contingent.

In a similar vein, Benjamin, writing on Schreber's memoirs, notes that "references to the 'countermeaning of primal words,' a theme treated sporadically by Freud, also appear in this remarkable document. 'Juice' is called 'poison,' 'poison' is called 'food,' 'reward' is called 'punishment,' and

so on" (SW2.1, 124).[27] Strikingly, Schreber's idiosyncratic schizophrenic
language seems to be following the findings of psychoanalysis.[28] Freud,
too, notes such similarity in Schreber's account of "divine rays," which are
in reality nothing else than a "concrete representation and projection outwards of libidinal cathexes" (SE12, 78): "these and many other details of
Schreber's delusional structure sound almost like endopsychic perceptions
of the processes whose existence I have assumed in these pages as the basis
of our explanation of paranoia" (SE12, 79). We can perhaps make sense of
this if, with Freud, we view Schreber's paranoia as an attempt at a cure. For
Freud recognizes that in the constructions of psychopathology, "the paranoiac
builds [the world] again, not more splendid, it is true, but at least so that he
can once more live in it. He builds it up by the work of his delusions. The
delusion-formation, which we take to be the pathological product, is in reality
an attempt at recovery, a process of reconstruction"(SE12, 70).[29] This links
Schreber to the "enigmatic satisfaction," the result of the masklike revival of
the empty world in mourning described in the *Trauerspiel* book,[30] where just
such a reconstruction of the world is attempted (OT, 139).

For Schreber, part of the attempt to regain his freedom from confinement
in psychiatric institutions was the publication of his memoirs. In sharing his
reconstruction with the world, he was not, as Freud notes, denying his psychopathology: Schreber emphasized "the importance of his ideas to religious
thought, and . . . their invulnerability to the attacks of modern science" (SE12,
16). For Schreber, delusion has become its own religion, its own truth-giver,
and its own therapy. This, then, is the complement to the melancholic revival
of the emptied-out world: it is revived, but, as Freud notes, "Such a reconstruction after the catastrophe is successful to a greater or lesser extent, but
never wholly so . . . the human subject has recaptured a relation, and often
a very intense one, to the people and things in the world, even though the
relation is a hostile one now" (SE12, 70–71). As in Benjamin's account of
baroque melancholia, this masking remains visible *as* a masking, and as a
marking: of the loss, different to its previous state, and lacking in comparison to
it. Such gestures also find an echo in Benjamin's *One-Way Street* (1928), where
in "To the Planetarium" the First World War is described as "an attempt at a
new and unprecedented commingling with the cosmic powers" (SW1, 486)—
an appeal to a revival of a pre-modern fullness of experience in catastrophic
form. At the same time, as Irving Wohlfarth (2002, 80) points out, "what *Zum
Planetarium* attempts to do—and actually, rhetorically, performs—is to span
the great world-historical divide that separates cosmogony from cosmology,
astrology from astronomy, myth from enlightenment, *Gemeinschaft* from
Gesellschaft, and thereby to heal the rift on which the modern world is built."

Where for Freud individual improvement of symptoms is the chief aim of analysis—however unstable and thus subject to an infinite process both may be—matters are thus even less straightforward for Benjamin. Pensky draws attention to the precarity of the position of the critical subject in relation to objective truth in Benjamin's early work. He suggests that Benjamin's "refusal to speculate on the role of subjectivity in the critical process" is grounded in his "reluctance to incorporate idealist philosophical baggage into an exploration of the metaphysical structure of truth, which, as he had been convinced from very early on, was objectively present and objectively discoverable in the phenomena themselves" (Pensky 1993, 61). Benjamin, Pensky suggests, transcends the impulse to expunge late idealism, embarking on what was to be a lifelong endeavour: the attempt to make visible, through the "right" critique, an objective truth already residing in the historical object, together with a wariness of the pitfalls of subjective speculation. The difficulty with this endeavour is already sketched out in the conclusion from the prologue to the *Trauerspiel* book, where "the discovery of (divine) meaning is distinguished from the imposition of (allegorical) meaning only by fiat" (Pensky 1993, 73). Pensky charts the tensions in Benjamin's concept of the critic as a conduit of "truth" from his early work to the *Trauerspiel* book, where the question of the critical subject and its objects reveal themselves as the problem of melancholia. Melancholia in the mourning plays thus serves as the dialectical mediation between subject and object, avoiding the pitfalls of the heroic individualism of the Kantian genius, "a process in which both 'objective' elements of a concrete world and dimensions of innermost subjectivity fuse and intertwine, illuminating in the process the theological grounds upon which the text, and indeed the very concepts of subjectivity and objectivity, originate" (Pensky 1993, 87). This "origin," as Pensky notes, is not about tracing a phenomenon back to its source, but precisely those "moments in which this same process is disrupted and crystallizes, monadically, into an image in which the entire course of historical happening lies encoded" (Pensky 1993, 87). Pensky acknowledges that this process of fusion in the melancholy gaze and the world is less than smooth: "the question concerning the critical subject, that is, whether the critic himself must be a melancholic, or whether this is just a vestige of historicism and demands the strict suppression of any 'subjective' states or temperaments by the critic, remains here wholly unanswered" (Pensky 1993, 94). Similar problems plague Benjamin's art historical categories. Benjamin's distinction between symbol and allegory parallels that between tragedy and *Trauerspiel*; the theological distinctions between both sets of poles refer back to the tension between myth and history. The aestheticisation of the essentially theological role of symbols is, for Benjamin, problematic, in that it makes exaggerated claims about the

artwork's ability to capture eternal (divine) "truth value," and simultaneously consigns allegory to the status of a deficient symbol, unsuccessful in
this grand venture. In reality, "just as the symbol bears indelible traces of its
own mythic origin, so allegory, dispersed into historical happening, comes to
acquire a petrifying power capable of 'blasting apart myth'" (Pensky 1993,
113). Benjamin's theory of art and art criticism in the *Trauerspiel* book re-
volves around the visibility of the immanent truth content of the object of criticism, which "should do nothing else than uncover the secret predisposition
of the work itself, complete its hidden intentions" (OT, 35). This language
of the work's "secret," the process of hiding, links this passage to Freud's
writing on the unconscious, which according to his records Benjamin had
read by the time he was writing *On the Origin of German Tragic Drama*. As
we have seen, such truth shines through in particular in the imperfect forms
of an age, in the expression of a generalised suffering in the production—of
fantasies, of texts—of psychopathology. Nevertheless, the critic too can fall
back into subjectivity through the imposition of his own subjective meaning
rather than an uncovering of the objective truth, and a "making absolute"
of the work itself. The question thus remains what happens to truth when
cultural forms, such as the baroque *Trauerspiele,* reflect and express the
symptoms of their age without finding resolution in analysis—and indeed,
when the tools of the analyst are not infallible.

This is precisely the moment where historical legibility comes into play,
for both Freud and Benjamin. For Freud, Haitzmann's neurosis is legible because we are so far removed from the objects of his fantasies that they seem
simple and easy to decode. For Benjamin, as we have seen, these unconscious
contents reside not just in historical "case studies" of the possessed or otherwise mentally ill, but are equally preserved in art and other cultural artefacts,
awaiting their analysis and deciphering by an "analyst" at a later date. Freud's
position is thus close to that of Benjamin, in that historical distance can be a
factor in cognition—we can know the neuroses of the past better now than
we could then. However, as I discuss in my last chapter, this is by no means
a straightforwardly linear development for Benjamin—the "flash of recognition" strikes only at a particular point in time, drawing together a specific
past and present moment into a constellation. As Stewart (2010, 84) states in
relation to the *Arcades Project*, "Benjamin made it his task to document as
well as explode the cocoon-like slumber of the nineteenth century by way of
reading and re-inscription processes and to recover the intricacies of linking
that constitute the experience of truly waking life. He saw such faculties as
individual defenses against fascist manipulation and fascistic narcissism."
However, as I discuss in my final chapter, what is at stake for Benjamin is
not merely an individual, but a collective awakening from the dream-sleep

of capitalism. Where Schreber escapes the thrall of the narcissism of fascism only through a withdrawal into an idiosyncratic system of psychopathology, his attempt to remain a subject in a world of his own construction costing him the world as it is, Benjamin is ultimately searching for a non-pathological, and thus, as we shall see, political, overcoming of the impasses of modernity.[31] In the following section, I will examine some of Benjamin's strategies for the distillation of truth beyond the sway of the mythic.

THE CRITIC, THE ANALYST, THE BAD NEW THINGS

For Freud, psychoanalysis has a pedagogic function for the analyst: he can safeguard against the subjectivist tendency towards censorship and partiality of memory only by undergoing analysis himself. It renders him capable of recognising potential blind spots and educates him to avoid them, in order to listen with the attitude of free-floating disinterestedness crucial to the analytic situation. For Freud, this attitude can and must be cultivated. In his 1912 "Recommendations to Physicians Practising Psycho-analysis," he also has strong words of warning for those who would begin analysing patients without undergoing analysis themselves: lacking self-knowledge, the analyst "will easily fall into the temptation of projecting outwards some of the peculiarities of his own personality, which he has dimly perceived, into the field of science, as a theory having universal validity; he will bring the psycho-analytic method into discredit, and lead the inexperienced astray" (SE12, 117). The danger of subjectivity here lies in its projection onto the world at large, a particularism that under the assumption of universal validity becomes narcissism, just as it ultimately does in melancholia. As Santner's comparison to the baroque sovereign highlights, this is a particular temptation for the analyst, as someone with the power to determine truth.

In *Berlin Childhood* (1934) we can begin to see Benjamin performing something similar to what Freud enjoins the analyst to do: taking precautions against the fall back into subjectivism. Where undergoing psychoanalysis performs this function for Freud, Benjamin's "inoculation" (SW3, 344) against nostalgia or homesickness in the form of writing down his childhood memories fulfils a similar task in distilling from these fragmentary personal impressions a generally-accessible, if specific, experience of a place (the city) at a certain time. In a similar way to psychoanalysis, which, seemingly paradoxically, brings up the past again and again in order to lay it to rest, relying on the psychoanalytic situation to bring about a process of working through rather than an acting out of memory,[32] for Benjamin the act of writing can itself be "therapeutic" if it is done with the clear aim not of indulging in homesickness, but precisely to counter it through a specific form of engagement with memories in order to drag them out of their context of meaning and cathect them differently. The point of this is to divest them of their subjective and idiosyncratic character; that is, the qualities that lead them to the ultimately pathological end point of the "illness" of homesickness, and to understand the irretrievability of the past "as it really was."[33] This is simultaneously to open up the possibility of a collective use of these individual impressions.

This is a practice of writing that is consciously posited in opposition to the left melancholia Benjamin deplores in some of his contemporaries: In "Left-Wing Melancholy" (1930), he writes that their stance "from the beginning, has nothing in mind but to enjoy itself in a negativistic quiet. The metamorphosis of political struggle from a compulsion to decision [*Zwang zur Entscheidung*] into an object of enjoyment, from a means of production to an article of consumption—that is this literature's latest hit" (GS3, 281, transl. mine). Benjamin thus hints at a Schmittian decisionism inherent to the political, eschewed by left melancholia, which results in an attitude of political quietism. Benjamin's own practice is precisely meant to counteract any tendency towards such languor. Although, as discussed above, Benjamin often links himself to melancholics and the mentally ill, he does not merely stop at acknowledging this characteristic; but rather uses his auto-diagnosis as a starting point for a "working through" of his own memories as well as those that reside at a more generalised, that is, cultural level, culminating in works such as the *Berlin Childhood* and its uncompleted precursor "Berlin Chronicle" (ca 1932). This coincides with the political call for an "organisation of pessimism" in Benjamin's Surrealism essay (1929)—what Alex Betancourt (2008, 78) terms Benjamin's "active pessimism." Of note is the intrusion of the political into Benjamin's account of homesickness as unwanted pathology against which one should vaccinate oneself. Were it not for the circumstances—the descent into fascism in 1930s Germany—and Benjamin's place within them, perhaps homesickness would not be such a threatening concept. Nevertheless, Benjamin is adamant in other texts that the gaze backwards into one's own or an imagined collective past can never be straightforward; it is not an issue of returning to the "good old days" but of embracing the "bad new" things (SW3, 340).

Ilit Ferber, drawing on Heidegger, claims that the melancholic mood is fundamental to "philosophical disclosure" per se (Ferber 2013, 31). Further linking Benjamin to Heidegger, she states that this is central to the "philosophical structure" of Benjamin's *Trauerspiel* book in particular and "determines its constitution" (Ferber 2013, 30). Ferber extrapolates that "melancholy has a far deeper affinity for Benjamin's philosophy than has yet been articulated—that beyond being a personal trait or choice of subject, melancholy represents a cornerstone of his epistemological and metaphysical claims" (Ferber 2013, 35). However, this disregards the fact that not only in his later production cycle, but even within the *Trauerspiel* book itself, Benjamin performs a movement *through* melancholia—a movement that requires a dwelling within and staying with the melancholic moment—but as a moment that is to be overcome.[34] Additionally, Benjamin's other writings, such as the *Berlin Childhood* and "Left-Wing Melancholia" briefly discussed here, further counter the notion of Benjamin as *a* melancholic, that is, some-one who has thoroughly embraced melancholia as not just an unalterable character trait but something that must necessarily inflect all action.

In Benjamin's early writings, the critic occupies the position that is later to be taken by the historical materialist, who appears in later chapters. In both these figures, as well as in his attitudes towards his own intellectual work, we see Benjamin grasping for a mode of cognition that does not fall prey to the pitfalls of subjectivity. In *One-Way Street*, Benjamin writes of his historical moment that "Fools lament the decay of criticism. For its day is long past. Criticism is a matter of correct distancing. It was at home in a world where perspectives and prospects counted and where it was still pos-sible to take a standpoint. Now things press too [closely] on human society" (SW1, 476). However, much as the baroque allegorist is under the spell of subjectively imposed meaning, and the critic likewise is threatened by its sway, these problems persist in the aftermath of the baroque. Margaret Cohen formulates this conundrum as follows: "How is critical demystification to be practiced in late capitalist society where all viewpoints are saturated by the phantasmagorical experience of commodity fetishism?" (Cohen 1993, 177). I shall investigate this in the following chapters. In this chapter, I traced how alongside melancholia, possession emerged as responses to a collective loss at the cultural level. At stake is the relation between self and other, world and humanity, and past and present forms. Implied is also struggle between a version of these relationships governed by myth or compensatory fantasies, premised on a subject that is somehow able to reconcile all these tensions within it, or an overcoming of such pathologies. Possession and neurosis ultimately emerge as effects of a social pathology—suggesting it is possible, even necessary, to read an epoch through its particular forms of psychopathology. How this plays out in the commodity-world of the nineteenth century examined in Benjamin's *Arcades Project* will form the subject of the following chapters.

NOTES

1. See also J. Butler, "Afterword: After Loss, What Then?" In D. Eng and D. Kazanjian (eds.), *Loss: The Politics of Mourning* (Los Angeles: University of California Press, 2003), 467–74; Julia R. Lupton and Kenneth Reinhard, *After Oedipus: Shakespeare in Psychoanalysis* (Ithaca, NY: Cornell University Press, 1993), 34–59; Rainer Nägele, "Beyond Psychology: Freud, Benjamin, and the Articulation of Modernity," in *Theater. Theory. Speculation: Walter Benjamin and the Scenes of Modernity* (Baltimore: Johns Hopkins University Press, 1991), 57.

2. "It has nothing to do with religious conceptions; the perfect martyr is no more released from the sphere of immanence than is the ideal image of the monarch" (OT, 73).

3. Freud here breaks off his analysis of mania, leaving the wound open for the time being. Further elaboration of the concept is to be found in *Group Psychology and the Analysis of the Ego* (1921c) [SE18, 130–33].

4. Sándor Ferenczi, drawing from mass psychology, later states in his 1926 "Present-Day Problems in Psychoanalysis" that mania for Freud is characterised by "a periodic or temporary attempt to overthrow the tyranny of the super-ego" (Ferenczi 2002, 31). Allthough this is Ferenczi's formulation, it is essentially consistent with Freud's conceptualisation of the relationship between the psychic faculties.

5. Transl. by Ley Roff (2004, 122). As Heinrich Kaulen, editor of volume 13 of Benjamin's *Werke und Nachlass*, points out, "Benjamins interest in the symptomatology of schizophrenia was also apparent in 1928 in his planned review of Alexander Mette's study" (WuN13.2, 145, transl. mine). The study in question is Mette's 1928 Über *Beziehungen zwischen Spracheigentümlichkeiten Schizophrener und dichterischer Produktion*.

6. As I discuss in my final chapter, Freud notes in the *Interpretation of Dreams* that the same holds true for wishes.

7. As discussed in particular in the next chapters, this runs counter to Benjamin's thought, for whom there must be no catharsis from within "guilt history." A line can be drawn from this to Benjamin's later interest in Brecht's plays, which eschew catharsis and resolution.

8. We can see, too, the proximity to Freud's concept of pathological gain. In his lecture on "The Common Neurotic State" from his *Introductory Lectures on Psycho-Analysis*, Freud writes of the formation of neuroses as an attempt of the ego to cure itself, displacing the experience of an inner conflict into symptoms. However, Freud notes that this easing of the conflict comes at a cost and speculates that the suffering attached to symptoms may be "an equivalent substitute for the torments of conflict, but they probably involve an increase in unpleasure. The ego would like to free itself from this unpleasure of the symptoms without giving up the gain from illness, and this is just what it cannot achieve. This shows, then, that it was not so entirely active as it thought it was" (SE 16, 383–84).

9. "Das alte Trauerspiel schlug seinen Bogen zwischen Kreatur und Christ. In dessen Scheitelhöhe steht der vollkommene Prinz. Wo Calderons christlicher Optimismus den sah, da zeigt sich der Wahrhaftigkeit des neueren Autors Untergang.

Sigismund geht zugrunde. Die dämonischen Gewalten des Turms werden sein Herr. Die Träume steigen aus der Erde auf und der christliche Himmel ist längst aus ihnen gewichen" (GS3, 33). This passage does not appear in Benjamin's 1928 review of the stage premiere of the play.

10. As discussed in the next chapter, this theme is fleshed out in relation to the gambler in the *Arcades Project* and other work of the 1930s.

11. For a discussion linking "Capitalism as Religion," *On the Origin of German Tragic Drama*, and "Books by the Mentally Ill" via the gnostic elements common to all, see Howard Caygill (2016, 144f). Also see Werner Hamacher's discussion in "Guilt History: Benjamin's Sketch 'Capitalism as Religion'" (2002).

12. In his "Five Lectures on Psycho-Analysis" (1910), which according to the *Verzeichnis* Benjamin had read, Freud likewise grounds *Hamlet* in the "incest complex" in the "Fourth Lecture" (SE11, 47), which is soon to become the Oedipus complex in his "Contributions to the Psychology of Love" (1910).

13. Hamlet also serves as an example of the difficulty of making visible this hidden truth: his 1905 "On Psychotherapy," Freud refers to Hamlet's soliloquy in 3.2, where Hamlet refuses to be "played like a pipe." He thus rebuffs Rosencrantz and Guildenstern's attempt to penetrate the mystery of his madness. For Freud, these words of "world-famous neurotic" Hamlet illustrate that "it is not so easy to play upon the instrument of the mind," thus serving as a cautionary note to psychoanalysts (SE7, 262). Unlike Benjamin, Freud ultimately grounds the appearance of this complex in the play in Shakespeare's own life. However, given the similar historical context and the parallels in the grounds of their symptoms—ambivalence in the aftermath of the death of the father—we can thus insert Hamlet into the lineage of baroque melancholics, in keeping with both Freud and Benjamin.

14. Indeed, Freud credits the Schreber's memoirs with making the psychoanalytic insights into the "feminine attitude" to the father speakable (SE 19, 91).

15. Haitzmann's solution to the *Handlungshemmung* is to appeal to the demonic side of God, becoming possessed by the devil, just as Schreber is possessed by an evil god who directs all of his actions.

16. An alternative reading of Schreber as experiencing gender dysphoria has emerged in recent scholarship. See for instance Trish Salah (2018).

17. For Freud, the example of Schreber also functions as a paradigmatic case of individual psychopathologies becoming symptomatic of a social prohibition. Freud notes the large amount of his contemporaries succumbing to paranoia as a means of warding off "homosexual desires," which to him is surprising as "Paranoia is precisely a disorder in which a sexual aetiology is by no means obvious; far from this, the strikingly prominent features in the causation of paranoia, especially among males, are social humiliations and slights" (SE12, 60). Thus the social comes to the fore in connection to the repression of homosexuality. Freud traces it back to the psyche: "delusions never fail to uncover these relations and to trace back the social feelings to their roots in a directly sensual erotic wish" (SE12, 60). Freud then postulates a teleology of sexuality via a sublimated homosexuality, which is channelled into fellow feeling for humanity as a whole.

If Scholem's account is to be believed, Benjamin found the original Schreber text more interesting than Freud's commentary, with its stress on the teleology of sexuality. Benjamin goes beyond Freud on the issue of homosexuality, too, in suggesting it might be treated as a political question of emancipation rather than pathology—or rather, recognising in the pathologisation of homosexual desire itself a larger, social pathology of modernity (see the discussion of lesbianism in "The Paris of the Second Empire in Baudelaire" (SW4, 58).

18. Freud touches on concepts found in his later *Totem and Taboo* in a 1912 letter to Ferenci. As in *Totem and Taboo*, in many ways Freud's *Urtext* of ambivalent filial relationship, the letter speaks of the "retrospect obedience" of the brother-clan to the murdered father. See E. Brabant et al. (eds.), *The Correspondence of Sigmund Freud and Sándor Ferenczi*, vol. 1, 1908–1914 (Cambridge, MA: Belnkap Press of Harvard University Press, 1993), 403–4.

19. As Freud notes, "In a footnote attached to the words *'contrary to the Order of Things'* in the above passage, the author foreshadows the subsequent transformation in his delusion of emasculation and in his relation to God: 'I shall show later on that emasculation for quite another purpose—a purpose *in consonance with the Order of Things—is* within the bounds of possibility, and, indeed, that it may quite probably afford the solution of the conflict.'" (SE12, 20). Thus, Schreber's initial victory over God is transformed into a compensatory fantasy of being emasculated *in keeping with the order of the world.* Just as masculinity itself is kept intact in Schreber's delusion, so the order of the world is not just followed, but later to be restored in his symptom, which he should—and does—experience as disorienting and disruptive of his body, but represses.

20. In connection to this, Santner stresses the importance of language in Schreber's delusions: "Schreber's experience of voices and fragments of speech being projected into his body by way of a kind of miraculous ventriloquism is among the torments that most directly endangers his capacity to experience himself as a source of individual agency and initiative" (Santner 1996, 33). Language here functions as a pathological link.

21. Freud also points to the inversion of a repressed narcissism in paranoia. Akin to the mechanism of love, where "das Ich, der finstere Despot" ("the ego, the gloomy despot" [transl. mine]) is made to die, paranoia likewise allows for an escape from demands of subjectivity (SE12, 65).

22. Freud here also notes, though he does not pursue further, the role of political power in the condensation of the father and the divine: "It is true that we cannot help feeling that there is an impassable gulf between the personality of God and that of any human being, however eminent he may be. But we must remember that this has not always been so. The gods of the peoples of antiquity stood in a closer human relationship to them. The Romans used to deify their dead emperors as a matter of routine" (SE12, 52). With Benjamin, we see how this re-emerges in the baroque where the sovereign acts as an intermediary between the divine and the creaturely, who is however doomed to remain fractured between these two poles.

23. Of course, the original document of Greek culture is *itself* a document of violence on this account.

24. Pensky notes Benjamin's proximity to cultural and art historian Aby Warburg here. Drawing from Warburg's successors Panofsky and Saxl, whom Pensky describes as "less encumbered by Warburg's obsession with the victory of rational self-control over the powers of myth" (Pensky 1993, 100), Benjamin transposes the Renaissance revival of melancholy heroism onto the baroque in the *Trauerspiel* book. In this move, Pensky suggests that "Benjamin bends the interpretation from the spirit if not the letter of the reflections of the Warburg Institute toward a reading of melancholy genius concentrating specifically on the propensity of the melancholy mind toward the fragmentary, the earthly, the decayed" (Pensky 1993, 103–4).

25. "Heidentum entsteht wenn die Sphäre des geniushaft Menschlichen . . . zur Sphäre der Geistigkeit selbst erhoben wird, zur dämonischen Gemeinschaft" (GS6, 90).

26. In his 1933 fragment "Agesilaus Santander," Benjamin wrote "I came into the world under the sign of Saturn, the planet of slow revolution, the star of hesitation and belatedness" (GS6, 521) [transl. mine]. Scholem suggests this is the only place where Benjamin reveals his own melancholic disposition (Scholem 1988, 58–59); however, as discussed here, it would appear to resurface repeatedly throughout his work.

27. A reference to Freud's 1914 text *"Gegensinn der Urworte"* ("The Antithetical Meaning of Primal Words").

28. See Santner (2001).

29. Santner (1996, 57) emphasizes the quasi-kabbalistic element at play in this process, conceptualizing paranoid world-building as a pathological version of *tikkun*, "the recollection of divine sparks scattered into earthly exile through the cosmic trauma of the 'breaking of the vessels.'"

30. The German—"rätselhaftes *Genügen*" [emphasis mine]—bears more overt similarity to Freud's characterisation of the world built up in psychopathology as less than splendid, merely adequate to survival.

31. Where Schreber creates his "private Germany" in psychopathology, Benjamin attempted to establish a "private Germany" of his own in opposition to the fascism engulfing the country. In *Deutsche Menschen* (1936), Benjamin collected some of the letters and comments he published between 1931 and 1932. Comprising twenty-five letters from German intellectuals, written in the period 1793–1883, Benjamin announces in an unpublished preface that "the purpose of this series is to show the countenance of a 'secret Germany'" (GS 4, 945). Benjamin thus implicitly presents a subversive, sidelined German tradition, but only by implication. Hanssen suggests it is the principle of montage that guides the "critical potential" of the collection; that Benjamin saw himself as part of this tradition and that the letters of exile therein served to demonstrate a link between previous periods of repression and national socialism (Hanssen 1998, 109). Crucially, where Santner suggests Schreber escaped the pressures and temptations of fascism into delusion and disconnection from the world, Benjamin's grounds his alternative in a collective, political tendency.

32. See Freud's "Remembering, Repeating and Working-Through" (1914).

33. See in particular Thesis VI in "On the Concept of History" (SW, 391), where Benjamin contests this Rankian dictum.

34. See also Pensky (1993, 108–9) for a discussion of the undialectical stasis of this reading of melancholy.

Chapter Three

Beyond the Pleasure Principle in the Arcades

In the *Trauerspiel* book, subjectivity emerged as an impossible demand from the moment of its inception and as a pitfall of false meaning that stands opposed to the truth, which for Benjamin is objective in character. The fractured baroque subject, suspended perilously between the two poles of the demand for decisive action and stable meaning and their impossibility, nevertheless endures, but endures changes over the course of its development in modernity. With Freud, it becomes possible for Benjamin to read the aftermath of the baroque as a continuation of its processes of mourning and melancholia. In the *Arcades Project* and the two "Exposés" he wrote for this work in 1935 and 1939, Benjamin investigates the way in which this process occurs within nineteenth-century capitalism, in the epicentre of trade: the imperial metropolis of Paris. In this analysis, Benjamin draws heavily from Freud's dream interpretation, as well as *Beyond the Pleasure Principle* (1920). Benjamin traces the reversal of agency that takes place, where the encounter with the object results not in its possession, but in a possession *by* it. Commodities take on a life of their own, structuring the experience of life in the "dream-world" (AP, 13) of nineteenth-century capitalism. In the *Arcades Project*, the subjectivity is thus mediated by capitalism: its tendencies towards massification and false individuation, its yearning for the forms of life of the past and its fixation on newness, the changing rhythms of work and life-transforming experience. Benjamin traces how political authoritarianism and the expansion of capitalist exchange and exploitation together create a space that is ultimately made almost uninhabitable for humanity: As Benjamin notes in the 1939 Expose, "the transformations made by Haussmann appear to Parisians as a monument of Napoleonic despotism. The inhabitants of the city no longer feel at home there; they start to become conscious of the inhuman character of the metropolis" (AP, 23). This process of "becoming conscious" foreshadows what will be dealt with in more detail in the final chapters: the nineteenth century as a dream and awakening as the interruption of its eternal return. Crucially, this moment of becoming conscious here occurs at a time of political foment, as a reaction against the unlivable, inhumane transformations wrought by the "detonation artist" Haussmann.

For Benjamin, the Paris arcades function like a microcosm of the nineteenth-century capitalist metropolis as a whole; they serve as both metaphor and actual site for the expression of its fractured subjects and their experience. As such, they do not only reflect the relations of production, but, as Benjamin stresses, they are infused with desire, becoming a repository of the "wish-images" (AP, 4) of the "dreaming collective" (AP, 546) of the nineteenth century. These wish-images of the arcades encapsulate an essentially collectivist, quasi-utopian impulse, thwarted by the social relations of capitalism that hold it back: "the collective seeks both to sublate and to transfigure the incompleteness of the social product and the deficiencies in the social order" (AP, 4).

Freud begins his 1913 *Totem and Taboo* with the assertion that "primitive" society is most emblematic of "prehistoric man," before interspersing examples drawn from Frazer's *Golden Bough* with those of his Viennese patients throughout the text. Freud's initial assertion of a teleology with developmental stages is thus complicated by his own text, in which the distinctions between "primitive" societies, turn-of-the-century neurotics, and the wider social mores of his era dissolve into ambivalence: the co-existing oppositional affects of love and hate. Benjamin radicalises this universalism in his examination of the resurfacing of archaic contents in the midst, and through the historically specific (socio/politico economic) forms, of modernity. Rather than the people it has colonized, it is the society of the nineteenth-century European metropolis that thus presents the epitome of the resurfacing of the mythic, and it does so due to its political and economic formation. Benjamin investigates the nineteenth century as the *Urgeschichte* of the twentieth, its primal history, whose elements only come to full fruition in a later historical moment. Indeed, as a Benjaminian origin, the central features of this age can be recognized only from the standpoint of a later one: origin is a category not of the past, but of a dynamic temporality that only finds its true form in that which it originates—an inversion of the idea that the true form can be traced back through history to an originary point in the past. *Urgeschichte* is informed by this temporal sliding, but in the *Arcades Project* it is more closely related to the category of myth. As Cornelia Zumbusch notes, at stake in Benjamin's *Urgeschichte* is not just a symptomatic return to past contents; "[r]ather, it seems to be the function of modernity itself to ceaselessly transform itself into *Urgeschichte*" (Zumbusch 2012, 149, transl. mine). As such, *Urgeschichte* represents remnants—

residues—of myth that not only reside in the past, but form something new in their reiteration in the present. Benjamin here draws on Freud's notion of prehistory as something that continuously interacts with the present, be it in the form of neurotic or childhood fantasies in *Totem and Taboo*, or in the *Urphantasien*, primal or original fantasies that he characterises as phyloge-netic in the *Introductory Lectures on Psycho-Analysis*, published in 1917. For Benjamin, however, there is something historically contingent about the ambivalences of modernity. I will examine Benjamin's use of Freud's *Beyond the Pleasure Principle* (1920) in his analysis of the philosophy of history of the nineteenth century and the resurgence of myth in modernity. It will become apparent that the nineteenth century remains under the sway of the mythic, resurfacing in capitalist forms—thus Benjamin also draws on Marx in his analysis.

THE UNCONSCIOUS CITY

In the *Arcades Project*, Benjamin conceptualises the city as a site of the entanglement of sleeping and waking states, city and psyche, antiquity and modernity. As Weigel notes, in the initial sketches for the *Arcades Project*, "the topography and architecture of the city are regarded as the memory-space (Gedächtnisraum) of the collective, so that already here we find a materialized memory-topography, in which the external topography, the city of modernity, and the topographical representation of memory in psycho-analysis converge" (Weigel 1996, 227). Benjamin compares the relationship between "waking existence," the conscious mind, and the unconscious, to ancient Greece, where access points to the chthonic underworld abound: "a land which, at certain hidden points, leads down into the underworld—a land full of inconspicuous places from which dreams arise. All day long, suspect-ing nothing, we pass them by, but no sooner has sleep come than we are eagerly groping our way back to lose ourselves in the dark corridors" (AP, 84). This passage bears clear traces of Benjamin's engagement with the Freudian model of conscious and unconscious states. He continues his reflec-tions on the city, in which,

> [b]y day, the labyrinth of urban dwellings resembles consciousness; the arcades (which are galleries leading into the city's past) issue unremarked onto the streets. At night, however, under the tenebrous mass of the houses, their denser darkness protrudes like a threat, and the nocturnal pedestrian hurries past— unless, that is, we have emboldened him to turn into the narrow lane. (AP, 84)

Cities function as the psyche of the social organism of the nineteenth century, identified with both the unconscious (the city at night) and the conscious, "waking" mind. The psychic structuring of the city forms the complement to the spatial and material structuring of the psyche. At stake is the overcoming of resistances to delving into the unconscious in order to unearth the source of dreams; in "emboldening" the dreamer to delve into the "narrow lane," the opening onto the "denser darkness" of the city's unconscious contents. Benjamin here also links the unconscious with the "underworld" of Greek antiquity. The many references throughout the *Arcades Project* to the underworld, the mythic, chthonic depths, and the importance of topography in shaping the people of the nineteenth century disclose themselves when read with—and against—Freud's architectural model and his own accounts of the palimpsest of layers of historical epochs that make up ancient cities.

Freud uses the same metaphor as Benjamin to render the psyche in a spatial idiom, taking Rome as an example of a city "in which nothing once constructed had perished, and all the earlier stages of development had survived alongside the latest . . . not merely in its latest form, moreover, as the Romans of the Caesars saw it, but also in its earliest shape" (SE21, 69). All it takes is for the onlooker "to shift the focus of his eyes, perhaps, or change his position, in order to call up a view of either the one or the other" (SE21, 69). Here, Freud introduces an archaeological model of the psyche, with Rome as the paradigmatic space of the endurance of historical contents. Against this, in a passage that seems to grapple with the above passage from *Civilisation and its Discontents*, Benjamin contrasts Paris and Rome: "Paris created the type of the flaneur. What is remarkable is that it wasn't Rome. And the reason? Does not dreaming itself take the high road in Rome? And isn't that city too full of temples, enclosed squares, national shrines, to be able to enter *undivided*—with every cobblestone, every shop sign, every step, and every gateway—into the passerby's dream?" (AP, 417). Paris as a city has a dialectical character: it is both interior and landscape. Rome lacks this; it is overdetermined by its history, and therefore unable to produce the modern subjectivity which encounters the ancient expressed precisely in the novel spaces of capitalist exchange. Antiquity must be present as citation, as a kind of raw material to be used in the dreamwork of the nineteenth century, in order to truly form a "phantasmagoria," which for Benjamin is a dialectical category, a semblance that combines two seemingly opposed poles—in this case, carrying within it elements of both the primordial and the novel. Paris as the metropolis of nineteenth-century capitalism exhibits both the weightiness of ancient and recent history, *and* the obsession with technological novelty. The city itself is layered like Freud's archaeological model: "The Passage du Caire is highly reminiscent, on a smaller scale, of the Passage du Saumon, which in the past existed on the Rue Montmartre, on the site of the present-day Rue Bachaumont" (AP, 40). It is a spatialised palimpsest of residues that functions for the collective like the psychic unconscious does at the individual level. Where for Freud, the architectural palimpsest of Rome becomes a metaphor for the psyche, Benjamin inverts this relationship, presenting a model of the psyche that is both colonised by architecture and expressed in it. It follows that "topography is the ground plan of this mythic space of tradition [*Traditionsraum*], as it is of every such space, and that it can become indeed its key—just as it was the key to Greece for Pausanias, and just as the history and situation of the Paris arcades are to become the key for the underworld of *this* century, into which Paris has sunk" (AP, 83). At the time of Benjamin's study, Paris is past its heyday, the ruined character of the arcades precisely what allows Benjamin to unlock its "underworld," the unconscious truths contained therein. For Freud, condensation in the dreamwork entails the fusion of things that are temporally separate. This is at play in the arcades when the most modern materials are expressed in the medium of the ancient—that is, the forms of ancient Greece.[1] Cities themselves become dreamlike for Benjamin: "Whoever sets foot in a city feels caught up as in a web of dreams, where the most remote past is linked to the events of today" (AP, 435). Crucially, "[t]hings which find no expression in political events . . . unfold in the cities: they are a superfine instrument, responsive as an Aeolian harp—despite their specific gravity—to the living historic vibrations of the air" (AP, 435). Like the unconscious, which registers things that are not consciously expressed, cities thus serve as a historical instrument, indicating both the most ancient and the most novel repressed contents that do not find "expression" in other spheres.

CULTURE AS SYMPTOM

Benjamin's method of reading the life-world of the nineteenth-century metropolis as a web of symptoms manifested in the arcades bears traces of Freud's way of conceptualising the social in the *Psychopathology of Everyday Life* (1901). This text, as its subtitle indicates, deals with "Forgetting, Slips of the Tongue, Bungled Actions, Superstitions and Errors." These are so characteristic of everyday life as to be unavoidable—hence the motto of the text reads "Now fills the air so many a haunting shape/ That no one knows how best he may escape"/ (SE6, vii). On the methodological issues of historical legibility and an analysis from fragments of everyday life, Benjamin's approach is informed by that of psychoanalysis—recognizing and diagnosing a pathology from a small part, the seemingly unimportant and unintentional revealed as a symptom. The nineteenth century itself here functions as an organism: decentring the individual subject, the pathology resides at the level of the social totality. Observations on the nineteenth century acting seemingly autonomously, without any reference to a human subject, are dotted throughout the *Arcades Project*. Benjamin quotes from Sigfried Giedion's *Bauen in Frankreich* that "'Wherever the nineteenth century feels itself to be unobserved, it grows bold' . . . In fact, this sentence holds good in the general form that it has here: the anonymous art of the illustrations in family magazines and children's books, for example, is proof of the point" (AP, 154). At stake is the age itself, the social body as a whole. This tendency is reflected in the literature of the nineteenth century, specifically that dealing with Paris: "We see a continuous stream of new works in which the city is the main character" (AP, 415). The physical body of the nineteenth-century city—its commercial spaces, of which the arcades are the most paradigmatic—demand a psychosomatic reading of its symptoms. Benjamin joins materialism and psychoanalysis to read the symptoms pointing to the psycho/pathology of the organism of the nineteenth century. At the same time as subjectivity is thus projected onto the age as a whole, fractured off from the human, the fracture of the modern subject comes to be expressed in the humans that populate the nineteenth century as they refract into types, as we shall see in the next chapter.

In the *Arcades Project*, Benjamin captures an impression of the arcades as a second nature, created by humanity to suit the needs of the specific socio-economic constellation of the nineteenth century. Thus, they are organised by the commodity form, adapting to basic human needs such as shelter almost as an afterthought. The many vignettes dealing with the absence of the elements in the arcades, their artificial light, the way they shelter the inhabitants of the city from unpredictable outside influence describe an artificial environment, which Benjamin reveals as far from the icon of progress it signified to contemporaries. This is illustrated in the following passage:

> Trade and traffic are the two components of the street. Now, in the arcades the second of these has effectively died out: the traffic there is rudimentary. The arcade is a street of lascivious commerce only; it is wholly adapted to arousing desires. Because in this street the juices slow to a standstill, the commodity proliferates along the margins and enters into fantastic combinations, like the tissue in tumours. (AP, 42)

The second nature of the arcade is likened to a cancerous growth, arousing desires it can never fulfil, arresting the dynamic flow of traffic, of life, its stagnation leading to unrestrained, purposeless growth in its dazzling display of "fantastic" combinations of commodities. In the arcades, the physically pathological (tumour) is brought into a constellation with the psychological (desire) and the commodity: "There was a Passage du Désir" (AP, 48)—repressed wishes and desires are expressed in the arcades, even as this expression remains partial and pathological.

Freud himself performs such a comparison in *Beyond the Pleasure Principle*, which Benjamin read at least twice, for the first time in or before 1928[2]—coinciding with the production of drafts of what was intended to become the *Arcades Project. A propos* the libido and the body, Freud speculates that the cells of an organism behave analogously to the psyche, in particular that germ cells act in a "completely 'narcissistic' fashion—to use the phrase we are accustomed to use in the theory of the neuroses to describe a whole individual who retains his libido in his ego and pays none of it out in object-cathexes" (BPP, 44). Freud takes this reflection further and considers that "the cells of the malignant neoplasms which destroy the organism should also perhaps be described as narcissistic in the same sense: pathology is prepared to regard their germs as innate and to ascribe embryonic attributes to them" (BPP, 44). Thus we see a slippage between the psychic and the physical at play in Freud's thought.[3]

Beyond the Pleasure Principle signified a watershed moment in Freud's model of the psyche. Previously, Freud described the psychic economy as subject to a constant cycle of a reduction in tension (when acting in accordance with the pleasure principle) or an increase in tension, or energy (*Unlust*, displeasure). The reality principle is introduced as a modifier on the pleasure principle, making possible the momentary acceptance of displeasure in the interest of self-preservation and long-term maximisation of pleasure. In *Beyond the Pleasure Principle*, Freud's focus shifts to the question of how it is possible that unpleasurable experiences often seem to be psychically repeated again and again, given the rule of the pleasure principle. After ruling our potential hidden sources of pleasure to be derived from this repetition, Freud is left with a "residue" that cannot be explained away. Among this he numbers dreams of accidents, as well as the return of repressed, painful experiences in analysis. These sometimes manifest as transference or are otherwise acted out and re-experienced as trauma in the analytical situation, rather than remembered, that is, narrated by the analysand.

The model of the psyche that underpins these processes is premised on an inner core of the unconscious, which is surrounded by consciousness as a protective mantle. Trauma occurs when this layer, the *Reizschutz*, is breached by a strong impression or shock (*Erregung*) from the outside. Crucially, in the chaos that ensues in the psychic economy of the organism as a result of this shock, the pleasure principle is at first disabled by the flooding of "the mental apparatus with large amounts of stimulus" (BPP, 23) and the subsequent attempt at "mastering," the "psychic binding" of the incoming stimuli in order to process them. Only after this urgent task of doing away with the stimulus is achieved can the pleasure—and the reality principle take over. Freud speculates that what facilitates the breaching of the *Reizschutz* is the insufficient preparedness for whatever stimulus (*Reiz*) causes the trauma. Based on this, Freud states that dreams, play, and the acting out of repressed traumatic experiences are belated attempts by the organism to achieve what it failed to do at the moment the traumatic wound was incurred. The death drive thus overpowers the two life-preserving principles in an attempt to belatedly restore a psychic balance that was disturbed. Freud describes the second aspect of repetition-compulsion as a tendency "*inherent in organic life to restore an earlier state of things* which the living entity has been obliged to abandon under the pressure of external disturbing forces; that is, a kind of organic elasticity, or, to put it another way, the expression of the inertia inherent in organic life" (BPP, 30). The hidden motivator of repetition-compulsion is thus the tendency of all things towards the restoration of an earlier state of homeostasis. Freud uses a real-life anecdote of child's play and a historical epic as examples, classing them all as repetition compulsion and concludes "that there really does exist in the mind a compulsion to repeat which goes beyond the pleasure principle" (BPP, 16). This repetition-compulsion is thus manifest across different aspects of life as well as reflected in cultural production, and it can have a variety of sources: Freud opens the text with observations about severe trauma resulting from accidents and wartime experience but quickly moves to a discussion of the trauma resulting from narcissistic injury in early childhood. Freud concludes that

> What psycho-analysis reveals in the transference phenomena of neurotics can also be observed in the lives of some normal people. The impression they give is of being pursued by a malignant fate or possessed by some "daemonic" power; but psycho-analysis has always taken the view that their fate is for the most part arranged by themselves and determined by early infantile influences.[4] (BPP, 15)

This passage posits the symptom as an expression of an internal conflict, an ambivalence. We can perceive the proximity to Benjamin's concept of phantasmagoria—the conjoining of two oppositional tendencies, resulting in something that is a distorted expression of them both. However, Freud notes that such symptoms are not displayed in all cases of repetition-compulsion: where in neurotic patients they are read as symptoms of their pathology, in the "normal person" these are explained as character traits or bad luck. The "psychical fixations" of traumas thus don't always express as symptoms, or at least, are not interpreted as such. The question remains open whether this absence of symptoms is truly the preferable state—as trauma and repetition-compulsion are then more forcefully relegated to the realm of the mythic, seen as unalterable "fate," and carrying something of the echo of demonic influence. In addition, repetition-compulsion is here linked to another term: *Schicksalszwang*, the compulsion to fate—which in Freud's interpretation is largely self-imposed but by no means conscious. Rather, it is in experiences such as this pursuit of fate that the subject is revealed as fractured, encountering aspects of its own self as strange and alien, an other within it, which may be acting counter to the interests represented by the pleasure principle and even the reality principle. Once again, we see that there is no clear, stable distinction between the pathological and the normal—both the neurotic and the "normal" person are subject to repetition-compulsion. As we shall see in the final two chapters, the phenomenon of dreams emerges as the paradigmatic case of the dissolution of the boundary between normal and psychopathological mental states. Extrapolating from this, we can see that the symptom comes to be a phenomenon which expresses more than just an individual pathology—or, rather, it expresses the generalised suffering of being an individual in society, which is always-already pathological, insofar as it causes tension between individual desires and their fulfilment in the world. In *The Future of an Illusion*, Freud traces the internalisation of that which denies the wish in the form of the superego. The subject thus takes the fracture between itself and the world *into* itself. Benjamin thus follows Freud in reading cultural production in modernity, and indeed all of the social world, as symptomatic.

OBSOLETE HUMANS: COMMODITY FETISH

Not only the city as a whole, but the material objects of the nineteenth century express this symptomatic character in Benjamin's text. Human agency has been divested into these things, thus they themselves exert a ghostly tenacity in the face of change, refusing to be supplanted easily by new technologies and products; they "resist" change. In the *Arcades Project*, Benjamin aims "to blaze a way into the heart of things abolished or superseded, in order to decipher the contours of the banal as picture puzzle" which, "as schemata of dreamwork, were long ago discovered by psycho-analysis. We, however, with a similar conviction, are less on the trail of the psyche than on the track of things" (AP, 212). The "similar conviction" Benjamin refers to here is that there are repressed, unconscious contents to be uncovered from the analysis of, in this case, the material object, which has undergone a process of deformation or encryption, becoming "picture-puzzles." This is a direct reference to Freud's *Interpretation of Dreams* (1900), where Freud *writes a propos* of the rebus: "A dream is a picture puzzle of this sort and our predecessors in the field of dream interpretation have made the mistake of treating the rebus as a pictorial composition: and as such it has seemed to them nonsensical and worthless" (SE4, 278). For Freud, the rebus is rather a way in which the latent dream content became deformed or disguised, something to be deciphered; understanding it as more than its parts: "we can only form a proper judgment of the rebus if we put aside criticisms such as these of the whole composition and its parts and if, instead, we try to replace each separate element in some way or other" (SE4, 278). What deciphers the rebus, then, is a transposition of its meaning into another register by way of replacing its components with something else—a translation, a making legible in analysis.[5]

Perhaps we can say that despite his assertion, Benjamin is not on the track of the thing *more* than that of the psyche; rather, he shows that their paths are interconnected: the object comes to contain unconscious residues—forming an "object-unconscious." Benjamin thus expands the Freudian notion of the unconscious beyond the individual, indeed beyond the human psychic apparatus, to encompass the material world.[6] Moreover, the "schemata of dream-work" is also at work in the nineteenth century as a whole, as the *Arcades Project* conceptualises its society as a "dreaming collective." Unconscious wishes are expressed in the marketplace of the arcades, in deformed forms—just as Freud saw the dream as a deformed expression of an unconscious wish. The dream-sleep is filled with elements that issue not from the inner workings of the individual psychic apparatus, but from the collective wish-images contained in material production. Human inwardness is not the only way in which interiority and subjectivity are expressed for Benjamin; rather, the entire world becomes symptomatic, and in- and outside are blurred: the psyche is colonised by objects and prevailing class relations, which, at the level of the collective, are turned outwards and stored in the objects produced by nineteenth-century society. The subjects' fracture makes it porous to such invasion, and at the same time, as we have seen in the previous chapter, also leads it to the projection of itself onto the world at large. This movement is at play in the commodity fetish in the spaces of the nineteenth century examined by Benjamin in the Exposes and the *Arcades Project*.

CONSUMPTION: EMPATHY WITH EXCHANGE VALUE

What, then, happens when the people of the nineteenth century encounter "fetish-commodities" in the sphere of consumption? To investigate this, Benjamin first looks to the world exhibitions in his 1935 Exposé. In this early version, Benjamin still retains a notion of actual consumption taking place:

"World exhibitions are places of pilgrimage to the commodity fetish . . . The worker occupies the foreground, as customer" and adds the Marxian concept of alienation: "The entertainment industry makes this easier by elevating the person to the level of the commodity. He surrenders to its manipulations while enjoying his alienation from himself and others" (AP, 7). In the later version of the expose of 1939, Benjamin seems to indicate that it is precisely the lack of consumption that engenders the phantasmagoria of its possibility. The point of this vacillation regarding the concept of consumption is grounded in the fact that consumption, in the sense of purchase and use, is not necessary for the *sensory* consumption of the object. Thus its power to shape human subjectivity, to "imbue" the masses with exchange value, is not contingent on becoming personal property. Benjamin continues:

> world exhibitions thus provide access to a phantasmagoria which a person enters in order to be distracted. Within these *divertissements*, to which the individual abandons himself in the framework of the entertainment industry, he remains always an element of a compactmass . . . in an attitude that is pure reaction. It is thus led to that state of subjection which propaganda, industrial as well as political, relies on. (AP, 18)

Worth noting is the conjunction of political and "industrial" propaganda (that is, advertising, but also events such as world exhibitions) in this passage—Benjamin recognises both as twin moments in capitalist domination. As Christine Blättler and Christian Voller write, "instead of describing the modern nation-state in the abstract as a function of capital . . ., [Benjamin] makes the glass- and iron constructions of the *grands magasins* of nineteenth-century Paris into the concrete indicators of the political tendencies of the time" (Blättler and Voller 2016, 10, transl. mine). Thus, in the arcades, the political is implied in the industrial, and in architectural fashion.

In section B, "Grandville, or the World Exhibitions" of the 1939 Expose, Benjamin examines the world exhibitions, whose modes of display find continuation in the arcades, department stores, and other spaces designed for masses, such as the amusement park. The mass of commodities on display comes to be reflected in the subjectivity brought about in these spaces: "World exhibitions glorify the exchange value of the commodity. They create aframework in which its use value becomes secondary. They are a school in which the masses, forcibly excluded from consumption, are imbued with the exchange value of commodities to the point of identifying with it" (AP, 18). Benjamin here describes a process of massification, where the individual is subjected through identifying with the commodity, and thus ultimately with exchange value itself.

Benjamin develops the concept of empathy from its use in nineteenth-century German art history. Robert Vischer, first outlining the concept in his doctoral dissertation "On the Optical Sense of Form: A Contribution to Aesthetics" in 1873, used it to refer to a process whereby an artwork is imbued with emotions by its creator, which can then be felt by the observer of the artwork. The observer then "enters" the work, by experiencing, or identifying with, these emotions. Wilhelm Worringer later identified naturalism and its depiction of the human figure and social life as the quintessential art of empathy (Worringer 1997, 33). Benjamin expands this concept of empathy to the commodity, identifying its display in the arcades as akin to the display and function of artworks.[7] The infusion of commodities with dead labour, that is, ultimately that which gives it its "sensuous-suprasensuous"[8] quality, is linked to the process of the infusion of a work of art with the emotions of the artist. Together, these qualities of the industrially produced and displayed commodity encourage identification and empathy in the spectator-consumer. The prohibition on touch, the way the items are displayed, seems to infuse them with the cultic value hitherto reserved for religious and art objects. This, then, opens up a lack: the injunction to consume as opposed to the practical inability to do so, resulting in a psychic state that is susceptible to identification with exchange value itself. This is the infinite potential of the commodity to become something else, its uncanny sensuous-suprasensuous quality, is not only a result of the dead human labour that fills the object, but the fact that as commodity, it always contains within itself something more than itself: its quality of exchangeability. This, in Benjamin's terms, is its mythic dimension, leading to an identification not only with the promise, but also, connected to it, the essential lack of the commodity: People themselves come to be exchangeable. The fractured subject of early modernity thus changes in the era of high capitalism: something alien is introduced in the form of empathy with an object; further fracturing the integrity of the subject. Simultaneously, as we shall see, these processes of disintegration which allow humanity to become a mass in the nineteenth century may also point the way beyond the fractured modern subject.

THE DEATH DRIVE IN THE ARCADES

Freud's death drive, as mentioned above, has a twofold effect: the compulsive repetition of past traumas and, at its root, the attempt to restore a previous state of homeostasis. This plays out for Benjamin in two ways: first, in the becoming-object, dead matter, of commodification. Second, in the compulsive repetition of previous memories, the revisiting of trauma.

In Convolute A of the collection of writings we know as the *Arcades Project*, "Arcades, Magasins de Nouveautés, Sales Clerks," Benjamin turns his attention from the world exhibitions to the department store. He writes that "with the establishment of department stores, consumers begin to consider themselves a mass. (Earlier it was only scarcity which taught them that.) Hence, the circus-like and theatrical element of commerce is quite extraordinarily heightened. [A4, 1]" (AP, 43). The encounter with the commodity world is a passive one in both the world exhibitions and the department store, and, mediated through the commodity form, so is the encounter with others that occurs in these spaces of consumption. As in the world exhibitions, it is the sensuous rather than the purely economic dimension of consumption that is at stake here; hence Benjamin likens this form of consumption to a spectacle viewed on stage. The arcades function as a metaphor for Paris and indeed Capitalist society in its entirety: As Benjamin suggests in the 1935 Expose, "the *passage* is a city, a world in miniature" (AP, 3), allowing Benjamin a condensed view on his object of study. In the arcades, like in the department shops and the world exhibitions, the phantasmagoric display of surplus commodity production is designed to engender desire for these objects of consumption in the worker—they bring the mode of experience of the world exhibition into everyday life in the city. Even when the masses are enjoined to consume and the world fairs are superseded by the arcade, the lack remains, needing to be filled with ever more distractions. This mass, as Benjamin writes, becomes vulnerable to the promise to make whole what is experienced as a lack under capitalism—this is what "propaganda" plays on. People may not be whole without possessing commodities, having alienated something of themselves in the products of their labour, which they then encounter as haunting objects not quite of themselves and not quite other. The object produced under capitalism can never truly be possessed, thus the masses are faced with the infinite insufficiency of the commodity in the quest for the satisfaction of desire.[9]

Freud's *Beyond the Pleasure Principle* is operative throughout in the *Arcades Project* in Benjamin's references to the "anorganic" and the way desire is bound up with death, nowhere more so than in fashion. This desire-death dualism is characteristic of nineteenth-century capitalism. New technologies and products emerge in this society and carry potential, but they are outgrowths of an organism that is pathological; as such, they function as symptoms. The tension between desire and death, expressed as ambivalence, is crucial for Benjamin's analysis. In Convolute B on fashion in particular, Benjamin delves deeper into the aspect of desire that links the commodity to both sexuality and death, as reification. Here, he sketches how "fashion has opened the business of dialectical exchange between woman and ware—

between carnal pleasure and the corpse" (AP, 62). In shaping desires, the commodity form fuses eros and thanatos—"the living body to the inorganic" (AP, 79).[10] In changing fashions, repressed, unconscious desires are expressed, but in being expressed through the "dead," "inorganic" commodity, this joins the libido with the death drive.[11] Commodity fetishism here becomes a sexual fetish, and vice versa. Benjamin thus fuses the concept of the fetish in Marx and Freud, while also retaining its religious—qua mythic—connotations, as formulated in "Capitalism as Religion." Benjamin writes of the different forms taken by the expression of these desires, his analysis allowing him to see all of them as part of the same struggle between social and aesthetic forms that have been overcome, and the possibilities opened up by new forms:

> Just as the first factory buildings cling to the traditional form of the residential dwelling, and just as the first automobile chassis imitate carriages, so in the clothing of the cyclist the sporting expression still wrestles with the inherited pattern of elegance, and the fruit of this struggle is the grim sadistic touch which made this ideal image of elegance so incomparably provocative to the male world in those days. (AP, 62)

Using the example of the then newly developed bicycle, Benjamin describes how (male) desire is shaped by new technological developments, in particular the tension that arises between these and the pre-existing social configuration. New technological developments directly affect the structuring of the libido, the choice of desirable object. Once again this unconscious process is linked, cryptically, to the dream: these early, hybrid forms are "dream prototypes" (AP, 62), expressing the disparate historical and stylistic elements they carry within themselves and the tension between them. These dream prototypes therefore function as dream images, waiting for interpretation. The obsolete social forms expressed in these dream-image technologies form a kind of nature; the second nature created by humanity for itself.[12] However, "[j]ust as technology is always revealing nature from a new perspective, so also, as it impinges on human beings, it constantly makes for variations in their inmost primordial passions, fears, and images of longing" (AP, 393). Human nature, then, is not a fixed, innate essence, but technologically mediated. This observation forms an important part of Benjamin's later writing. The potential of the camera and film were of particular interest to Benjamin for what they make visible: As he notes in the artwork essay, "film has enriched our field of perception with methods that can be illustrated by those of Freudian theory" (SW4, 265). Notably, Benjamin links this to the perspective opened up by Freud, whose *On the Psychopathology of Everyday Life* profoundly changed perception, "isolated and made analyzable things which had previously floated unnoticed on the broad stream of perception. A similar deepening of apperception throughout the entire spectrum of optical—and now also auditory—impressions has been accomplished by film" (SW4, 265). Film, like psychoanalysis, affords an observer or listener the opportunity to pause and analyse the stream of events, of words, of objects, extending the human sensory apparatus and making a different form of understanding possible.

Benjamin here joins the Marxian notion of the "naturally-grown relations" with Freudian concepts of desire, fear, and primordial drives. On a more extreme formulation borrowed from Paul Valery, under capitalism "Man is himself, is man, only at the surface. Lift the skin, dissect: here begin the machines" (AP, 404). Technologies go beyond shaping desire, or, rather, what is revealed is desire shaped by technologies as constitutive of human beings. It is clear that this "man" of nineteenth-century capitalism, permeated by empathy with the commodity, that is, with value, the inorganic, and ultimately the death drive; thoroughly objectified not only through labour, but through desire, is just as fractured as the baroque sovereign-subject.

Where in the 1935 Expose the "prostitute" in her ambiguity is for Benjamin a dialectical image that fuses the seller and the sold, and is, as such, connected to death, another female figure linked to the death drive appears in this passage—the femme fatale. Benjamin quotes French sociologist Roger Caillois on this "woman-machine, artificial, mechanical, at variance with all living creatures, and above all murderous. No doubt psycho-analysis would not hesitate to explain this representation in its own terms by envisaging the relations between death and sexuality and, more precisely, by finding each ambiguously intimated in the other. [Z2a, 1]" (AP, 696). This is yet another instance of the "coupling of the living body with the inorganic"—the femme fatale is a type, defined only by her sexuality and her relationship to death. Unlike the figure of the prostitute, she is *both* dead and death-dealing.[13] This attraction to "the corpse" or the un-life of machines that resemble humans is another aspect of the fracturing of the subject in modernity, once again along gendered lines. Like the inauguration of the fractured subject, this linking of femininity and sexuality with the corpse dates back to baroque poetry:

> The detailing of feminine beauties so dear to the poetry of the Baroque, a process in which each single part is exalted through a trope, secretly links up with the image of the corpse. This parceling out of feminine beauty into its noteworthy constituents resembles a dissection, and the popular comparisons of bodily parts to alabaster, snow, precious stones, or other (mostly inorganic) formations makes the same point. (Such dismemberment occurs also in Baudelaire: "Le Beau Navire.") (AP, 79–80)

The ambiguous intimation of sexuality and death is explicitly linked to psychoanalysis here: not only does it draw from the interrelation of the drives;
it occurs "secretly," remains repressed and thus unconscious. A link is established between this tendency in the baroque, and Baudelaire, the epitome of
the nineteenth-century poet. This brings us back to the cultural milieu that
also informed Schreber's neuroses: fears about female sexuality, the inversion of the identification of femininity with reproductive/gestational capacity
into its nightmarish obverse, the death-dealing woman-machine. Women are
not subjects in being thus objectified, denied interiority, identified with death.
In the above-mentioned passage from the 1935 Expose, the prostitute is
accompanied by the fetish of the commodity and the arcade as one of a tri-
fecta of "dialectical images" characterised by their ambiguous arrest of "the
law of dialectics": they embody a moment in the circulation of value, represent a snapshot of the movement of capital at a given point in time and space,
and as such they are in a sense impossible—because this circulation never
stands still. Thus, "this standstill is utopia, and the dialectical image therefore
dream-image" (AP, 10): the arcades, the prostitute and the commodity per se
are representations of impossible states, juxtapositions or montages of things
that cannot rightfully coexist in the same entity, but nevertheless do. Thus,
the question for Benjamin becomes, where are such appearances possible?
And the answer, of course: In utopia—a fantasy of wish-fulfilment—and in
the constructions of dreamwork.

These passages clearly demonstrate that Benjamin drew on Freud in his
concept of ambiguity, especially as it relates to the question of the connection
of libidinal and thanatic drives. Freud writes in *Beyond the Pleasure Principle*
that psychoanalysis has always "recognized the presence of a sadistic component in the sexual instinct" (BPP, 48). Questioning how such an instinct
can be derived from the life-preserving principle of eros, Freud speculates
that "this sadism is in fact a death-instinct which under the influence of the
narcissistic libido, has been forced away from the ego and has consequently
only emerged in relation to the object" (BPP, 48). Sadism, aggression directed at the libidinally-cathected, or love object, is revealed on this analysis
as a self-destructive drive rechannelled onto something outside of the self.
This process, for Benjamin, is embodied in fashion, by which he refers both
to fashion in garments and more general stylistic elements. In the former
sense, "Fashion couples the living body to the inorganic"; that is, fashion
stokes desire for the "living body" through the mediation of the "inorganic,"
clothing, and moreover the dead labour as well as the social meaning contained in a given garment within its socio-historical context. As in the above
quote, where the cyclist is a threshold-figure caught between the constricting
elegance of the past and the new technology of cycling, Benjamin is alert to

the "sadistic" elements of much of the fashion of the nineteenth century—it expresses the semblance of desire that is mediated by the commodity form: "Every fashion is to some extent a bitter satire on love; all sexual perversities are suggested in every fashion by the most ruthless means; every fashion is filled with secret resistances to love" (AP, 64). These "resistances," again, are drawn from a Freudian idiom, where the process of cathexis, or choice of love-object, involves a management of the redirection not only of the libido, but also the death drive.

The intermingling of the erotic and the thanatic in fashion serves an ideological function, is directly political: fashion is "a witness to the history of the great world only, for in every country . . . the poor people have fashions as little as they have a history, and their ideas, their tastes, even their lives barely change" [B4, 6] (AP, 72). What fashion documents is thus not merely "history" *in toto*, but *class* history, specifically the history of the ruling class. The following remark by Brecht, quoted in Convolute B, makes it possible to recognize how fashion functions as camouflage for their particular interests:

> Rulers have a great aversion to violent changes. They want everything to stay the same—if possible for a thousand years. If possible, the moon should stand still and the sun move no farther in its course. Then no one would get hungry any more and want dinner. And when the rulers have fired their shot, the adversary should no longer be permitted to fire; their own shot should be the last. (AP, 71)

Thus, the semblance of change in fashion obscures that the fundamentals, in other words, class relations, remain the same. The stasis-preserving or -seeking aspect of the death drive functions in the interests of the ruling class. Where for Freud, writing in the "Three Essays on Sexuality" (1905), perversion is a universal feature of sexuality, for Benjamin, performing a kind of Freudo-Marxian class analysis, the perversion that joins the libido and the thanatic together in fashion is revealed as belonging to the bourgeoisie. The death drive is thus revealed as not neutral. Under Capitalism, its function of aiming to preserve homeostasis serves the ruling class in preventing change to the social organism.

In the era of industrial capitalism, class thus emerges as a factor forcefully structuring the experience of the fractured subject. Benjamin delves into the "inhuman character" of the sphere of production and the changing forms of work in the nineteenth century. He quotes Conrad on this point, where a clerk describes his role for the harbour master, a "deputy Neptune," as

merely a subject for official writing, filling up of forms with all the artificial
superiority of a man of pen and ink to the men who grapple with realities outside
the consecrated walls of official buildings. What ghosts we must have been to
him! Mere symbols to juggle with in books and heavy registers, without brains
and muscles and perplexities; something hardly useful and decidedly inferior.[14]

The harbour master's function as a "deputy-Neptune" signals the resurfacing
of the mythic in the nineteenth-century workplace, where workers become
abstracted through their labour. Where Marx writes of the ghostly aspects
of the commodity, here the workers themselves become ghosts, "mere
symbols"—thoroughly reified. Benjamin elaborates on what this quote
encapsulates for him: the obsolescence of the "human element" in the labour
process: "Practice is eliminated from the productive process by machinery. In
the process of administration, something analogous occurs with heightened
organization. Knowledge of human nature, such as the senior employee could
acquire through practice, ceases to be decisive" (AP, 227). Where in the eighteenth century, the human element still proved crucial, factory labour serves
as the paradigmatic form of nineteenth-century production. It is here that the
human skills, qualities, and experience that previously formed an important
part of work cease to be of relevance, and human labour is dissected into units
of abstract labour time. Conversely, the factory is the emblematic space of the
divestment of human qualities into objects, where commodities are infused
with dead labour, as noted by Jules Michelet: "The head turns and the heart
tightens when, for the first time, we visit those fairy halls where polished
iron and dazzling copper seem to move and think by themselves, while pale
and feeble man is only the humble servant of those steel giants" [F7a, 6] (AP,
168). Humanity is subordinated to the production process, the methods of
production, and ultimately its own products. In this context, Benjamin refers
to Michelet's indictment of the first factories as "true hells of boredom" (AP,
109). This adjustment to the machine rhythms of modern life is experienced
as hellish, repetitive suffering by the workers,[15] who come to embody its patterns and thus become machine-like themselves: subjects fractured not only
from God, and their own bodies, but now also characterised by the fracture
of the labourer from his capacity to labour. In his sketch "Capitalism as
Religion," Benjamin wrote "Freud's theory, too, belongs to the hegemony of
the priests of this cult. Its conception is capitalist through and through. By
virtue of a profound analogy, which has still to be illuminated, what has
been repressed, the idea of sin, is capital itself, which pays interest on the
hell of the unconscious" (SW1, 289). By the time Benjamin was assembling
materials for the *Arcades Project*, this theory had come to be a useful tool
for the understanding of the hell of capitalism.

INDIVIDUAL VERSUS COLLECTIVIST TENDENCIES

In opposition to the machine-rhythm of factory labour, and alongside the tendencies of massification and reification, individualism comes to the fore in consumption, in the private sphere. This is the flip side of the fractured proletarian subject: an ostensibly hyperindividualised bourgeoisie. Despite his awe at factory production, to Michelet the realm of consumption seems to vouchsafe the endurance of individuality: As Benjamin notes, "the author in no way fears that mechanical production will gain the upper hand over human beings. The individualism of the consumer seems to him to speak against this: each 'man now . . . wants to be himself'" (AP, 168). For Benjamin, in contrast, this individuality is primarily a bourgeois phenomenon. The subject remains fractured between the semblance of individuality and the actual reification and loss of individuality in the mass. The public/private split of the citizen, ushered in with the political changes introduced by Louis Philippe, allows for a symbiotic relationship between the realities of capitalism and the illusions afforded by the interior. Capitalism needs the private individual in order to continue unabated, relies on the private sphere in which the phantasmagoria of autonomy and individuality can exist. This is the root cause for the proliferation of knickknacks and the stuffy interiors Benjamin describes in great detail in the *Arcades Project*, summarising in the 1939 Expose that "[t]he private individual, who in the office has to deal with realities, needs the domestic interior to sustain him in his illusions . . . he has no intention of grafting onto his business interests a clear perception of his social function. In the arrangement of his private surroundings, he suppresses both of these concerns" (AP, 19). This suppression, or repression, points to Benjamin's fusion of Marx and Freud: the repression of the true social function of classed individuals is what allows capitalism to flourish, and what sustains the deformed subjectivity of the bourgeoisie. Thus, where interiority appears, it is a smokescreen for—or semblance of—the emptiness of the subject fractured between the demand to be a subject, an individual with interiority, and the reality of commodification in capitalism.

This, of course, draws from Freud's pronouncements on the interiority of the melancholic in *Civilisation and Its Discontents* (1930), the withdrawal into one's own inner world, which is also present in neurosis: "an intention of making oneself independent of the external world by seeking satisfaction in internal psychic processes" (SE21, 79).

The withdrawal into the interior does not stop, ultimately, at the private sphere—despite the proliferation of gates, borders, and thresholds in nineteenth-century Paris, the interior swallows up spaces outside of itself. Benjamin is attuned to the psychoanalytic import of this movement and recognises it as an attempt to return to the womb. The arcades, too, are part of this: "'Whoever enters an arcade passes through the gate-way in the opposite direction.' (Or rather, he ventures into the intrauterine world)" [L5, 1] (AP, 415). Here, again, Freud's conceptualisation of life as aiming at a return to the inorganic returns in Benjamin's writing.

However, Benjamin notes in the 1939 Expose that this process itself is subject to a historical dialectic, whereby the reality of capitalism expands into the private sphere, leading to a crisis:

> The liquidation of the interior took place during the last years of the nine-teenth century, in the work of Jugendstil, but it had been coming for a long time . . . Henceforth, as Fourier had foreseen, the true framework for the life of the private citizen must be sought increasingly in offices and commercial centers. The fictional framework for the individual's life is constituted in the private home. (AP, 20)

Thus, this development into the separate public and private spheres is a mere moment in the spread of capitalism, exemplified in the phantasma-goria of Jugendstil. Ostensibly triumphantly individualistic, it is revealed rather as a kind of *Nottrieb* of an individualism faced with its demise in the introduction of new technologies. The fixation on individuality is thus no safeguard against encroaching commodification. It culminates in the fusion of the human with the object, the becoming-object, expressed thus by the *poete maudit* Leon Deubel, whom Benjamin quotes in the section C. Louis Philippe, or the Interior of the 1939 Expose: "I believe . . . in my soul: the thing."[16] The very metaphysical essence of the individual human comes to be experienced as objectified: in submitting to the machine rhythms of the factory in the sphere of consumption, in the structuring of experience by commodity consumption in the private sphere, and in the projection of empa-thy onto material objects. It is only on later analysis that this individuality is revealed as a smokescreen for the actual massification of nineteenth-century society. Benjamin quotes Giedion's description of the nineteenth century as a

> singular fusion of individualistic and collectivist tendencies. Unlike virtually every previous age, it labels all actions "individualistic" (ego, nation, art) while subterraneanly, in despised everyday domains, it necessarily furnishes, as in a delirium, the elements for a collective formation . . . With this raw material, we must occupy ourselves—with gray buildings, market halls, department stores, exhibitions. (AP, 390)[17]

Again, we see how the "subterranean," "despised everyday domains" come to function as an unconscious—the spaces of commodity consumption furnish the material building blocks of the experience of the "dreaming collective" throughout the *Arcades Project*. It follows from Benjamin's characterisation of this collective as a dreaming one that this experience remains unconscious.

Further to the temporal condensation that occurs in the nineteenth-century city, a spatial one is at play in the arcade: One of its central features is the condensation of outside and inside, veiling its street character through the semblance of being an *interieur*. As Jutta Wiegmann observes, what is repressed in the arcades are the twin features of massification and isolation (1989, 63). She traces how in the street, the individual is confronted with the fact that their perceived individuality is a mere semblance (*Schein*) in "representing, despite all eccentric singularity, only a specific type" (Wiegmann 1989, 65). Benjamin writes in the *Arcades Project* and both *Baudelaire* texts that in the street, types like the flaneur and the *privatier* are "as much at home among house facades as a citizen is within his four walls" (SW4, 19).[18] In the arcades, we see the apotheosis of the fusion of the semblance of public and private, as "The arcades are something [*ein Mittelding*] between a street and an interieur" (SW4, 19).[19] This ambivalence is what gives them their dreamlike character, but is also an indication of the dialectical tension at their heart. Wiegmann links this back to the compensatory function of the arcades: "To subordinate the street to the *interieur* serves the purpose of making the visitor of the arcade believe that he was in a space which—despite being populated by the crowd—allows for the unfolding/development [*Entfaltung*] of his individuality" (Wiegmann 1989, 66). Thus in the semblance of an interior, private space that is actually public and thronged by crowds, a semblance of subjectivity is created, which itself arises as a compensation for an emptiness. Wiegmann points to the wealth of mirrors in the arcades as illustrative of this; an attempt to artificially create "ego-consciousness" (Wiegmann 1989, 67), to reflect back at the subject the semblance of wholeness in its encounter with its mirror image. However, what is at stake in the proliferation of mirrors is not merely the creation of the semblance of individuality and thus the enduring possibility of subjectivity, but the becoming-narcissism and egocentricity of that subjectivity. Benjamin notes "Egoistic—that is what one becomes in Paris, where you can hardly take a step without catching sight of your dearly beloved self. Mirror after mirror!" (AP, 539), substituting a multitude of self-images and a pathological fixation on this self as compensation. This connects the fractured subject dwelling in the nineteenth-century city to the inward gaze of the baroque melancholic, and the inward-outward reach of narcissism, discussed in chapter 2. The narcissism of the nineteenth century becomes apparent in the mirrors of Paris. They reveal that the gaze is connected to the erotic—first and foremost autoerotic:

> Paris is the city of mirrors . . . Women here look at themselves more than elsewhere, and from this comes the distinctive beauty of the Parisienne. Before any

man catches sight of her, she already sees herself ten times reflected. But the
man, too, sees his own physiognomy flash by. He gains his image more quickly
here than elsewhere and also sees himself more quickly merged with this, his
image. Even the eyes of passersby are veiled mirrors, and over that wide bed of
the Seine, over Paris, the sky is spread out like the crystal mirror hanging over
the drab beds in brothels. (AP, 537).

The sky itself here becomes a mirror, endlessly reflecting the world of the
nineteenth century back onto itself, but it does so sordidly. Like its panoramas, which make everything visible as though on a flat plane, the mirrors of
nineteenth-century Paris reflect a will to domination, an expansionist narcissism that will know no outside. In the mass, people do not encounter each
other as subjects capable of intersubjective recognition, but merely as mirrors
to reflect the semblance of self in a multitudinous flow of images. What is
ultimately at stake in the multitudes of mirrors in the spaces of nineteenth-
century capitalism is the death drive:

> although this mirror world may have many aspects, indeed infinitely many, it
> remains ambiguous, double-edged . . . In its tarnished, dirty mirrors, things ex-
> change a Kaspar-Hauser-look with the nothing. It is like an equivocal wink com-
> ing from nirvana . . . The whispering of gazes fills the arcades. There is nothing
> here that does not, where one least expects it, open a fugitive eye, blinking it
> shut again; but if you look more closely, it is gone. (AP, 542)[20]

What is reflected in the mirrors of the arcade is thus the mere semblance
of a subject, along with the uncanny agency of things. Benjamin's mention
of Odilon Redon in this context, who "caught, like no one else, this look of
things in the mirror of nothingness, and who understood, like no one else,
how to join with things in their collusion with nonbeing" (AP, 542) also connects the cryptic "Kaspar-Hauser-look" to Verlaine's poem "Gaspard Hauser
Chante," in which the lines *"Suis-je né trop tôt ou trop tard?/ Qu'est-ce que
je fais en ce monde?* (Am I born too early or too late? What am I doing in
this world?" express Verlaine's identification of Hauser with Redon, the up-
rooted poet of modernity. Benjamin's fascination with Hauser also emerges
in his 1930 radio broadcast about him and follows the line taken by Verlaine:
Kaspar Hauser as a figure emblematic of the condition of modern man,
disconnected from history, even language itself.

Thus the "Kaspar-Hauser-look" exchanged by things in the mirrors of the
arcades adds layers upon layers of the non-being of a subject on top of each
other: the subject is a semblance, disconnected from all the things that could
conceivably make it a subject; this semblance is taken on by commodities
themselves in the arcades, but their glances, too, are only a reflection, in tar-
nished and dirty mirrors incapable of even rendering that reflection clearly,

and directed at: nothingness. Underneath all the layers of semblance in the nineteenth-century arcade is thus the death drive, which Freud also referred to as the "nirvana principle" (BPP, 50). This connection is further stressed by the next line, in which the gaze of things is likened to "an equivocal wink coming from nirvana": In this ambiguity, death itself becomes a mere semblance in the arcades, just as it does, as I discuss above, in fashion.[21] In the "whispering of gazes" of the ensouled objects that fill the arcades, Benjamin describes an atmosphere of menace and paranoia, linking the demonic and thus mythic ambiguity with the psychological, as well as a Marxist analysis of the dual nature of the commodity. The visitor of the arcades is not sure whether the whispering of the gazes is addressed to her, or indeed, who that addressee of the "I" might even be, given the multitude of reflections and refractions of the self in the arcades. This picks up on themes from *Civilisation and Its Discontents*, where Freud mentions examples of pathological states "in which the boundary lines between the ego and the external world become uncertain or in which they are actually drawn incorrectly" (SW21, 66). Ambiguity is thus a feature of psychopathology—and it is a constitutive feature of capitalism.

FRACTURED BODIES AND DOPPELGÄNGER

In his 1919 text "The Uncanny," Freud takes up this theme of ambiguity again in relation to the *Doppelgänger* or double. He states that while doublings or multiplications arise in primary narcissism, where they serve a compensatory function in signifying the endurance of life, they later become "harbinger[s] of death" (SE17, 235). The idea of the *Doppelgänger* draws its energy from the development of a faculty capable of observing and judging the rest of the ego—to treat it like an object. Freud here terms this faculty "conscience" and was later to name it the superego. Freud writes that this "renders it possible to invest the old idea of a 'double' with a new meaning and to ascribe a number of things to it—above all, those things which seem to self-criticism to belong to the old surmounted narcissism of earliest times" (SE17, 235). Freud concludes that the uncanny character of the double stems from its creation at a stage of "primitive" psychic development, its originally benign meaning having become inverted: "The double has become a thing of terror, just as, after the collapse of their religion, the gods turned into demons" (SE17, 236). The uncanny is grounded in the demonic character of the reiteration of something believed to belong to the past and laid to rest. Freud writes that this repetition "does undoubtedly, subject to certain conditions and combined with certain circumstances, arouse an uncanny feeling, which, furthermore, recalls the sense of helplessness experienced in some dream-states" (SE17, 236–37).

This, then, is the source of the uncanny phantasmagoric atmosphere of the arcades, with their ambiguous blurring of old and new, inside and out, and its endless multiplication of images of the self. The doctrine of eternal return forms the temporal equivalent to this in representing the moment of the repetition of similarityin the nineteenth century. For Benjamin, a specific form of doubles appears in industrial capitalism: "Neurosis creates the mass-produced article in the psychic economy. There it takes the form of the obsessional idea, which, manufactured in countless copies, appears in the household of the neurotic mind as the ever selfsame. Conversely, in Blanqui the idea of eternal return itself takes the form of an obsessional idea" (SW4, 166). Benjamin makes a direct reference to psychoanalysis in linking neurosis and the commodity-form. Eternal return is here revealed as itself a repetition-compulsion. Conversely, the psychic economy is linked to the material one in the figure of the compulsive neurosis—the compulsive thought resembles the commodity in its simultaneous massification and sameness.

MISSED OPPORTUNITIES

As we have seen, Capitalist processes lead to the massification of individuals in cities: as a mass of workers, but also a mass of observers of the commodity, and, if not direct consumers as a result of their immiseration, they still consume through their senses and their psyche, which is shaped by the commodity-form. This subject is a subjected one—vulnerable to propaganda, both commercial and political. The needs of the organism of capitalist society as a whole have thus shaped human subjectivity to the point where it is useful for its own ends—the continuation of the system, the ability of value to remain in circulation. The individuals in this mass are mere "elements," compressed together in a "compact mass," barely distinguishable from the point of view of the social organism in its totality, fungible and interchangeable. The expansionist drive of this capitalist organism, meanwhile, draws from Freud's assimilationist orientation of the libido, first conceptualised in *Beyond the Pleasure Principle*, here manifested at the collective level in the pulling together of humanity into a mass or collective. Simultaneously, as I discuss above, this mass is striated by different class positions, which relate to these tendencies of massification differently. The classes are locked in a struggle with each other; a struggle that the winning side seeks to continually suppress.

Like the psyche of an individual, Paris as the nineteenth-century capitalist metropolisis riven between the most modern and the archaic. This sets it apart from London and Rome, which for Benjamin each respectively are associated with one of these poles. A subterranean counter-network where information is disseminated exists, forming a counterpoint to the arcades— "another system of galleries runs underground through Paris: the Metro, where at dusk glowing red lights point the way into the underworld" (AP, 84). Sporadically, Benjamin alludes to the potential of the ostensibly capitalist space of the arcades themselves to become instead spaces of subterfuge for the poor, criminality, political resistance, and even barricade fighting. After all, the arcades and world exhibitions host worker's delegations as much as the displays of the fetish-commodity (AP, 186), and indeed harbour Marx and Engels as much as the rebellious masses: The nineteenth century "produced not only imperialism but also the Marxism that interrogates it with such useful questions" (SW3, 9), as Benjamin notes in "Brecht's *Threepenny Novel.*"[22] The arcades are thus spaces of contestation where the tensions of its age become visible. As phantasmagoric spaces, the arcades function as the unconscious of the nineteenth century: they are a repository of drives, desires, repressed knowledge, trauma. To expose their content to the analytical gaze is to set the social organism on the road to recovery. However, the failed revolutions of the eighteenth and nineteenth century—failed insofar as they are followed by a period of reaction and remain incomplete—mean that it was "the experience of this generation: that capitalism will die no natural death" (AP, 667). There is no automatism, no teleological unfolding of liberation in history for Benjamin. Of the three delegations of workers that were sent to the world exhibition in London in 1851, Benjamin writes that none "accomplished anything significant" [G8, 4] (AP, 188). They had official blessing and were thus subject to appeasement, taken in by the phantasmagoria of the exhibitions. This, then, is part of the ambiguity of the nineteenth century—its forms contain the potential for liberation, but whether this is recognized in awakening or again falls into the dream is a matter of the gaze, of one's standpoint— and of one's collective tactics. This, of course, is intimately bound up with the philosophy of history.

As we have seen, Freud grounds one pole of repetition-compulsion in the trauma of the missed event. In the context of Benjamin's *Arcades Project*, a major source of this historical trauma is the *revolutionary* moment that was missed and the disavowal of this trauma, much as the baroque was a response to the trauma of the rupturing of Christian cosmology. This also opens up the possibility of reading the *Trauerspiele* in light of a political failure: Just as the *Arcades Project* is written in the shadow of the failed commune, with the question of its making possible twentieth-century fascism implicit in the text, the baroque affect of mourning functions not just as the result of the rending of a cosmological totality, but as an index of the unfulfilled egalitarian promises of the Reformation and the historical failure of the peasant revolts.[23] In Benjamin's evocation of the nineteenth century, the city of Paris emerges as analogue to the human psyche. It is a repository of "revolution" and libidinal desire, which is repressed and emerges in symptomatic form as production, art, and culture-making. Freud and Benjamin part ways here— for Freud, aggressive, destructive individual instincts and drives must be restrained in the interest of society. While for Freud, the drives often work against civilisation, and no emancipation can be expected from them on their own, this taming is a more explicitly negative thing from Benjamin's perspective of collective liberation. The *Arcades Project* thus functions as a history of reaction in France, while at the same time raising the question of the possibility of overcoming this temporality.

Freud's concept of repetition-compulsion is operative in Benjamin's critique of historicism and the experience of time in the nineteenth century, where seemingly nothing is new and everything is repeated in the attempt to regain an original state of homeostasis. Following Freud, Benjamin points to a tension at the level of drives, the "mutually contradictory tendencies of desire: that of repetition and that of eternity"(AP, 117) which results in the idea of eternal recurrence attributed to Nietzsche, Blanqui, and Proust by Benjamin. We need to differentiate carefully between Benjamin's own position and the philosophy of history he depicts in the *Arcades Project* in order to critique it: It is the perception particular to the bourgeoisie that the world is ending, that the decline of the life-world of one's own class is synonymous with a general downfall of the era. At the same time, the dialectical antithesis of this belief is that in the true novelty of the new, which on Benjamin's analysis is revealed as merely being the newest mediation of that which has always been—domination by the mythic, and relations of domination. This fixation on novelty also functions as the opposite pole to the death drive—the expression of libido in partial form: "Why does everyone share the newest thing with someone else? Presumably, in order to triumph over the dead. This only where there is nothing really new" [D5a, 5] (AP, 112). Novelty is here identified with life and taken to stand in opposition to death.

However, the philosophy of history that experiences everything as repetition, and that which sees the present era as a break with history in its novelty, are two sides of the same coin when viewed as oppositional drives of the same organism—and, just like the life-preserving drives are "circuitous routes to death" for Freud, the opposition between life and death drives in the nineteenth century is destabilised by Benjamin's dialectical view: The fascination with new technologies and the conviction that they were a sign of a new era coexisted with the nihilistic outlook provoked by the perception of the impossibility of change. The pessimists of the nineteenth century, Benjamin seems to suggest, were partially accurate in their perception. They were right in the empirical observation of ostensible continuity of "the time of hell" (AP,

936) in nineteenth-century capitalist modernity but wrong about the ontological impossibility of change. They also, as a consequence, suggested the wrong strategies for effecting change and interrupting this temporality. On Benjamin's reading, a paradigmatic example of misguided utopianism turning to utter resignation is present in the thought of Auguste Blanqui.[24]

BLANQUI'S ETERNAL RETURN: *URGESCHICHTE*, MYTH AND ANTIQUITY

In the nineteenth century, capitalism presents itself as the newest form taken by class society, manifesting in the sensorium of the arcades. Given that the arcades were already outmoded by the time Benjamin wrote about them, this is illustrative of his point about the cyclical nature of the new and the ever-same: "the pomp and the splendor with which commodity-producing society surrounds itself, as well as its illusory sense of security, are not immune to dangers; the collapse of the Second Empire and the Commune of Paris remind it of that" (AP, 15). The form of the arcades, once experienced as so novel, has become archaic, but what they express is not, as it is still present at the moment of writing in the twentieth century: class society, exploitation, the commodity form. On Benjamin's view, Blanqui is correct in identifying this but commits the error of eternalising or ontologising this temporality, when Benjamin is concerned with interrupting it: Blanqui's "extreme hallucinatory power" is "anything but triumphant; it leaves, on the contrary, a feeling of oppression. Blanqui . . . strives to trace an image of progress that (immemorial antiquity parading as up-to-date novelty) turns out to be the phantasmagoria of history itself" (AP, 25). This phantasmagoria—that change is impossible and eternal recurrence is fated, not only on this earth, but on other planets—forecloses alternate imaginaries and the possibility of revolution. Thus, "Blanqui's cosmic speculation conveys this lesson: that humanity will be prey to a mythic anguish so long as phantasmagoria occupies a place in it" (AP, 15). This passage from the Expose of 1939 makes it Benjamin's task to dispel the phantasmagoria that tie humanity to "mythic anguish." Blanqui correctly diagnosed the problem but did not offer a solution, instead falling prey to it himself: blinded by "cosmic spleen" (AP, 5), Blanqui's "terrible indictment . . . against society takes the form of an unqualified submission to its results" (AP, 112). Blanqui paints a vision of a lateral unfolding of parallel universes rather than any vision of progress, projecting what was to become Nietzsche's eternal return onto a cosmic scale, years before Nietzsche himself. True liberation is contrasted with the finitude of Blanqui's vision, which is really just a recombination of fixed sets or types. Blanqui, to Benjamin, thus presents a claustrophobic utopia of closing in, an infernal interiority. He withdraws into his private hell, the hell of the capitalist society that imprisoned him, in the very moment of expanding his vision to a universe which is conceived as nothing but carceral, and—crucially—without any hope of escape. Thus, Blanqui writes his last work "in order to open new doors in his dungeon" [D5a, I] (AP, 111). Rather than liberatory, Blanqui's vision of eternal repetition on a cosmic scale is revealed as a capitulation to the philosophy of history of the nineteenth century. Benjamin concludes that "[t]he century was incapable of responding to the new technological possibilities with a new social order. That is why the last word was left to the errant negotiators between old and new who are at the heart of these phantasmagorias. The world dominated by its phantasmagorias, to make use of Baudelaire's term, is 'modernity'" (AP, 26). On this view, the people of the nineteenth century appear frozen in time, incapable of conceiving of anything beyond capitalism's use of technology or anything but its attendant, objectified subjectivity. Conversely, Benjamin's approach, with the twin analytic tools of Marxism and Freudian psychoanalysis, aims to perform a reality-testing of these phantasmagorias, in order to dispel the forces that hold back the possibility of a "new social order."

This is also at the root of the reiteration of Hellenic antiquity in the nineteenth century, and the return of *Urgeschichte*, primal, mythic history, in the midst of modern capitalist methods and relations of production. Benjamin quotes Karl Löwith on this: "'The existence that has lost its stability and its direction, and the world that has lost its coherence and its significance, come together in the will of the 'eternal recurrence of the same' as the attempt to repeat—on the peak of modernity, in a symbol—'the life which the Greeks lived within the living cosmos of the visible world'" (AP, 116). Just as the baroque appealed to it in its time of crisis, in the face of the seeming meaninglessness of the nineteenth century, an appeal is made to the imagined golden age of the past: classical antiquity. Eternal return and the idea of linear progress are both aspects of "the mythic mode of thought," that is, the facts of human history being fated to remain entirely outside the control of humanity.

Benjamin traces how this plays out in architecture in Convolute D: "The flexible and animated classical style was succeeded by the systematic and rigid pseudoclassical style . . . The Arc de Triomphe echoes the gate of Louis XIV; the Vendome column is copied from Rome; the Church of the Madeleine, the Stock Exchange, the Palais-Bourbon are so many Greco-Roman temples" (AP, 107). As in other fashions, nineteenth-century architecture is distinguished by the repetition of historical styles—specifically those of eras seen as triumphant and stable. The ancient resurfaces precisely in what is most modern about the city, in the nineteenth century as much as in Benjamin's own memories:

Other European cities admit colonnades into their urban perspective, Berlin setting the style with its city gates. Particularly characteristic is the Halle Gate—unforgettable for me on a blue picture postcard representing Belle-Alliance Platz by night. The card was transparent, and when you held it up to the light, all its windows were illuminated with the very same glow that came from the full moon up in the sky. [D2, 1] (AP, 104)

This passage, rich in allusions to perspectives and vision, itself opens up the possibility of seeing the conflux of *Urgeschichte* and nature in an artifact produced under industrial capitalism: it is modern production technologies, the mass production of souvenirs, that allows the postcard to be made. It renders it transparent, and that, paradoxically, is what allows the moonlight—elementary and mythic—to shine out of the windows of the modern city buildings. Tensions between these contradictory elements remain in these nineteenth-century vistas, in a similar fashion to the way allegory emerges in the baroque as a new form of accounting for the tension between the image of heroic antiquity of the Renaissance and the demonic side revived in the Middle Ages. The baroque embodies the tension not just between the Christian and the pagan, but between their tradition and revival in the Middle Ages, the Renaissance, and the Counter-Reformation. The nineteenth century cites triumphalist moments of history in its art forms and architecture but cannot control the return of the repressed in the form of the mythic.

Urgeschichte is not only linked to Hellenic antiquity, but also to nature: "As rocks of the Miocene or Eocene in places bear the imprint of monstrous creatures from those ages, so today arcades dot the metropolitan landscape like caves containing the fossil remains of a vanished monster: the consumer of the pre-industrial era of capitalism, the last dinosaur of Europe"—natural history resurfacing in modernity. Benjamin's metaphor is mirrored in Freud's observation that the neurotic's mind resembles "a prehistoric landscape, e.g. the Jurassic. The great dinosaurs still mill about, and the snake grass is as high as palm trees" (GW17, 151, transl. mine).[25] For Freud, it is in the symptoms of the neurotic that these "prehistoric" residues become most apparent. Benjamin reads the ruins, the residues of the arcades in the same way: they bear the imprints of the creatures that inhabited them, the consumers of previous eras of capitalism. It is in capitalist modernity that the mythic domination of humanity by heteronomous nature resurfaces via the commodity fetish: The subtleties of Grandville aptly express what Marx calls the "'theological niceties' of the commodity" [G5a, 2] (AP, 182), thus "if the commodity was a fetish, then Grandville was the tribal sorcerer" [G7, 2] (AP, 186). Once more, we see the proximity to the language of *Totem and Taboo* here. As Benjamin writes, "Capitalism was a natural phenomenon with which a new dream-filled sleep came over Europe, and, through it, a reactivation of mythic forces" (AP, 391). Nature—determination—the mythic, and sleep, are thus conjoined. This is what links the arcades to antiquity: the persistence of the mythic, of that which is passed down, unreflected, which Benjamin also likens to dreaming. The arcades, for all their novelty, emerge as closer to ancient caves or mythic entrances to hell than anything modern, and it is in the forms of capitalism that this structure devoid of human agency, of collective delibera-tion, finds expression: "The rebirth of the archaic drama of the Greeks in the booths of the trade fair" (AP, 88). What in the baroque was expressed in the *Trauerspiele*—the impossibility of recreating the ethical community of the Greeks and its tragic mode—is now mediated by the economic. Tradition is revealed as repetition-compulsion, passed from one generation to the next:

> In the idea of eternal recurrence, the historicism of the nineteenth century cap-sizes. As a result, every tradition, even the most recent, becomes the legacy of something that has already run its course in the immemorial night of the ages. Tradition henceforth assumes the character of a phantasmagoria in which primal history enters the scene in ultramodern get-up. [D8a, 2] (AP, 116)

Phantasmagoria are characterised by uniting dialectical opposites within themselves while obscuring the tension between them, in this case that of primal history and the "ultramodern" in the form of tradition. Benjamin here points to a tension at the level of the philosophy of history of the nineteenth century: between historicism and eternal return. This reveals both progress and tradition into a phantasmagoria, because they present a contradiction that the nineteenth century cannot do anything other than express, in other words, it presents it as symptoms without consciousness of a solution. Benjamin is as scathing about the liberal idea of progress—"an infinite perfectibility under-stood as an infinite ethical task"—as that of conservative eternal return. They are "complementary," "the indissoluble antinomies" against which Benjamin posits his own "dialectical conception of historical time." To this bourgeois philosophy of history, "the idea of eternal return appears precisely as that 'shallow rationalism' which the belief in progress is accused of being, while faith in progress seems no less to belong to the mythic mode of thought than does the idea of eternal return" [D10a, 5] (AP, 119). Benjamin thus inverts the notion of progress as the shedding of the mythic. Benjamin's understanding of *Urgeschichte* draws from the "psychic residue" of previous ages discussed by Freud, who in "Analysis Terminable or Interminable" writes of a similar historical residue:

> There is not one of the erroneous and superstitious beliefs of mankind that are supposed to have been left behind but has left a residue at the present day in the

lower strata of civilized peoples or even in the highest strata of cultivated society. All that has once lived clings tenaciously to life. Sometimes we are inclined to doubt whether the dragons of primeval times are really extinct. (SE23, 229)

This is in keeping with Freud's conceptualisation of the libido in *Beyond the Pleasure Principle* and views put forward in *Totem and Taboo*. However, Benjamin historicises the reappearance of this mythic residue. It is the specific forms social organisation of an epoch that bring about its reiteration of antiquity in the modern: "But precisely modernity is always citing primal history. Here, this occurs through the ambiguity peculiar to the social relations and products of this epoch" (AP, 10), that is, in capitalism. The stakes are high: As Stewart points out, Benjamin in part turns to the *Trauerspiel* "because he detects a mimetic relationship between the baroque and his own Weimar. At key moments, his treatise illuminates the usefulness of an understanding of the baroque for his own historical moment, the collapse of democracy, that is, and the rise of totalitarianism" (Stewart 2010, 16). The consequences of a failure to break out of the continuum of mythic history are catastrophic, but in order to effect this break, the movement of origin must be followed: forward and backward into history and, at the same time, disrupting the concept of linearity—as in psychoanalysis, so in Benjamin's philosophy of history.

In the *Trauerspiel* book, Benjamin investigated the resurfacing of ancient concepts such as acedia and *taedium vitae* in the early modern era. In the *Arcades Project* and the Baudelaire project, this is transposed into the nineteenth century. Here, baroque melancholia becomes spleen. As Benjamin outlines in "Central Park," it "interposes centuries between the present moment and the one just lived. It is spleen that tirelessly generates 'antiquity'" (SW4, 166). In what follows, I will investigate the way in which these processes bring about the types Benjamin examines in the *Arcades Project*, beginning with the figure most emblematic of spleen: Baudelaire.

NOTES

1. See also Wiegmann (1989, 61) on this point.
2. See also Weigel's detailed reconstruction of which of Freud's works Benjamin read (e.g., Weigel 2016, 91).
3. Indeed, Freud himself expands the libido to encompass the concepts of philosophical and literary tradition: "In this way the libido of our sexual instincts would coincide with the Eros of the poets and philosophers which holds all living things together" (BPP, 44).

4. The translation elides that the "daemonic" resides in the "experience or life" (*Erleben*).

5. A detailed engagement with Benjamin's dream theory in the context of Freudian dream interpretation will follow in the final chapters of this book.

6. That Benjamin's thinking here is not entirely opposed to a Freudian logic is hinted at in Freud's note on the mystic writing pad from 1925: Freud here likens the human memory apparatus to a new invention, the "*Wunderblock*" which can simultaneously store writing and present a clean slate for new inscriptions. While important as an early elaboration on Freud's theory of memory and experience, discussed below, of interest here is his comment on traditional writing methods: "the surface upon which this note is preserved, the pocket-book or sheet of paper, is as it were a materialized portion of my mnemic apparatus [memory apparatus], the rest of which I carry about with me invisible [which I otherwise carry invisibly within myself]. I have only to bear in mind the place where this 'memory' has been deposited and I can then 'reproduce' it at any time I like, with the certainty that it will have remained unaltered and so have escaped the possible distortions to which it might have been subjected in my actual memory" (SE19, 225). Thus, a sort of object-memory is presupposed by Freud himself, even if he does not pursue this line of thinking. See also N. Werner (2015) for a detailed discussion of this passage in Freud in the context of its influence on Benjamin.

7. We can see the links to Benjamin's work on aura in the artwork essay here. See also A. Conty (2013) for a discussion of what she terms the "optical unconscious" which touches on some of the issues presented here.

8. Translation of Marx's term "*sinnlich-übersinnliches Ding*" (MEW23, 85) by Sami Khatib (2017, 56). See also the discussion of the role of the commodity-form in the *Arcades Project* as an allegorical form of perception in the same article.

9. See the below discussion on gambling—at stake is an addiction to the potential, not the fulfilment, of desire.

10. The same formulation appears in both Exposés, indicating its centrality to Benjamin's thought around the *Arcades Project*.

11. In a 1938 letter to Adorno, Benjamin again stresses that "Empathy with the commodity presents itself to self-observation or internal experience as empathy with inorganic matter" (C, 592).

12. First nature, too, frequently appears in the arcades, and Benjamin traces how they themselves come to look like the sea, or recreate natural environments in other ways. Indeed, the arcades, Benjamin notes, were originally modelled on hothouses. Thus at their root, just like Paxman's crystal palace design for the world exhibition, they are an architectural form not made for humans, but houses made for plants.

13. In later Convolutes, the same process of the combination of death drive and libido resulting in a fusion of human and artificial reappears in automata and uncanny dolls.

14. We can see a link here to Kafka's short story "Poseidon" (1920), where the sea-god himself is portrayed as a disgruntled administrator, making obscure calculations in his office while never seeing the sea himself. Kafka here satirises a profane age where the divinity of the sea-god is no longer possible, and he has been reduced to the

status of a manager. We can read Benjamin's use of Conrad as performing a similar gesture to Kafka in its emphasis on the emptied-out, ghostly shells of the harbour administrators, robbed by the process of nineteenth-century Capitalist labour of even the semblance of full subjecthood.

15. Of note is Benjamin's inclusion of the observation by Georges Friedman, a sociologist and contemporary of Benjamin's: "Often the remarks of Michelet (for example, on reverie and the rhythms of different occupations) anticipate, on an intuitive level, the experimental analyses of modern psychologists" (AP, 109–10). This linking of the boredom caused by the work rhythm of capitalist labour to experimental psychology resonates with Benjamin's interest in not only the psychic dimension of the experience of capitalism in the nineteenth century, but specifically the insights gained from the discipline of psychoanalysis.

16. This is also the reason for Benjamin's interest in the figure of "the prostitute" who, like the flaneur, "takes him [or her]self to market." Thus, for Benjamin, "Love for the prostitute is the apotheosis of empathy with the commodity" (AP, 511).

17. In a letter to Giedion of February 1929, Benjamin writes "Your book constitutes one of those rare cases that everyone knows: that we know in advance of the *Berührung* with something (or someone: writing, house, human, etc) that it will be meaningful to the highest degree" GB III, 444 (letter no. 631). And indeed, Benjamin refers to Giedion's book throughout the *Arcades Project*, in particular to his theory of construction, discussed below.

18. "ebenso häuslich wie der Spießbürger in seinen vier Wänden" (GS1, 628). It should be noted that the *Spießbürger* is not primarily a citizen at all, but rather a specific type of stuffy, conservative *petit bourgeois*, who in Benjamin's time was linked to the rise of fascism.

19. "Die Passagen sind ein Mittelding zwischen Straße und Interieur" (GS1, 539).

20. Arianne Conty (2013, 476) links this to aura: "Nature, like the cult object, has an aura to the extent that it has been invested or endowed with the capacity to return our gaze. On this reading, it is this investment of the imagination that empowers the cult object and can explain the sacralisation and anthropomorphisation or personification of nature in many ancient cultures. Aura would thus illustrate a theory of projection, the projection of consciousness, of familiarity, and hence of intentionality, to the non-human world of nature. Aura would come to signify the projection of the known onto the unknown, and find a place alongside projection theories of religion."

21. Caspar Hauser also appears in Benjamin's review of Hugo von Hoffmansthal's *Der Turm*, which Benjamin saw as a successful contemporary reiteration of the baroque *Trauerspiel*. Its prince, he writes, is of the type of Caspar Hauser: "In the newly-formed hero, too, words break only fleetingly through the churning sound-sea, looking about themselves with an alienated naiad's gaze. It is the same which today affects us so deeply in the language of children, visionaries or the mad" (GS3, 99, transl. mine). It is here, in its *Urlaute*, in its breaks and failures, that language is at its strongest for Benjamin. We encounter it in the speech of those whose experience and perception, their different relation to language and detachment from social conventions is for Benjamin encapsulated in their gaze, estranged from the world.

22. However, Marxist doctrine is not exempt from the bad historicism and economic determinism of the milieu of the nineteenth century in which it was brought

about. Benjamin refers to an anecdote from Lafargue to illustrate this: "Engels told me that it was in Paris in 1848, at the Cafe de la Regence (one of the earliest centers of the Revolution of 1789), that Marx first laid out for him the economic determinism of his materialist theory of history" [D3, 6] (AP, 108).

23. Also see Rebecca Comay (2011) for a discussion of the reception of the French Revolution in Germany, specifically German Idealism.

24. See Peter Hallward's work on a contesting reading of Blanqui's understanding of history (Hallward 2014).

25. On this point see also Freud's 1916 *Mythologische Parallele zu einer plastischen Zwangsvorstellung* on the imagistic parallels between neurotic fantasies and ancient myth.

Chapter Four

The Types of the Nineteenth Century

Benjamin's Case Studies

At the same time as functioning as a collective organism, the nineteenth century also brings forth individuals who grapple with the forms of their age as fractured subjects, refracted into types. Of note is the relationship of Benjamin's investigation of these types to Freud's case studies. In their insertion into the canon of psychoanalytic literature, the latter become ideal-typical figures, chosen for making most apparent something Freud seeks to highlight about his method. Beyond the specificity of their individual psychopathology, they are thus made into emblematic figures for the human psyche and psychoanalysis as a discipline. While stressing the importance of the psychoanalytic situation (with analyst and analysand present in the same room), Freud also goes against this in "analysing" cases that are historical or fictional in character—as we saw in chapter 2, Schreber and Haitzmann are two such cases, and even literary figures such as Hamlet appear in his writing. In his 1895 *Studies on Hysteria*, Freud notes how strange it appears to him that his case histories "read like stories" (SE2, 160)—the literary dimension of narrative surfaces almost against Freud's will, even as he emphasizes his reluctance to extend psychoanalytic methods to literature. Benjamin draws on Freud in his account of nineteenth-century types but also complicates psychoanalytic methods: Where Freud is surprised by the narrative form his case stories take, and narration and re-narration form the crux of his "talking cure," Benjamin examines the tension between a collective, narratable form of experience and the increasing impossibility of this in Capitalist modernity. His types present an alternative form of case studies that uses episodic glosses, citations, and textual montage, exploring ways to illustrate both specific neuroses and states of mental distress and those common to nineteenth-century fractured subjects.[1] As types, they distil the general from the specific and present case studies that are composites of individual cases as well as literary figures and cultural fragments.

Benjamin's method in analysing his types draws from Freud, most explicitly in the case of the gambler, and in his writings on Baudelaire. Both Benjamin's types and Freud's Schreber are trapped in the nineteenth century, their symptoms expressive of the particular psychopathology of individuals of this society and thus of the psychopathological character *of* that society itself. Here, the fractured post-baroque subject, torn between commodification, massification, and the demand to remain an individual, experiences melancholia as spleen, re-enacting the traumatic loss of cosmological integrity. Spleen expresses the fracture of the subject in high modernity: it emerges as the main form in which Baudelaire, the paradigmatic poet of this era, casts the modern, "and is usually counterposed to ('it fractures') the *ideal*" (SW3, 40). Spleen fractures the ideal—and as I discuss below, it is the recasting of the baroque melancholia of the fractured subject in the era of rapidly-developing capitalism. Benjamin connects spleen to the interlinked loss of collective experience and the change in memory in modernity.

MEN OF THE CROWD? MODERN MELANCHOLIA: BAUDELAIRE'S SPLEEN

In a letter to Horkheimer of 16 April 1938, Benjamin describes the Baudelaire work as "an extensive treatment in which the most important motifs of the *Arcades* project converge," a "miniature" model for the whole *Arcades Project* (C, 556). Agamben draws attention to the fact that Benjamin's notes and correspondence imply that the Baudelaire "chapter is in reality functioning as a principle of disaggregation for the entire structural unity of the book on Paris" (Agamben 2016, 221). Far from merely constituting a text dealing with Baudelaire the person, the Baudelaire project in its final form portrays the subject of Baudelaire as a manifestation of the nineteenth century as a whole: a figure in which the melancholia of the nineteenth century crystallises as boredom and spleen. Benjamin quotes a variety of commentators on Baudelaire, his selection focusing on the inwardness of Baudelaire's writing and his person. Baudelaire's confessional style, that is, the subjectivism of his writing, is noted: "He was the first to write about himself in a moderate confessional manner, and to leave off the inspired tone . . . The first also who accuses himself rather than appearing triumphant, who shows his wounds, his laziness, his bored uselessness at the heart of this dedicated, workaday century . . . spleen and illness, without ever once using the word (AP, 246)." This melancholia is explicitly characterised as symptomatic and linked to psychoanalytic categories. Baudelaire's writing is thus characterised as the obverse of the protestant work ethic. His inward gaze leads him not to narcissistic exuberance but to his traumas ("wounds") and displays all the hallmarks of a melancholic, conceiving of himself as lacking and inadequate. Indeed, another commentator quoted by Benjamin notes that "Baudelaire is as incapable of love as of labor. He loves as he writes, by fits and starts, and then relapses into the dissolute egoism of a flaneur. Never does he show the slightest curiosity about human affairs or the slightest consciousness of human evolution" (AP, 249). Baudelaire's egoism is "dissolute" as he is focusing inward, but this merely yields a retrenchment of his melancholia.

Benjamin's characterisation of Baudelaire as the quintessential modern melancholic culminates in a comparison to Hamlet: "I asked myself whether Baudelaire . . . had not sought, through histrionics and psychic transfer, to revive the adventures of the prince of Denmark" (AP, 245). This ties his figure to the *Trauerspiel* book, and indeed forms the link between nineteenth-century subjectivity and that inaugurated in the baroque. Baudelaire is a type of modern subject which is not one: refractured into types, experiencing and expressing different forms of the pathology of subjecthood particular to its era. Just as in the baroque, the individual in the nineteenth century suffers from the injunction to act as a subject under conditions which make this impossible. Benjamin writes that while Baudelaire liked to portray himself as a quasi-demonic figure of menace outside the social order, his death cast him as a martyr. This dualism also speaks for reading Baudelaire as the modern equivalent of the baroque sovereign, of which Hamlet is the seventeenth-century epitome. He is fractured along the same lines, into the martyr and the tyrant. With Freud, we can see him oscillating between outward and inward directed destructiveness, rendering him at times melancholic, at times psychotic—just as in the figure of the baroque sovereign, melancholia, far from being successfully worked through, turns outwards and flips into its obverse, madness and rage.

Benjamin is interested in the deeper motivations of Baudelaire as unveiled by the psychoanalytic understanding of the centrality of the familial relationship, especially that with the mother, as it relates to the poet's later stance on sexuality. Benjamin employs psychoanalytic vocabulary here, writing of the "rationalisations" of Baudelaire's unconscious, repressed wish for his mother's love. At the same time, Benjamin stresses that "His artificially maintained dependence on his mother had not only a psychological cause (underscored by psychoanalysts) but a social one" (SW4, 179). Of course, as discussed in chapter 2, psychoanalysis understands the psychic as inflected by the interplay of the individual and the social, an intra-psychic conflict arising when a need is not being met by the world. Freud points to this gap between wish and reality, the unmet needs and desires in the life of an individual, as the trigger for neuroses in modernity: "To-day neurosis takes the place of the monasteries which used to be the refuge of all whom life had disappointed or who felt too weak to face it" (SW11, 50). These reflections on the changing character of the responses to an unresolved conflict between individual and world can be read against seventeenth-century Haitzmann's decision to take holy orders. Where Haitzmann was still capable of entering a monastery in order to resolve this conflict (though, as we have seen, uneasily so), modernity has instead supplied neurosis as an alternative space for withdrawal, this time into the self. Just as Haitzmann unconsciously tested the world and himself and judged himself inadequate, Benjamin writes that in the attitude of "someone dependent on handouts, Baudelaire put his society continuously to the test" (SW4, 179). Both assume a passive, helpless attitude towards the world and express their experience of being incapable of enacting their wishes on the world in historically specific forms of psychic suffering. Where Haitzmann assumes a feminine role towards the devil in his delusion, Baudelaire expresses the inability to act as sexual impotence. For Benjamin, this expresses the condition of the modern, fractured, subject. Baudelaire follows a socially determined path due to the social character of the reasons for male impotence, and "Only this explains why, to sustain him on his travels, he received a precious old coin from the treasury amassed by European society. On its face it showed the figure of Death; on its reverse, Melancholia sunk in brooding meditation. This coin was allegory" (SW4, 185). Melancholia and the death drive are revealed as that which feeds Baudelaire's work.[2] In this, he is emblematic of his age: The masculine subject, enjoined to lead a *vita activa* and be a heroic subject, is not tenable in the nineteenth century, just as he was not tenable in the baroque. With the declaration of the rights of man, with the advent of democracy, all men are enjoined to be sovereigns, and none of them can be. The anxieties about masculinity reflected in the delusions of Schreber and Haitzmann thus also play out in the figure of Baudelaire. He carries on the legacy of the baroque in the form of the "treasure" of European culture, the coin spinning between death and melancholia. By the nineteenth century, modern melancholia has utterly entrapped the subject within itself:

> The decisively new ferment that enters the *taedium vitae* and turns it into spleen is self-estrangement. In Baudelaire's melancholy [*Trauer*], all that is left of the infinite regress of reflection—which in Romanticism playfully expanded the space of life into ever-wider circles and reduced it within ever narrower frames—is the "somber and lucid tete-a-tete" of the subject with itself. (SW4, 163)

Again, we see the effects of the loss of transcendence in modernity: Like the bottomless reflection of the baroque brooder, the nineteenth-century melancholic encounters not truth, or knowledge, or God, but is entrapped by subjectivism. The constitutive fracture of the modern subject—its foundation on loss—is expressed in this self-centred circling. The truth of the "precious old coin" of the history of the modern European subject is thus revealed in its ceaseless movement, death drive and melancholia blurring into one in the form of spleen: "From the perspective of spleen, the buried man is the 'transcendental subject' of historical consciousness" (SW4, 165). Like baroque allegory, the product of a world that has lost is eschatological referent, the decay of experience expressed in the *ennui* of modernity makes all of history appear as decay. Robbed of transcendence, the fractured modern subject is entrapped by the constraints of the demand of subjecthood and lapses further into subjectivism. The ultimate destination of his ever-smaller concentric circles is death. At the same time, as Salzani observes, "This is the dialectical potential of allegory and thus of spleen: it destroys the *Schein*, the deceptive appearance of organic wholeness, and exposes the naked truth of the demise of experience" (Salzani 2009, 138). Only in thus revealing the semblance of experience in modernity for what it is—the doomed attempt by fractured subjects to integrate their experience of the world in order to create meaning—is there a potential for the redemption of experience and the overcoming of the fractured subject. At the same time, the "self-estragement" of humanity in the nineteenth century, as we saw in the previous chapter, is mediated by the commodity form, its inorganic matter binding human libidinal energies to itself.

Benjamin thus establishes a link between the baroque melancholic and the allegorist of the nineteenth century, positing Baudelaire as the zenith of the conflux of inwardness and intense concentration on the (material) fragment. What links the allegory of the baroque and the nineteenth century, despite the latter's ostensibly much more "optimistic" historical character, is historically specific melancholy—this time as a response, the "motorial reaction," to the commodity form. Just as in baroque poetry, stereotypes proliferate in Baudelaire's writing, and he returns to the same motifs again and again. This marks him as a melancholic:

> The magnetic attraction which a few basic situations continually exerted on the poet is one of the symptoms of his melancholy. Baudelaire's imagination is occupied by stereotyped images. He seems to have been subject to a very general compulsion to return at least once to each of his motifs. This is doubtless comparable to the compulsion which repeatedly draws the felon back to the scene of his crime. Baudelaire's allegories are sites where he atoned for his destructive drive. (SW4, 172)

Baudelaire's destructive impulse results in a constant return of the same in his poetry, driven by a traumatic compulsion to revisit that which was destroyed. There are thus historical differences between the allegories of the baroque and those of the nineteenth century. The disintegrating force of allegory in capitalist modernity is locked in a struggle with the semblance that would disguise the commodity character of the objective world and the stereotyped images it produces. Allegory works against this: "What resists the mendacious transfiguration of the commodity world is its distortion into allegory. The commodity wants to look itself in the face" (SW4, 173).[3] As commodities, objects under capitalism are imbued with agency, further challenging the centrality of the human element in the subjective process of allegoresis by becoming capable of it itself. Benjamin notes the changing function of allegory in a "commodity-producing economy" and suggests that Baudelaire's poetry reflects this process in attempting to making apparent the "peculiar aura" of the commodity: "He sought to humanize the commodity heroically. This endeavour has its counterpart in the concurrent bourgeois attempt to humanize the commodity sentimentally: to give it, like the human being, a home" (SW4, 173). In this, Baudelaire submits to the same principle at play in production, and in the bourgeois home: the humanisation of the commodity in "etuis, covers, and cases in which the domestic utensils of the time were sheathed" (SW4, 173).

As a stylistic medium, allegoresis no longer occupies the centrality it did in the seventeenth century, leaving Baudelaire isolated and out of time. Benjamin grounds this in the socio-economic formation of capitalism, which was not yet the determining factor for allegory in the baroque. Thus, "[t]he devaluation of the world of things in allegory is surpassed within the world of things itself by the commodity" (SW4, 64). As Pensky observes, allegory in the nineteenth century

> confronts a world of a priori objects that themselves have already been allegorized by the advent of the commodity. Exchange value, in which the object is hollowed out, to be rendered "meaningful" only by the arbitrary assignation of price, is a "devaluing" force far more powerful than the *Trauer* with which the baroque playwrights contemplated their world. (Pensky 1993, 166–67)

The contradictory character of nineteenth-century melancholy becomes manifest in its poet, Baudelaire, whose poetic gift—the melancholic gaze that allows him to capture the commodity nature of nineteenth-century metropolitan life—is simultaneously what prevents him from realising the true nature of his insight. The opposition between correspondences and allegory, never developed in Baudelaire, once again leads to the re-emergence of critical subjectivity, as the truth content of the fragments of social life cannot be reconstructed by the artist, but must involve critical incisiveness. Its attempt to deliberately grasp and make manifest "moments of transcendent meaning from within the continuum of natural history" (Pensky 1993, 180) is doomed to failure. Ultimately, then, Baudelaire's allegory, supposedly more faithful to the "realm of things" than the baroque, falls victim to the same process. Proust emerges as another paradigmatic nineteenth-century literary figure who attempts to overcome the fracture of the subject, iterating the conflict of experience in modernity through his writing on the objects of memory.

PROUST'S MEMOIRE (IN)VOLONTAIRE, EXPERIENCE AND THE PSYCHOANALYTIC THEORY OF MEMORY

Written from March to June 1929 concurrently with the *Arcades Project*, "On the Image of Proust" initially functioned as a "breakaway" piece, just as the Baudelaire texts were intended to be.[4] Benjamin here conceptualises two types of life: the life lived or experienced and the life recollected by the one experiencing it, which forms the object of Proust's work. The main aspect of Proust's investigation, however, is not the recollection of the facts that were experienced, but the construction of memory—the "weaving" of it in the "Penelope work of remembrance" (SW2, 238) [*Eingedenken*]. However, Benjamin immediately complicates this picture of the "Penelope work": Its "weaving" is not a consciously willed, deliberate act, but rather a *memoire involontaire*, a memory that remains largely unconscious—a remembrance that appears "spontaneously," and thus much more intimately entwined with forgetting, the unconscious. Thus, Benjamin poses the question whether this form of remembrance is not rather a counterpart to the work of Penelope, the construction of something—the day unravelling what the night fashioned; in other words, the conscious mind unpicking what the unconscious made visible in dreams. Rather than the conscious mind dredging up specific memories, Benjamin here inverts the relationship between subject and memory—*Erinnerung* dictates the pattern of this weave, rather than the other way around. Strikingly, the very unity of Proust's text is only provided through memory, rather than the person of the author or the actual plot. They are revealed as only effects or functions of the process of memory, "the reverse of the continuum of memory" (SW2.1, 238). Thus, the centrality of memory serves to destabilise the subject in Proust's work. This is also what forms the kernel of Benjamin's interest in it. However, in order to flesh out what is at stake in Proust's memory theory, Benjamin looks to Freud.

For Freud in *Beyond the Pleasure Principle*, psychoanalysis reveals consciousness as a function of a particular psychic system. This part of the system does not preserve, it merely has the capacity for constant reception of sensory data. The psychic apparatus is thus divided into two functions, one of the reception of perceptions, one of the storing of them. Crucially, at the point of the reception of a stimulus in the perception-consciousness (W-Bw), this stimulus is either registered by consciousness (Bw), *or* it circumvents the Bw part of the system and is channelled towards the unconscious, where it is stored as a memory-trace.[5] With Freud's model of perception and memory-formation, Benjamin can thus explain how a memory is formed when the psychic shield is breached by a shock and the shocking stimulus is stored in the unconscious.[6] Benjamin and Freud part ways on the possibility of experience in modernity; where for Freud, this remains possible, Benjamin is increasingly convinced that the life-world of the nineteenth century foreshadows a poverty of experience, culminating in Benjamin's own day. In the *Arcades Project*, he notes that in the daily experience of life in the capitalist metropolis, these shocks are more and more frequent, forcing modern man to adapt psychologically, as the overcrowded city forces people into a proximity with others that would be intolerable without "psychological distance" [M17, 2] (AP, 447). Benjamin thus assumes a habitual hardening to these shocks in modernity. Benjamin looks to Freud to account for this, quoting the attempt to belatedly process the traumatic experience in dreams and repetition-compulsion. Benjamin takes this to mean that the shock-reception of consciousness trains its ability to process impulses in dreams and memory. He speculates "[t]hat the shock is thus cushioned, parried by consciousness, would lend the incident that occasions it the character of an isolated experience [*Erlebnis*], in the strict sense" (SW4, 318). Crucially, Benjamin needs this notion of a "training" of consciousness in order to arrive at his central point: the downfall of collective experience, *Erfahrung* in modernity. Thus, he writes that "The greater the shock factor in particular in particular impressions, the more vigilant consciousness has to be in screening stimuli; the more efficiently it does so, the less these impressions enter long experience [*Erfahrung*] and the more they correspond to the isolated experience [*Erlebnis*]" (SW4, 319). *Erlebnis* is the conscious experiencing of impressions, caused by the chocs of modern life. These are individual rather than collective, occurring at a specific point in time rather than over a duration. Thus, Freud helps Benjamin account for the non-linear temporality of experience.

Benjamin relates this to Proust: "For an experienced event is finite—at any rate, confined to one sphere of experience; a remembered event is infinite, because it is merely a key to everything that happened before it and after it" (SW2.1, 238). Thus memory is a type of origin, in accordance with the way origin works in the *Trauerspiel* book. We see here the contrast between *Erlebnis* and *Erfahrung* that is not quite formulated in the *Arcades*

Project: *Erlebnis* is committed to the unconscious and as such a "limitlessly remembered" one. It is not self-contained, or rather, it is self-contained in the way of a monad, in that it contains within itself everything else—including its pre- and post-history. A memory of an *Erlebnis* is thus a key with which to unlock the entirety of what is stored in the unconscious—everything before and after it. Benjamin's reading of Proust is thus influenced by a Freudian understanding of the psyche, where the individual memory can be made sense of only in the context of the entire life.

In "On Some Motifs in Baudelaire," Benjamin seeks to put Freud's "hypothesis" about the "correlation between memory (in the sense of a *memoire involontaire*) and consciousness" (SW4, 316) to work "in situations far removed from the ones he had in mind when he wrote" (SW4, 317). Attentive to the accelerated pace of the disintegration of experience in modernity, even when compared to Freud's time, Benjamin looks to Reik once more: "the function of memory [the author identifies the sphere of 'forgetfulness' with 'unconscious memory' . . .] is to protect our impressions; reminiscence aims at their dissolution" (AP, 402). Investigating what happens to the sensory input once it is committed to the unconscious, this sets up a division between two types of memory: one remains at the level of the unconscious; from the standpoint of consciousness, it can be equated with "being forgotten," as it is not attainable by it. As soon as it is dragged up again, it becomes reminiscence, the second type of memory, which like the atmospheric exposure that corrodes archaeological artifacts dissolves the original memory-trace: "Put in Proustian terms, this means that only what has not been experienced explicitly and consciously, what has not happened to the subject as an isolated experience [*Erlebnis*], can become a component of *memoire involontaire*" (SW4, 317). Thus, a conscious attempt at recapturing the original inscription of the memory-trace is doomed to fail, as it will destroy it. An unbidden "flashing up" of the memory in a *memoire involontaire* does not follow the same pattern, however, as once again the active involvement of consciousness is circumnavigated and the content of the memory is preserved.

This is also the conception of unconscious memory operative in Benjamin's autobiographical "Bullrich salt" anecdote. In Convolute G "Exhibitions, Advertising, Grandville," there is a sudden irruption into the succession of aphoristic quotes that mirrors the shock of its content: an account of Benjamin's own experience of seeing a striking advertisement. He writes "As is sometimes the case with very deep, unexpected impressions, however, the shock was too violent: the impression . . . struck with such force that it broke through the bottom of my consciousness and for years lay irrecoverable somewhere in the darkness" (AP, 174). The poster, an advert

for "Bullrich salt," struck Benjamin so strongly it was contained unconsciously for years, until it resurfaced years later, when he was confronted
again with the slogan of the brand. As Benjamin recounts, the lettering
alone was enough to bring his visual memory of the original poster into full
consciousness—"I had it once more." In this, Benjamin follows Freud's
account of the formation of trauma in *Beyond the Pleasure Principle*,
discussed above, in which the different strata of the psychic apparatus have
different functions relating to the processing and storing of sensory data, and
the unconscious is only reached by impulses strong enough to breach the protective layer of consciousness. Here, a different aspect of this process comes
to the fore: The formation of memories from the contents of the unconscious.

Crucially, this memory is stored in an object—as it is for Proust, writing on
the attempt to deliberately recapture the past: "all the efforts of our intellect
must prove futile. The past is hidden somewhere outside the realm, beyond
the reach, of intellect, in some material object . . . And as for that object, it
depends on chance whether we come upon it or not before we ourselves must
die" [K8a, 1] (AP, 403). Arianne Conty comments: "In Benjamin's historical
materialism, memory thus becomes an imminently political entity, because
the control of artefacts and their mediation is the key not only to our past, but
also to the future of that past which brings us, for a brief instant, the image of
our present" (Conty 2013, 478). Benjamin thus looks to Proust to supplement
the Freudian model of memory, in order to allow for a type of remembrance
that is not purely destructive, but preserves something of the character of
the past precisely because it does not seek to recreate it in full. In the realm
of the philosophy of history, this is opposed to bourgeois historicism, which
seeks to capture the past "as it really was" and which is thus doomed only
to project onto the past what it *assumes* of it. Proust, for Benjamin, attempts
to "synthetically" create experience in the sense of *Erfahrung* under the
conditions of modernity in his work. *Memoire involontaire* is thus already a
hybrid form situated between pre-modern and modern forms of
remembrance: experience proper encompasses a collective, from which the
modern private individual is more and more detached. It increasingly encounters memory-traces in material objects rather than collective practices.[7]

THE COLLECTOR

Benjamin contrasts the collector's way of relating to objects with the
memoire volontaire, which "is a registry providing the object with a classifi-
catory number behind which it disappears. 'So now we've been there' ('I've
had an experience.')" (AP, 211). In this example, something of Benjamin's

concept of *Erlebnis*, developed further in the writings on Proust and Baude-laire, is foreshadowed: what is experienced is spent in the moment without being committed to the unconscious. Benjamin contrasts the psychoanalytic concept of *Erlebnis* with this quotidian one, the "[e]xperiences emptied out and deprived of their substance" (AP, 326) described by Baudelaire. Benjamin links this to Freud's account of experience: "'To experience [*Erleben*] means to master an impression inwardly that was so strong we could not grasp it at once.' This definition of experience in Freud's sense is something very different from what is meant by those who speak of having 'had an experience' [*Erlebnis*]" [K8, 2] (AP, 402). Quoting Freud's student Theodor Reik, Benjamin suggests that this becomes most apparent in grief, as it "reveals its depths only long after we think that we have got the better of it.' The 'forgotten' grief persists and gains ground" (AP, 402). Grief thus reveals something about the unconscious nature and belatedness of experi-ence itself. The fluctuation between the meanings of *Erlebnis* and *Erfahrung* in the *Arcades Project* show that Benjamin here had not yet arrived at the hard and fast differentiation between the two characteristic of his 1933 *Experience and Poverty*; nevertheless, these reflections were becoming apparent and fleshed out in his work on Baudelaire and Proust.

Benjamin's types are fractured modern subjects seeking to resist the anonymity of the crowd and the commodification of human life intrinsic to capitalism. They are caught in the same double bind as baroque humanity, enjoined to be subjects and failing in the impossible demand of subjecthood. One such type brought about by the nineteenth century is the collector, who seeks to overcome this antinomy of subjectivity by investing himself in objects *differently*. Benjamin unearths a repressed layer in his analysis: at the heart of the collector's hoarding, his "most deeply hidden motive" is "the struggle against dispersion." In this, he resists the chaos of human life and the material world: "the great collector is struck by the confusion, by the scatter, in which the things of the world are found" (AP, 211).[8] The obverse of the massification in the urban crowd and the industrial production process are the dispersion and isolation of individual elements within it. The tension between these two poles is characteristic of the nineteenth century and its fractured subject.

This motif of countering dispersion is consistent with Freud's characterisa-tion of the libido as seeking to integrate elements into ever-greater wholes. The "hidden motive" of the collector, his unconscious motivation, is the attempt to repair the lack experienced in modernity, and to thus preserve life, express-ing the libidinal pull of units of life together into an ever-greater network. At the same time, just as Freud characterises the libidinal drive as "circuitous paths to death" (BPP, 33), death is also the ultimate aim of collecting: it attempts to stabilise everything in its order. The inchoate world presents to the collector "the same spectacle that so preoccupied the men of the baroque; in particular, the world image of the allegorist cannot be explained apart from the passionate, distraught concern with this spectacle" (AP, 211). Just like the mortifying melancholy gaze of the baroque allegorist, the collector cannot bear the disorder of the world. However, his attempt at the completion of his collection is always overshadowed by the knowledge that one missing piece would render it incomplete—only provisional completeness is ever possible for the true collector. Crucially, it is also this incompleteness at the level of the individual that makes intersubjectivity possible, even necessary, as Benjamin's quotation from Proust demonstrates:

> I had already lived long enough so that, for more than one of the human beings with whom I had come in contact, I found in antipodal regions of my past memories another being to complete the picture . . . In much the same way, when an art lover is shown a panel of an altar screen, he remembers in what church . . . and private collection the other panels are dispersed. (AP, 211)

At stake is a relational way of being that seeks completion through an other—which in capitalist modernity is mediated by the commodity. This is also expressed in the fragmentary note "Broken-down matter: the elevation of the commodity to the status of allegory. Allegory and the fetish character of the commodity" [H2, 6] (AP, 207). The frequent linking between the collector and the allegorist—Benjamin's positioning of "the collector *as* allegorist" [H2, 1] (AP, 206 [emphasis mine])—stress the lack central to this nineteenth-century subjectivity. Nevertheless, there is in the collector and in Proust's art lover an echo of the way of relating that involves memory and life experience—the very human qualities capitalist production processes are rendering obsolete. Much as in the case of the baroque allegorist, at the root of the nineteenth-century's drive to collect is an attempt to fill an empty world with material objects. At the same time, with the advent of industrial capitalism and Benjamin's own turn to Marx, the account of the function of this *Sammeltrieb*, the drive to collect, in the nineteenth century goes beyond the *horror vacui* of the baroque. Where allegorical intention in the seventeenth century was grounded in an attempt to fill up the loss of the holistic cosmological horizon that was riven, the nineteenth century represses the truth of the capitalist production process: the fetish character of the commodity and the commodification of fractured human subjects. Thus, "the collector actualizes latent archaic representations of property. These representations may in fact be connected with taboo" (AP, 209). With Henri Lefebvre, Benjamin speculates that "declaring something taboo would have constituted a title.

To appropriate to oneself an object is to render it sacred and redoubtable to others; it is to make it 'participate' in oneself."[9] [H3a, 6] (AP, 210). Here we see again the inversion of subject and object of commodity fetishism in the concept of property. This is not entirely novel, however; rather, it only "actualizes" the latent archaic nature of the category of property: In reviving the archaic function of objects as cultic, the collector makes visible the conflux of commodity-fetishism and older forms of religious veneration of fetish-objects. Fundamentally, Benjamin writes, "the true collector detaches the object from its functional relations." Additionally, "for the collector, the world is present, and indeed ordered, in each of his objects. Ordered, however, according to a surprising and, for the profane understanding, incomprehensible collection" (AP, 207). This likens the collector's understanding of the objects he has amassed and ordered to the sacred—an attempt to reconstruct sacrality in post-baroque modernity. Benjamin's nod to the "surprising" nature of the arrangement and selection of objects in the collection is also redolent of the taxonomies of the mad in "Books by the Mentally Ill," discussed in a previous chapter. In the attempt to overcome both the alienation of self and that of objects, the collector creates a subjective order of things, which, Benjamin hints, attempts to re-erect a quasi-religious level of validity and truth in the "'magic encyclopedia' of their collection" (AP, 207). Collecting can thus border on pathology. Unsurprisingly, then, it relates not just to the pursuit and fulfilment of pleasure, but also the death drive: "With individuals as with societies, the need to accumulate is one of the signs of approaching death. This is confirmed in the acute stages of preparalysis. There is also the mania for collection, known in neurology as 'collectionism' . . . But compare collecting done by children!" [H2a, 3] (AP, 208). Benjamin thus conceptualises two modes of collecting: The one which expresses the death drive, "borders on pathology" even in the normal person, and is on a continuum with the "mania" of "collectionism"—and that of the child. The collector is a figure suspended between these two poles of pathology and possibility. It is the vision afforded by intoxication that allows the collector to become an allegorist. His gaze inserts the object-as-commodity into the totality of meaning created by his collection, thereby tearing it out of circulation and its "mere presence at hand," allowing it to become allegorical; that is, suffused with particular historical meaning and the transience of history itself. In the *Arcades Project*, this mode of signification is transposed from the baroque into high modernity in the commodity form. The fetish character of the commodity in capitalism makes it amenable to such allegorisation.

In the 1935 Expose, Benjamin writes "The collector delights in evoking a world that is not just distant and long gone but also better—a world in which, to be sure, human beings are no better provided with what they need than in the *real* world, but in which things are freed from the drudgery of being useful."[10] The collector displays a perverse utopian imagination where a "better world" is not considered superior on account of lessening human suffering, but merely because material objects are taken out of a means-ends relationship of fulfilling human needs. The emphasis for the collector is not of divesting things of their exchange value, but infusing them with a semblance of individuality, and indeed humanity, through connoisseur value: "He makes his concern the transfiguration of things. To him falls the Sisyphean task of divesting things of their commodity character by taking possession of them" (AP, 9). This kind of utopianism, then, signifies the apotheosis of commodity fetishism for Benjamin, pointing to the utter enmeshment of the individual and the commodity—giving rise to an imagination that cannot fathom human beings freed from necessity, but only commodities freed from the necessity of humanity.[11] Like Schreber, who creates his private language and system of meaning, the collector strives to bring about an idiosyncratic model of relating to objects in the midst of Capitalist modernity. His fantasy of "rescuing" the object by "possessing" it, imbuing it with a metaphysical quality, can at best restore cultic value to it—and further obscures the actual "sensory-suprasensory" quality of the commodity, which cannot be erased under capitalism. Where Schreber still attempted a narration of his world and his symptoms, storytelling for Benjamin was an increasingly impossible mode in modernity, resulting in the attempt to save, salve, and salvage the self (and through it, the world) through objects. Rather than transmitting experience and *Lebensgefuehl* through the craft of storytelling, these human qualities become embedded into objects in nineteenth-century capitalism.

One of the last writers to attempt a narrative transmission of experience is Proust, but already the object forms the kernel of his writing: It expresses the centrality of commodities to human psychic life under capitalism. Drawing on Hoffmannsthal's reading of Proust in *Buch der Freunde* (1929), Benjamin names "the fidelity to things that have crossed our path in life" as Proust's crucial subject. As such, "Proust, in the deepest sense, 'perhaps ranges himself on the side of death.' His cosmos has its sun, perhaps, in death, around which orbit the lived moments, the gathered things." It follows that "'Beyond the Pleasure Principle' is probably the best commentary there is on Proust's works. In order to understand Proust . . . it is perhaps necessary to begin with the fact that his subject is the obverse side, *le revers*, 'not so much of the world but of life itself'" [S2, 3] (AP, 547).[12] Benjamin is here referring to Freud's twin formula from *Beyond the Pleasure Principle*: "'the aim of all life is death' and 'inanimate things existed before living ones'" (BPP, 32). Freud's analysis offers Benjamin insights into the death-driven nature of Proust's writing, which in turn expresses the thanatic tendency of the nineteenth century as a whole. Crucially, where Freud speaks of the "unwelcome fidelity" of repetition-compulsion, a fidelity to the traumatic event, in Proust this is supplemented with a fidelity to material objects. These objects are of interest from the standpoint of Benjamin's theory of memory precisely because they are invested with unconscious desires, and in turn come to constitute the unconscious itself. The coexisting of material and immaterial objects in memory—"things that have crossed our path in life an afternoon, a tree, a spot of sun on the carpet; fidelity to garments, pieces of furniture, to perfumes or landscapes" (AP 547)—and the externalisation of memory into material objects thus point to the circulation between life and death, psychic economy and political economy.[13]

These collected objects overwhelmingly inhabit the bourgeois homes of the nineteenth century. Benjamin suggests that "One need only study with due exactitude the physiognomy of the homes of great . . . collectors. Then one would have the key to the nineteenth-century interior" (AP, 218). This is a further point of connection to Freud, who in his 1937 "Constructions in Analysis" writes of the transfer of memory to objects as a compromise between remembering and repression. Confronted with such a construction, that is, a plausible scenario pieced together by the analyst, the analysand responds with a sudden, vivid memory. Not, however, a memory of the event described in the construction, but in details connected to it: "the faces of the people involved in the construction or the rooms in which something of the sort might have happened, or . . . the furniture in such rooms" (SW23, 266). Freud concludes that these memories must be the result of a compromise between the repressed, which, buoyed by the construction, aims to make conscious the obscured "memory-traces," while the resistance to this movement diverts or displaces it to "adjacent, objects of minor significance" (SW23, 266). Memory and the attempt at forgetting thus leave their traces on material objects, which can in turn become a trigger for remembrance.

In the 1935 Expose, Benjamin states: "The interior is not just the universe but also the etui of the private individual. To dwell means to leave traces" (AP, 9). The concept of the memory-trace also links Freud to Convolute I "The Interior, the Trace."[14] In Benjamin's account, furniture placement serves as an unconscious expression of the defensiveness of the bourgeoisie, thus manifesting class struggle in interior design and style. Benjamin quotes George Lukac's "universal" observation that "from the perspective of the philosophy of history, it is characteristic of the middle classes that their new opponent, the proletariat, should have entered the arena at a moment when the old adversary, feudalism, was not yet vanquished. And they will never quite have done with feudalism" [12, 3J] (AP, 215). Thus, the bourgeoisie's repressed desire to be like the feudal lords of old manifests itself in its unconscious actions—most especially in the decoration of their interior spaces. The interior thus emerges as a space full of clues to be deciphered—akin to a crime scene, or indeed as a symptomatic space. What is repressed, unconscious, is revealed as class struggle: "the unconscious retention of a posture of struggle and defense" (AP, 215) on the part of the bourgeoisie grounded in their repressed knowledge of the persistence of oppositional class interests.

In language strikingly similar to that of Benjamin, Freud concludes in "Constructions in Analysis" that "therapeutic work . . . would consist in liberating the fragment of historical truth from its distortions." Where for Freud this liberation is directed into the analysand's individual past—loosening "its attachments to the actual present day and in leading it back to the point in the past to which it belongs" (SW23, 268), as we shall see, the movement of liberation is not a straightforwardly retrograde one for Benjamin. However, Benjamin does draw from Freud's methodology presented here: the "deeper explanation" (AP, 215), that is, the tools furnished by psychoanalysis allows Benjamin to make visible this repressed factum of class struggle that is expressed in the object-unconscious.

THE FLANEUR

Benjamin contrasts the crowd, "with its abrupt and intermittent movements" (AP, 337), more akin to the machines they operate, with the flaneur, who "forms an obstacle in its path." In his nonchalance, Benjamin detects "an unconscious protest against the tempo of the production process" (AP, 338). The flaneur thus attempts another protest of heroic individuality against the rhythms of industrial capitalism, which leak from the production process into the movement of the crowds in the modern city. Ultimately, his protest remains futile, and he does not escape subsumption. The flaneur thus functions as another characteristic expression of fractured nineteenth-century subjectivity: "Empathy with the commodity is fundamentally empathy with exchange value itself. The flaneur is the virtuoso of this empathy. He takes the concept of marketability itself for a stroll" (AP, 448). For Benjamin, the flaneur's wanderings around the nineteenth-century capitalist metropolis signify not just mere walking, but a circumnavigation of the boundaries of public and private space, past and present, encapsulating the impossibility of remaining outside of rapidly expanding capitalism. Just as the products of the nineteenth century linger on the "threshold" of capitalism—becoming commodities but carrying the semblance of previous social forms—the flaneur walks on the precipice, the "threshold" of the soon-to-be total capitalist system, carrying within himself vestiges of the old ruling class, the aristocracy. He is on the way, he "takes himself to market." In this figure, Benjamin can observe—and typecast—the move from aristocratic detachment to full immersion in the "world of things," total commodification. As such, Benjamin writes "The attitude of the flaneur—epitome of the political attitude of the middle classes during the Second Empire" [M2, 5] (AP, 420), on the cusp of becoming the dominant class while still mimicking—repeating—the styles of their aristocratic forebears. Here, as throughout the *Arcades Project*, Benjamin highlights the class position of his types. Their experience, their subjectivity is not neutral.

Empathy with the commodity signifies an altered state of consciousness, an "intoxication," a form of madness provoked by the sensorium of nineteenth-century capitalism, the presence of both past and present social formations and the residue of the aspirations of the past. The experience of the flaneur extends not merely to commodities produced in factories and displayed in the arcades, but comes to encompass the natural world as it too becomes subsumed by the commodity form, and ultimately all of experience suffers the same fate: "Today, for instance, as man and woman, both lover and mistress, I rode in a forest on an autumn afternoon under the yellow leaves, and I was also the horses, the leaves, the wind, the words my people uttered, even the red sun that made them almost close their love-drowned eyes" [MI7a, 4] (AP, 449). The entire outside world here comes to be subsumed by the semblance of the subject, mirroring the subsumption taking place in the sphere of exchange. The intoxication of this form of empathy extends across epochs, allowing the flaneur to feel in detail as though he had been present at various points in history, as Benjamin writes in Convolute M. The quasi-mystical experience of oneness with the world is revealed as a product not of a spiritual epiphany, true religious experience, but of capitalism. It draws close to the paranoid reconstruction of the world discussed in chapter 2 and, as we shall see in the final chapter, it hints at an attempt to recover the lost experience of childhood. At the same time, Benjamin contrasts the individuality of the flaneur with the "rubberneck, who is absorbed by the external world . . . which moves him to the point of intoxication and ecstasy." He thus "becomes an impersonal being. He is no longer a man—he is the public; he is the crowd" [M6, 5] (AP, 429). In opposition to the rubberneck, who has been utterly absorbed by the mass, the flaneur clings to the last vestiges of individualism, even as he is ultimately unable to resist commodification. In this, he is related to the dandy, who forms the last bastion of the heroic subject.

THE DANDY: BOREDOM'S HERO

In Baudelaire's words, quoted in Convolute D "Boredom, Eternal Return," "Dandyism is a mysterious institution . . . It is of great antiquity, Caesar, Catiline, and Alcibiades providing us with dazzling examples; and very widespread, Chateaubriand having found it in the forests and by the lakes of the New World" [D4a, 4] (AP, 110). Dandyism is thus associated with aristocratic characters from Antiquity, becoming a transhistorical category, and at the same time a global phenomenon: "Dandyism is the last spark of heroism amid decadence; and the type of dandy discovered by our traveler in North America does nothing to invalidate this idea; for how can we be sure that those tribes which we call 'savage' may not in fact be the *disjecta membra* of great extinct civilizations?" [D5, 1] (AP, 111). Dandyism, on this view, is an ancient remnant in modernity, a fragment of the past. While the flaneur and the dandy are closely related, the former is a dynamic character who moves from the aristocratic mode of life to the shop floor, becoming subsumed by capitalism. The latter is a dying breed, embodying that same aristocratic existence which the flaneur is shedding. Baudelaire laments this state of affairs: "Dandyism is a sunset; like the declining daystar, it is glorious, without heat and full of melancholy. But alas, the rising tide of democracy . . . is daily overwhelming these last representatives of human pride" (AP, 239). Thus, the melancholia of the baroque finds expression in the type of the dandy in the nineteenth century, via Baudelaire's representation. Just as that of the baroque sovereign, the subjectivity of the ruling class is revealed as pathological here, torn by the desire for omnipotence and the melancholic realisation of its impossibility. It is noteworthy that it is democracy that is blamed by Baudelaire for this downfall, for making the aristocratic subjectivity of the dandy obsolete. Holding democracy responsible for this decline is, of course, an example of the aristocratic mindset itself, linking Baudelaire with the dandy.

The dandy, Benjamin writes, makes a "show of boredom." He speculates that this might be grounded in boredom's function as an "index to participation in the sleep of the collective" (AP, 108): The upper classes can only display a collective affect in the form of tedium. Benjamin quotes Engels on "[f]actory labor as economic infrastructure of the ideological boredom of the upper classes" (AP, 106). The do-nothing ennui of the moneyed and idle class is the pendant to the repetitive tedium of factory work. As Peter Osborne notes, Benjamin's Convolute D provides a social history of boredom in the nineteenth century (Osborne 2006, 37): Benjamin's study of the affect of boredom and the psychology of the bored thus allow him to diagnose the material organisation of society.[15] However, boredom functions as a symptom not only of the way the social world is structured, but as a repository of energies for its overcoming. Osborne notes the utopian potential "of boredom in modernity as the basis of a distinctive experience of possibility" (Osborne 2006, 36). This is encapsulated in particular in Benjamin's "The Storyteller," where boredom is described as "the dream bird that hatches the egg of experience" (SW3, 149). It is also in this text that Benjamin links boredom to the decay of experience and pre-industrial activities (storytelling as well as manual practices such as weaving and spinning) in particular. As Salzani notes, "*Langeweile, ennui, taedium vitae . . .* if the roots are in medieval *acedia*—almost equated with *melancholia* in the Renaissance—*ennui, Langeweile* and *boredom* took a very specific connotation after the industrial revolution and are therefore strictly connected to modernity" (Salzani 2009, 127). As noted in the discussion of Benjamin's writing on Baudelaire, the specificity of modern boredom lies in its connection to the decay of experience, which in the nineteenth century is mediated by Capitalist forms. Thus, as Osborne notes, "boredom becomes a central part of that form of subjectivity constituted by the dynamics of the commodity form" (Osborne 2006, 42). This also means it is mediated by class: It is the decay of bourgeois experience that is at stake for the dandy, the flaneur, and the collector. Both the worker and the bourgeois are bored, but bored differently. Where the boredom of one is grounded in idleness and a further deepening of subjectivism, the boredom of the other is grounded in the rhythms of the factory, Michelet's "true hells of boredom."

Andrew Benjamin also draws attention to the historical specificity of this modern subjectivity characterised by boredom (Benjamin 2005, 156). He frames his discussion of boredom through the concept of moods, which mediate between modernity and its subjects, organising experience: the people of the nineteenth century are bored because their century is boring. Boredom thus transcends the individual subject and is, as indicated above, symptomatic of what Andrew Benjamin terms "the world"; that is, the social world of the nineteenth century. Andrew Benjamin groups boredom together with distraction as moods that subvert any simple opposition between individual and mass, pointing instead to a differential relation between the two in modernity. Not "the individual as opposed to the mass, nor the mass in opposition to the individual" (Benjamin 2005, 162), but an individual as *mass* individual "both dispersed across, though also articulated within, this matrix" of the mass (Benjamin 2005, 163).[16] Andrew Benjamin thus links the utopian potential of boredom identified by Osborne and Salzani to an overcoming of the constraints of subjectivity. Locating boredom at the structural level, as opposed to a boredom that "merely" exists for an individual, allows for a different politics, Andrew Benjamin suggests: changing the structures through mass action, rather than placating the boredom of an individual. The latter attempt is precisely what characterises the eternal return of the nineteenth century; the endless search for novelty rendered futile by its lapse back into the ever- same. As Osborne notes, this type of "[b]oredom drives subjectivity forward in the search for social content, much as, in psychoanalytical accounts, boredom is associated with the 'suspended animation of desire'" (Osborne 2006, 41). This leads us to the last main type of nineteenth-century fractured subject to be discussed: the gambler, who fuses the protest against boredom in his desire for novelty with the inevitability of repetition-compulsion.

THE GAMBLER

The many notes on the psychology—specifically the psychopathology—of the gambler demonstrate that Benjamin found the psychoanalytic perspective more relevant to him than to any of the other types. In a lengthy quote from Paul Lafargue, Benjamin introduces gambling as paradigmatic for modern capitalism, "a giant international gambling house, where the bourgeois wins and loses capital in consequence of events which remain unknown to him." Here, we also see how the mythic resurfaces in the form of gambling, that is, capitalism in toto: "The inexplicable is enthroned in bourgeois society as in a gambling hall . . . Successes and failures, thus arising from causes that are unanticipated, generally unintelligible, and seemingly dependent on chance, predispose the bourgeois to the gambler's frame of mind" (AP, 497). Like the gambler, the bourgeois is connected to the mythic in his submission to something inhuman and inexplicable—the rule of chance. His attempts to gain control over this process are themselves part of the mythic: "The habitues of gambling casinos always possess magic formulas to conjure the Fates . . . The inexplicable in society envelops the bourgeois, as the inexplicable in nature the savage" (AP, 497). Here, again, Capitalist domination is likened to nature insofar as it signifies the rule of the mythic, which both the gambler and the bourgeois are governed by.

Benjamin here frequently quotes from Edmund Bergler's article "*Zur Psychologie des Hasardspielers*," published in *Imago* in 1936. Via Bergler, a Freudian psychoanalyst, Freudian themes play out strongly in Benjamin's characterisation of the gambler. First, he notes that "The gambler is driven by essentially narcissistic and aggressive desires for omnipotence" (AP, 510) which exceed the satisfaction of genital sexuality and are projected or sublimated in gambling. This is also taken up in Benjamin's summary of Ernst Simmel's take on the psychopathology of the gambler: "The insatiable greed that finds no rest within an unending vicious circle, where loss becomes gain and gain becomes loss, is said to arise from the narcissistic compulsion to fertilize and give birth to oneself in an anal birth fantasy, surpassing and replacing one's own father and mother in an endlessly escalating process" (AP, 511). Benjamin here delves deeply into the psychology of capitalist individualism, revealed as grounded in a fantasy of omnipotence and self-sufficiency, characterised by boundless narcissism displayed in the "autoerotic satisfaction" of gambling. This links the gambler to Schreber and Haitzmann, who also fantasized about having the capacity for pregnancy and birth. However, in the nineteenth-century gambler, the narcissistic aspect of this fantasy of—male—self-sufficiency becomes more apparent: "Thus, in the last analysis, the passion for gambling satisfies the claim of the bisexual ideal, which the narcissist discovers in himself" (AP, 511). It is worth noting that "bisexual" here refers not to the later usage, but the original Freudian meaning of combining male and female sexuality in one organism; in other words, to be "complete" in the schema of the nineteenth century.

Again, this fractured subject is a classed one: what is being analysed here is the psyche of the bourgeois. However, with the total domination of capitalism that is inaugurated in the nineteenth century, Benjamin elaborates that this subjectivity is perceived as extending beyond the bourgeois, becoming paradigmatic for "the human," and leading to the apocalyptic mood of nineteenth-century culture. He relates a conversation with Berthold Brecht regarding this:

> A propos of Freud's conjecture that sexuality is a dwindling function "of" the human being, Brecht remarked on how the bourgeoisie in decline differs from the feudal class at the time of its downfall: it feels itself to be in all things the quintessence of humankind in general, and hence can equate its own decline with the death of humanity. (This equation, moreover, can play a part in the unmistakable crisis of sexuality within the bourgeoisie.) The feudal class, by virtue of privileges, felt itself to be a class apart, which corresponded to the reality.[17] (AP, 511)

Again, we see Benjamin joining class analysis and psychoanalysis to investigate the object of his study more thoroughly. The two approaches compensate for each other's shortcomings and thus allow a fuller picture of the nineteenth century to emerge: Brecht's Marxian analysis supplements Freud's universalism with the specificity of the class to whom the analysis applies, while Freud's psychoanalysis of the dwindling function of sexuality reveals an aspect of the apparent "decline" of the bourgeoisie not made visible by class analysis alone. Taken together, they show how the psyche of the bourgeoisie is enmeshed with the "spirit of the age" of the nineteenth century and differentiate it from the previous class formations which gave rise to a different subjectivity on account of their differing politico-legal structure. The dwindling sexuality that Benjamin attests the bourgeoisie thus becomes a symptom of its lack of special privileges, such as possessed by the feudal nobility, expressed in the phantasmagoria of constituting a universal subject. Benjamin turns to Bergler again in relating the drives and principles Freud delineates in *Beyond the Pleasure Principle* to the psychology of the gambler. Bergler singles out games of chance as the only instance in which the reality principle does not supersede the pleasure principle "and the omnipotence of its thoughts and desires" (AP, 510). He identifies this as the "retention of the infantile fiction of omnipotence" and notes that it contains "posthumous aggression against the . . . authority which has 'inculcated' the reality principle in the child. This unconscious aggression, together with the operation of the omnipotence of ideas and the experience of the socially viable repressed exhibition, conspires to form a triad of pleasures in gambling" and concludes that "[a]t the deepest level, the game of chance is love's will to be extorted by an unconscious masochistic design. This is why the gambler always loses in the long run" (AP, 510). Gambling is thus revealed as a dialectic between the pleasure principle and masochism, of libidinal and death drives. As also seen in the analysis of fashion, this is typical of the nineteenth century, which submits to the domination of the market as previous ages have to the mythic. Benjamin quotes Anatole France: "The fascination of danger is at the bottom of all great passions . . . It is the mingling of terror with delight that intoxicates. And what more terrifying than gambling? It gives and takes away; its logic is not our logic. It is dumb and blind and deaf. It is almighty. It is a God" (AP, 498). The "intoxication" of gambling is grounded in its phantasmagoric, ambivalent character: the fusing of pleasure and terror, and the experience of submitting to a principle outside of human control and "logic."[18]

On the face of it, gambling differs from capitalist labour in one important respect: its temporality, defined by a lack of a past, in the fact that every round is independent of the previous one. Benjamin quotes, "Gambling strenuously denies all acquired conditions, all antecedents . . . pointing to previous actions; and that is what distinguishes it from work. Gambling rejects . . . this weighty past which is the mainstay of work and which makes for seriousness of purpose, for attention to the long term, for right, and for power" (AP, 512). Unlike traditional forms of labour, gambling lacks a past—but, given Benjamin's pronouncements on the changing nature of work under capitalism, which sees experience and other "human" qualities becoming obsolete in the face of modern methods of mass production, it is again apparent how even this aspect of gambling becomes typical of capitalism. Benjamin speculates on the implication of this temporality for experience: "The lack of consequences that defines the character of the isolated experience (*Erlebnis*) found drastic expression in gambling. During the feudal age, the latter was essentially a privilege of the feudal class, which did not participate directly in the production process. What is new is that in the nineteenth century the bourgeois gambles" (AP, 512). Thus, the change in experience—the replacement of *Erfahrung* with *Erlebnis*[19]—under the conditions of nineteenth-century capitalism are a consequence of the ruling class no longer being exempt from production, as the feudal class was, but becoming subject to its rhythms and structures even as it attempts to hold on to the obsolete feudal forms of existence in the private sphere. Gambling's relationship to temporality is also touched upon in Benjamin's initial quote from Bergler: "whoever . . . has experienced the mechanism of pleasure as abreacted in games of chance, and possessing, as it were, eternal value, succumbs the more readily to it in proportion as he is committed to the 'neurotic pleasure in duration' (Pfeifer)" (AP, 512). This emphasises the psychoanalytic dimension of gambling's temporality—Bergler is here referring to the desire for omnipotence manifested in gambling that seeks to eternalise its satisfaction in its endless repetition and simultaneous newness.

In *Beyond the Pleasure Principle*, Freud also refers to Pfeifer's then-recent study of 1919: "These theories endeavour to conjecture the motives of children's play, though without placing any special stress on the 'economic' point of view, i.e. consideration of the attainment of pleasure." For Freud, the child's *fort-da* game is another example of an attempt at omnipotence—to compensate for the displeasure of the loss ("*fort*") in restaging dis- and reappearance in a way that is subject to the child's control in the game, ultimately restoring balance to its psychic economy. Even though at base, both the gambler and the child are driven by the same desire, what differentiates Benjamin's gambler from the child is the pathological and compulsive nature of the expression of this desire, his "neurotic pleasure in duration," once again a symptom of the repetition-compulsion and the desire for eternity of the nineteenth century. Benjamin is clear on the destructive nature of gambling and its attendant mode of experience: "The ideal of the shock-engendered experience [*Erlebnis*] is the catastrophe. This becomes very clear in gambling; by constantly raising the stakes, in hopes of getting back what is lost, the gambler steers toward absolute ruin" [O14, 4] (AP, 515). This is not to be taken in purely financial terms; rather, it is the attempt to return to his previous fullness of experience that characterises the self-destructive behaviour of the gambler. This peculiar experience of temporality and constant exposure to shock contributes to his sense of intoxication: "the greater the component of chance in a game, the more speedily it elapses" (AP, 512). The sense of ever-increasing speed in gambling is a function of the element of chance, the greater the less control the gambler has over the outcome of the game. Nevertheless, this provokes a response of increased "presence of mind," of focus, which is broken the instant the stakes change and the game begins anew, only to be built up again, and so on. In this way, gambling ultimately functions almost like a bodily reflex—a way of responding that "rules out an 'interpretation' of chance" (AP, 513), circumvents ratio. Thus, the body comes to the fore once again, but through it also the unconscious— the gambler reacts through reflex rather than reflection, instinct governs his decision.[20]

The gambler's attempt at satisfying the narcissistic desire for omnipotence is ultimately doomed to failure: "money and riches, otherwise the most massive and burdensome things in the world, come to him from the fates like a joyous embrace returned to the full. They can be compared to words of love from a woman altogether satisfied by her man. Gamblers are types to whom it is not given to satisfy the woman. Isn't Don Juan a gambler?" [013, 4] (AP, 513). Thus, there is a lack at the root of the psyche of the gambler, for which gambling attempts to compensate. It is, as an ambivalent, dialectical phenomenon, characterised by both the aggressive desire for omnipotence and a sense of incompleteness. Benjamin's speculation on the lack of sexual satisfaction here connect the gambler to Baudelaire, and to the insistence on the waning sexuality of the bourgeoisie as a symptom of its melancholic sense of decline. This points to a centrality of these reflections in his analysis of the subjectivity of the bourgeoisie of the nineteenth century in toto. Taken together with the other psychoanalytic aspects of the section on the gambler—his narcissistic desire for omnipotence, his relationship to time as grounded in repetition-compulsion, the ensuing model of his experience, and the endurance of mythic thinking in gambling thus demonstrate the importance of Freudian psychoanalysis for the analysis of this type, and by extension the entire *Arcades Project*. It is also present in its offshoots: Benjamin writes in "Central Park" (1939) of "[g]ames of chance, flanerie, collecting—activities pitted against spleen" (SW4, 1). All the activities that come to characterise these nineteenth-century types are thus attempts to counter melancholia. Their attempts to encounter something truly novel, to have an experience, are foiled in modernity—only death, the ultimate caesura, can provide this. All novelty within the nineteenth century is revealed as semblance, a reflection of nothing but the age itself. All of Benjamin's types make attempts at having an experience: The collector attempts to retain a fullness of experience through his collection, the flaneur seeks to experience the city in his meanderings, the gambler seeks out liminal experiences in his play with chance, the dandy seeks to eternalise the experience of the *Lebensgefuehl* of the aristocracy. They are all dynamic, in the process of historically- driven change.

All the types of the nineteenth century are incapable of having a real experience. Like Freud's hysterics, this means the past instead resurfaces in pathological form: In the first of his "Five Lectures on Psycho-Analysis" (1909), which Benjamin had noted in his *Verzeichnis*, Freud reprises his conclusion to his 1895 *Studies on Hysteria*: *"our hysterical patients suffer from reminiscences.* Their symptoms are residues and mnemic symbols [*Erinnerungssymbole*] of particular (traumatic) experiences" (SE11, 16). Strikingly, Freud draws close to Benjamin in linking this pathological mode of remembrance to material memory-culture: "We may perhaps obtain a deeper understanding of this kind of symbolism if we compare them with other mnemic symbols in other fields. The monuments and memorials with which large cities are adorned are also mnemic symbols" (SE11, 16). Like the hysterics, nineteenth-century culture does not merely remember past experiences, they are still cathected: "Not only do they remember painful experiences of the remote past, but they still cling to them emotionally; they cannot get free of the past and for its sake they neglect what is real and immediate" (SE11, 17). Benjamin drew from this in conceptualising how mythic domination resurfaces time and again in capitalism, and specifically in the modern city. The social world under capitalism increasingly functions like a pathological psyche, simultaneously appealing to a vision of fullness which is unattainable, and re-stages the losses of the past. These losses are thus still present in the nineteenth century, mediated by the commodity-form. The fractured post-baroque subject remains melancholic, torn between the semblance of individuality in the private sphere and the reality of increasing commodification: in production, as consumer, in the urban mass.

As we have seen, all the types into which the fractured baroque subject refracts in modernity contain a truth within their untruth for Benjamin; that is, just like allegories, and the ruins of the arcades themselves, the truth they reveal is precisely the ambiguity, and thus untruth, of the world that brought them about. Just like the symptom in Freud, they function as an indication of a pathology. In the *Arcades Project*, the loss of the conditions of experience is being resisted by figures such as the collector. However, in his solitary pursuit of the objects of his collection, he too ultimately succumbs to empathy with the commodity. His relationships to others, as we have seen, are characterised by the same alienation as that of the flaneur and other types—thus he seeks refuge in making it his aim to liberate "things from the drudgery of being useful" by inserting them into a taxonomy that is ultimately subjective—and false. The nineteenth-century individual, like the collector, has no defence against the shocks of perception; everything "strikes" him, as Benjamin says. He can be said to "live a dream life" where nothing is stable, all his experience is permeated by the things he encounters, the rhythm of his life subject to surprising impressions *vis a vis* which he is passive, just like the mass of which he forms a part. All things and events are given equal attention, as in a dream. As such, just like the flaneur, who dreamily walks down sloping streets that all lead to regression, the collector is emblematic of the nineteenth century. In the next chapters, I investigate Benjamin's conceptualisation of this "dream-world" in relation to Freud's dream theory, and the question of awakening.

NOTES

1. Benjamin notes that the psychoanalytic approach is analogous to the conventional approach of literary history (SW4, 161): Psychoanalysis and other theoretical approaches can thus yield similar insights, while Benjamin repurposes these methods.

2. The German denotes this coin as Baudelaire's "Zehrpfennig" (GS1, 684), that is, money intended to sustain him on his travels.

3. In the use of the word "*Verklärung*," here translated as "transfiguration," we see again the link to Benjamin's "Capitalism as Religion."

4. See Agamben (2016) for a reconstruction of the genesis of this work.

5. See also Weigel (1996) and Werner (2015) for a detailed reconstruction of this process. Additionally, Porath highlights the centrality of technology for Freud in these speculations: "the models that Freud sketched for the so-called 'psychic apparatus' often use technical metaphors and cannot be thought without being related to communication media and the building of models in the sciences in Freud's day" (Porath 2005, 12, transl. mine).

6. It is worth noting that in discussions in the literature on Freud, notions of trauma and shock are sometimes posited as opposites, as for instance by Tim Armstrong (2000). He contrasts Freud's trauma theory with what Freud himself terms the "old, naïve theory of shock" as a response to physical violence. However, as also noted by Matus (2009), the opposition Armstrong suggests between the economic model of shock and "the timelessness of the unconscious wound" (Armstrong 2000, 64) is not as stark in Freud. In *Beyond the Pleasure Principle*, Freud's innovation is the transposition of the economic model to the psychic apparatus *as it concerns its capacity to process experiences* rather than its wholesale replacement with an exclusively innerpsychic generation of trauma.

7. These reflections form part of Benjamin's larger corpus of writing on the change of tradition and experience in modernity, such as "The Storyteller" (1936).

8. We can detect here a theological, specifically Jewish, allusion to the scattered state of the world, with implied the goal of Tikkun Olam, repairing the world, and recovering the shards of the broken vessel of Kabbalism. This could be conceptualised as an answer to the sadness of baroque subjectivity's lament over a broken world, transposing the ruptured cosmological horizon of Christianity into a Jewish one in which the Messiah is yet to come. Scholem's *Walter Benjamin. The Story of a*

Friendship and "Walter Benjamin and His Angel" are of course the foundational texts for a reading of Benjamin's theological impulses. In a 1935 letter to Werner Kraft, Benjamin suggests the theological has been absorbed in his thinking, referring to "the far distant period of my immediately metaphysical, indeed theological thinking, and the upheaval was necessary so that they could nourish with their full force my present disposition" (C, 486). Nevertheless, the relation of truth to the theological remains prominent, right to the 1940 "On the Concept of History," where the language of theology is to be taken into the service of historical materialism. Recent scholarship, such as the 2016 collection of essays on *Walter Benjamin and Theology*, and Judith Butler's 2012 *Parting Ways*, pursue this further. For the role of Jewish theology in Freud see for instance Santner, who makes a brief reference to *tikkun* in Freud's interpretation of Schreber's paranoid world building (1996, 57). See also D. Klein, *Jewish Origins of the Psychoanalytic Movement* (Chicago: University of Chicago Press, 1985), and Peter Gay, *A Godless Jew: Freud, Atheism and the Making of Psychoanalysis* (New Haven: Yale University Press, 1987).

9. The English "redoubtable" misses the meaning of the French "redoutable," better translated as "fearful" or "abhorrent"—the repellent function of the taboo.

10. The collector "dreams his way not only into a distant or bygone world but also into a better one"—pointing again to the centrality of the dream as a metaphor for this mode of life.

11. A supplement to Benjamin's characterisation of the collector appears in [H3a, 1]: "The positive countertype to the collector—which also, insofar as it entails the liberation of things from the drudgery of being useful, represents the consummation of the collector—can be deduced from these words of Marx: 'Private property has made us so stupid and inert that an object is ours only when we have it, when it exists as capital for us, or when . . . we use it.'" There is thus something in the symptomatic relation of the collector to his objects that points beyond pathology, a truth that can be gleaned only negatively.

12. Note also that immediately preceding this passage, the quote states that "Proust never heightened but rather analyzed humanity" (AP, 547), which can be taken as another oblique reference to psychoanalysis, as it is immediately followed by the reflections on the centrality of the death drive in Proust.

13. As I discuss in more detail in the section "Death Drive in the Arcades," Benjamin takes Freud literally on the grounding of life in the inanimate, supplementing it with a Marxian understanding of the material object as commodity and historicising Freud's universal claim as a particularity of capitalism.

14. Benjamin also refers to the "theory of the trace" in his investigation of the changing nature of work in capitalist modernity (AP, 227).

15. Benjamin was not alone in investigating the centrality of boredom in modernity around this time: this question was also addressed prominently by Martin Heidegger in his 1938 *Fundamental Concepts of Metaphysics: World, Finitude, Solitude* and Siegfried Kracauer in his 1927 essay on boredom in the *Mass Ornament*.

16. As Andrew Benjamin notes, in the dandy, the contradictions between mass and individual come to the fore, and thus the dandy is not yet the mass individual (Benjamin 2006, 166).

17. The conversation that gave rise to this note in the *Arcades Project* is also documented by Brecht—see the discussion in Edmund Wizisla (2004, 68–70).

18. It is difficult to overlook the closeness of this quote to other pronouncements in the *Arcades Project* on the nature of the capitalist economy, the commodity fetish and the value form, and Benjamin's text "Capitalism as Religion."

19. The change in experience is discussed in more detail below.

20. This is taken up again in "On Some Motifs in Baudelaire," where Benjamin posits the gambler as the mirror of "the reflexive mechanism that the machine triggers in the workman" (SW4, 329). Labour under industrial capitalism is thus similar to gambling, right down to the gestural level (SW4, 330).

Chapter Five

Dreaming

As shown in the previous chapter, the dream is a pivotal concept for the *Arcades Project* and associated writings. In this chapter, I examine in more detail the Freudian inheritance in Benjamin's use of the concepts of dreaming and awakening in the *Arcades Project* and some adjacent texts such as *One-Way Street*. I investigate the similarities as well as some differences between Benjamin's and Freud's thought on the dream, with particular reference to the status of the body in the dream theory of both thinkers. From this discussion, it will emerge that Benjamin pushes Freud's thought on the unconscious with respect to the fracturing of the subject, using insights from dream analysis to move beyond the individual psyche to the collective.

I then turn to the centrality of the concept of awakening, both false and true. Benjamin's engagement with Surrealism will be discussed in the context of the former, along with Art Nouveau. At stake is the question whether these artistic movements provide enough to move beyond the dream-consciousness of the nineteenth century and break the spell of post-baroque subjectivity that lingers there. Finally, I turn to the tensions within the arcades, alongside a consideration of the centrality of the "tears and cracks" of the dream for Freud—the question of a "counter-arcade" or, that aspect of capitalist modernity which harbours potential for its own undoing.

Like the mourning plays of the baroque, the arcades have become ruins of their cultural moment when examined from the standpoint of the twentieth-century observer, revealing in their decline something that was invisible during their heyday. By the time of Benjamin's account, they have fallen out of fashion and been reduced to "residues of a dream-world" (AP, 13). Thus it becomes possible to analyse them as one would a dream. Benjamin here reprises Freud's notion of "day-residues," conscious thoughts and experiences that become enmeshed with and stimulate unconscious wishes. Benjamin reverses this movement and sees "dream elements" themselves as residues, waiting to be analysed.

Dream themes proliferate in the *Arcades Project* and adjacent writing. Prior to the genesis of what has come to be referred to as the *Passagenwerk* in German, Benjamin originally conceived of a work entitled "Paris Passages. A Dialectical Fairytale," which was to be closer to *One-Way Street* in volume and intended to "transpose dream experience to historical cognition" (Lindner 2008, 162). In exile in 1934, Benjamin wrote to Gretel Adorno that he had abandoned this project as it was of an "impermissible 'poetic'" nature (C, 507). Referring to Benjamin's short text "Dream Kitsch: Gloss on Surrealism" (1926), where Benjamin asserts that "[t]he history of the dream remains to be written," Burkhardt Lindner concludes that the original intention remained: "The *Arcades Project* was the attempt to write the unwritable history of the dream" (Lindner 2008, 168 [transl. mine]). In the course of this project, super-stition was to be dispelled by historical enlightenment. Elissa Marder is in agreement with Lindner on this point, suggesting that the *Arcades Project* is connected to a larger project on the dream, including the "Surrealism" essay (1929) and "On the Image of Proust": "In this sense, the *Passagen-Werk* ex-plicitly makes the dream central to the philosophy of history" (Marder 2006, 186). While Marder suggests that "Convolute K of the *Passagen-Werk* can be read as an implicit critical commentary on Freud's *Interpretation of Dreams*" (Marder 2006, 186), Lindner (2008, 151–52) sees Benjamin as not taking a direct position vis a vis Freud's dream interpretation and states that there are few traces of an intensive engagement with it discernible in Benjamin's work.

Conversely, I will argue that the motif of the dream in the *Arcades* and adjoining work does display a strong engagement with the *Interpreta-tion of Dreams* (1900) throughout. While Marder is correct in stating that Benjamin most explicitly deals with the Freudian concept of the dream in Convolute K, under the headings "Dream City and Dream House, Dreams of the Future, Anthropological Nihilism, Jung," Benjamin's engagement with this text and dream themes more generally is not restricted to this Convolute and indeed inflects the *Arcades Project* as a whole.

FREUD VIA MARX, MARX VIA FREUD

As Rolf Tiedemann concludes in his afterword to the text, "Under capitalist relationships of production, history could be likened to the unconscious ac-tions of the dreaming individual, at least insofar as history is man-made, yet without consciousness or design, as if in a dream" (AP, 933). This points once more to the conflux of Marxian and Freudian themes in Benjamin's work, already highlighted in the previous chapter. In a 1937 letter to Horkheimer, Benjamin wrote *a propos* the *Arcades Project*:

> I imagine that the definitive and binding plan of the book . . . would have to emerge from two fundamental methodological investigations. One would have to do with the critique of pragmatic history on the one hand and of cultural history on the other, as it presents itself to the materialist; the other with the significance of psychoanalysis for the subject of materialist historiography. (cited in Cohen 1993, 6)

This announcement of Benjamin's theoretical grounding of the *Arcades Project* in both materialist and psychoanalytic thought already hints at the fusion of materialist, specifically Marxist, concepts with those inherited from Freud. We also find clues to the centrality of Freud as a point of connection between Benjamin and Marx in Benjamin's 1930 review of Siegfried Kracauer's study *Die Angestellten*, published the same year. Here, too, Benjamin stresses the fall back into mythic nature in the "false consciousness" of capitalism and suggests the Marxist "doctrine of the superstructure" must be supplemented with the "schema of repression" in order to grasp contradictory consciousness.[1] Unconscious, involuntary action and dreaming are thus conceptualised as a resurgence of nature, which Benjamin also attributes to Freud: in his notes for the *Arcades Project*, he writes of the "doctrine of the natural dream of Freud. Dream as historical phenomenon" (GS5, 1214, transl. mine). This line of thought is carried over into the *Arcades Project*. In Convolute K, Benjamin writes: "Capitalism was a natural phenomenon with which a new dream-filled sleep came over Europe, and, through it, a reactivation of mythic forces" [K1a, 8] (AP, 391). Equal exchange is an example of mythic thought which comes to the fore in capitalism. To break out of the "dream-filled sleep," the second nature created by capitalism and dispel the mythic forces, Benjamin proposes an analysis that fuses Marxian as well as Freudian categories in order to identify the causes, symptoms, and mechanisms of repression. We thus see the conflux of Freud and Marx in Benjamin's thinking; together, they make visible the constellation dream-nature-history-myth. As we shall see, analysis is to serve as an emancipatory process that allows the explosion of this constellation.

Unlike the baroque, which for Benjamin was still largely under the sway of feudalism and found the source of its conflicts in religious strife, the pathology of the nineteenth century is mediated by capitalism. The "working through" of memories in mourning is repressed in the arcades, manifesting as symptoms in the cultural production of the nineteenth century, such as its architecture, utopias, advertising, and shops. Benjamin's symptomatic reading does not distinguish between these different spheres of culture, or indeed between art and commercial cultural forms. From the perspective of the twentieth-century analyst, using the approaches of both historical materialism and Freudian psychoanalysis, they reveal themselves as not distinct spheres, but as expressions of the totality of nineteenth-century capitalism in its epicentre the metropolis. Thus, on nineteenth-century German writer Friedrich Gerstäcker's tale "Die versunkene Stadt" (1852), which depicts a city sunken underwater, populated by near-anthropomorphic fish, Benjamin writes

> If a work of literature, an imaginative composition, could arise from repressed economic contents in the consciousness of a collective, as Freud says it can from sexual contents in an individual consciousness, then [here] we would have before our eyes the consummate sublimation of the arcades, with their bric-a-brac growing rankly out of their showcases. Even the vitreous radiance of the globes of the street lamps, the utter pomp and splendor of gas lighting, enters into this undersea world. [R2, 2] (AP, 540)

Benjamin makes a dual point here. On the one hand, Gerstäcker's tale itself functions for Benjamin as an expression of repressed, unconscious collective wishes—in other words, it sublimates the objects and dreamlike atmosphere encountered in the arcades. Benjamin bases his reflections on his reading of Freud, speculating that in the transposition of the analysis of repression from the individual to the collective, what is at stake is no longer (just) sexual or libidinal contents, but economic ones.[2] In turn, we might speculate that this is because, as individual libido is concerned with survival and pleasure, these drives or principles are collectively expressed in the economic sphere, which mediates the meeting of needs and thus the survival of the social body. The unconscious of the collective, then, is a repository of the economic form of its age. Art and other cultural production thus emerge as a sublimation of this repressed economic sphere, analogous to the way sexual impulses are sublimated in individuals in Freud. This is the second aspect of Benjamin's speculation.

This shows us how central Marx is to not only the theoretical underpinnings of the *Arcades Project*, but specifically the Freudian, psychoanalytic dimension of Benjamin's engagement with the nineteenth century: in the unconscious of the collective, the economic is repressed; that is, the mode and relations of their production, and cultural products as deformed expressions of this repressed content. At the same time, Benjamin is interested in the way in which psychoanalytic themes are also latently present in Marx, as evinced in the following passage:

Reform of consciousness not through dogmas but through the analysis of mystical consciousness that is unclear to itself, whether it appears in a religious or a political form. Then people will see [then it will become apparent] that the world has long possessed the dream of a thing [of which it only needs to possess the consciousness in order really to possess it]. [N5a, 1] (AP, 467)[3]

This quote contains some of the elements that Benjamin also takes from Freud's *Interpretation of Dreams*: analysis of unconscious contents, which are repressed, and subsequently expressed in a deformed fashion in social forms; as well as a conceptualisation of this process as a dream. It follows that Benjamin in the *Arcades Project*, starting with the expose of 1935, conceptualises his attempt to analyse the whole of the nineteenth century as a "dreaming collective" and its "wish images" as a form of historical materialism. Benjamin thus fuses together a heterodox reading of both the Marxist dynamism of dialectics and the psychic dynamism of conflicting drives in Freud.[4] In what follows, I examine some aspects of Freud's account in the *Interpretation of Dreams* that point to the text's fracturing of the subject, before tracing Benjamin's reworking of Freud's concept of the dream and dream analysis in the move from an individual to a collective dream. I also discuss the tension between Freud and Benjamin on the status of dream content/images relative to dream work/analysis. As we shall see, while Benjamin at times seems to be drawing from a pre-Freudian psychology that sees dreams as originating in somatic function, he ultimately transforms both, taking us far away from the merely somatic, or rather, the somatic conceptualised as nothing but bodily functions that translate directly into dream images. Rather, via Freud, Benjamin comes to expand the psychic to encompass the body, without therefore fully psychologising the somatic.

FREUD'S DREAM

One of the most puzzling features of dreams, Freud notes, is that they are abnormal psychical phenomena but nevertheless form part of every normal person's psychic life. This is one of many indications of the slippage between the normal and psychopathological in his work. Dreams point to the central split of the subject into conscious and unconscious; they reveal that we are not "master in our own house" (SE16, 43). On this contradiction, Freud writes,

Our scientific consideration of dreams starts off from the assumption that they are products of our own mental activity. Nevertheless the finished dream strikes us as something alien to us. We are so little obliged to acknowledge our responsibil-

ity for it that [in German] we are just as ready to say "*mir hat geträumt*" ["I
had a dream" literally "a dream came to me" or "it dreamed me"] as "*ich habe
geträumt*" ["I dreamt"]. (SE4, 48)

This observation sets the scene for his introduction of the unconscious
generation of dreams—rooted in a psychic agency we can never fully
encounter, or "know," dreams carry with them something of the strangeness
of that psychic faculty. Freud stresses the uncontrollable, involuntary character of dream images. This cognition in images is typical of the dream and
delineates it from deliberate, waking mental activity, characterised by thinking in concepts. Dream images arise unbidden, as "involuntary ideas" (SE4,
71), which may strike the waking mind as absurd or even immoral. While the
latter in particular are experienced as running counter to the waking moral
compass of the dreamer, all dream images are characterised by their strangeness. This is at the root of the sense of the alien quality of dreams: they seem
to originate from elsewhere, indicating an other, beyond and sometimes running counter to the subject's own, conscious volition. Rather than "willing"
the dream, it comes to one, calling into question intentionality, and thus the
conscious mind, or what Freud was to later call the ego. The main characteristic of the dream is thus the subject's inability to control its mental images. In
this, the dream operates akin to perception—the dreamer experiences dreams
as something that unfolds, a process to which she is exposed. Instead of
constituting intentional, rational thought, the dream hallucinates, that is, it
replaces thoughts with hallucinations—experiences that are perceived as real,
even though they are not. This again points to the limits and fallibility of
consciousness and the existence of other agencies within the psyche.

     As Mikkel Borch-Jacobsen (1988, 3) observes, the proposal that the sub-
ject is split from the start is the "fundamental hypothesis of psychoanalysis."
Analysis reveals the conscious mind as being far from the originary source
of ideas—and not all of them are present to or even directly accessible by
it. In this unconscious, an alien element is introduced into the subject: "The
cogitatio—Freud's term for it is the psychical—exceeds and overflows consciousness at every turn, where consciousness is understood as certainty and
presence of self in representation. This thinking thinks *without me*, without
ceasing to think, moreover (as we see, for example, when it calculates or
makes a joke)" (Borch-Jacobsen 1988, 4). Nevertheless, "that other subject
is simultaneously the *same* as the subject-of-consciousness. The otherness
labelled 'unconscious' is an intimate otherness, if only because the unconscious (or the unconsciousness) *of* the subject is at stake" (Borch-Jacobsen
1988, 6). He claims this does not indicate that there is no (one) subject; rather
we are dealing with a unitary, yet split, subject: "In this sense, the cleav-
age or division of the subject that psychoanalysis keeps talking about takes

place against a background of unity, a *unitary* subject" and points to *The Interpretation of Dreams* where the dreamer, in relation to the dream-wish, is characterised by Freud as "'an amalgamation of two separate people who are linked by some important common element'" (*Dreams*, pp. 580–81, I) (Borch-Jacobsen 1988, 6–7).

Freud's step-by-step revelation of the other actors on the psychic stage besides consciousness—the unconscious, which provides the dream-wish and the material used to illustrate it, the pre-conscious, whose censorship leads to its deformation, and later the id-ego-superego model—all constitute fractures in the concept of the subject. At the same time, dreams and other unconsciously grounded psychic phenomena such as the many "everyday" psychopathologies (e.g., slips of the tongue) have a relationship to reality; that is, waking life, consciousness. However, as we have seen, this relationship is not a straightforward one. The further "agencies" and processes are introduced to account for the circuitous route taken by the dream-wish in its path to consciousness—chief among them repression and censorship.

The proximity of these concepts to the political arena is not lost on Freud, who more than once takes recourse to analogies of sovereigns and subjects to illustrate the workings of the psyche, such as when he formulates the address of psychoanalysis to the subject in the following terms: "You behave like an absolute ruler who is content with the information supplied him by his highest officials and never goes among the people to hear their voice. Turn your eyes inward, look into your own depths, learn first to know yourself! Then you will understand why you were bound to fall ill; and perhaps, you will avoid falling ill in future" (SE17, 143). We see here in Freud's writing the connection between the subject, always teetering on the brink of a relapse into the narcissism that characterised its first state of being, and Benjamin's writing on the inauguration of the subject in the figure of the baroque sovereign, discussed in chapter 1.[5]

The unconscious stores infinitely more than is accessible directly by the psychic tyrant of consciousness and finds ways around its repression. Freud speaks of the hypermnesia of dreams, revealed in analysis: "dreams have at their command memories which are inaccessible in waking life" (SE4, 12). Thus, what surfaces in the dream is not *mere* hallucinations in the sense of bearing no relation to waking life. Rather, they express something of it—but in distorted form. This distortion relates to the form as much as the contents of the dream—"Dreams yield no more than fragments [*Bruchstücke*] of reproductions; and this is so general a rule that theoretical considerations may be based on it" (SE4, 21). The dreamwork's fourfold mechanisms of condensation, displacement, censorship, and presentability include a fifth—that of fragmentation. For Freud, "dream memory" is thus infinitely more than mimesis, that is, the mere reproduction of memory-contents. Indeed, recall in dream is often fragmentary (with the notable exception of traumatic experience). This is in part due to the dreamwork's imperative to distort the latent wish and its use of "day residues" as raw materials to express something else, but also relates to memory itself—the unconscious stores contents in such a way that they require translation to be integrated into the order of the waking mind.

The crucial distinction introduced by Freud concerns the manifest content of the dream, which is not the same as the latent dream-thoughts. As discussed above, this is the result of the interaction of the different psychic agencies involved in the formation—and subsequent interpretation—of the dream. Freud names as the central and most peculiar characteristic of his dream theory "the derivation of dream-distortion from an internal conflict, a kind of inner dishonesty" (SE14, 20). The subject is not true to itself. Lindner suggests that "in this manner, Freud's *Interpretation* opens a suggestive way to enable one to read oneself, so to speak insidiously, via one's own unconscious" (Lindner 2008, 153, transl. mine). Analysis "dismembers" the manifest dream content in order to allow the latent content to become intelligible.

Freud wavers on the relative status of manifest dream images versus latent dream-thoughts. While he sometimes dismisses the dream itself in favour of what lies "behind" or "underneath" it in the latent wish, the importance of the manifest material frequently resurfaces in his own writing. Importantly, there is no instrumental rationality to be found in dreams—the dream may express something, but this "something" is not in itself rational, it does not obey the same laws as conscious thought, and neither is the dream-wishes' path to expression governed by a straightforward teleology. Dreams are more than the latent dream-thoughts which they process, and Freud notes "how far removed it is from the purpose of a dream to produce attempted solutions of the life-task. Dreams are only a form of thinking; one can never reach an understanding of this form by reference to the content of the thoughts; only an appreciation of the dream-work will lead to that understanding" (SE14, 65). The dream itself is thus always in excess; any insight into it is not immanent to the content of the dream-thoughts alone. Freud highlights the central importance of dreamwork—not just the static content but the dynamic process of their generation, and what they obscure. What matters is precisely not the dream images in themselves; rather, they present a riddle, something to be solved—consciously. At the same time, this "solving" of the puzzle does not result in the dream being revealed as taking part in a grand project of individual improvement, or bringing the subject closer to the generation of "meaning" in its life. Rather, it reveals a glimpse of the unconscious, and more besides: the dream expresses the latent wish in distorted form, but also the work of the different agencies, and the intra-psychic conflict itself, thus demonstrating the fractured status of the subject. Stella Sandford identifies two types of dream interpretation that run parallel in the *Interpretation of Dreams*: "that based on the archaeological model and that in which the dream itself (as a finished piece, rather than a collection of broken-up bits) is understood as a fragment in the Romantic sense" (Sandford 2016, 29). The former model aims at a reconstructive analysis that can be made into a synthesis: "the perfectly intelligible, rational kernel of the dream which can become an object of knowledge" (Sandford 2016, 29). As Freud summarises, it is the task of the interpretation of dreams to restore "the connections which the dream-work has destroyed" (SE4, 312) and thus allow the latent meaning of the dream to come to the fore.

Sandford also identifies a second view of dreams in the *Interpretation*, which "accepts none of these distinctions or conceptions. On this second view, 'the dream's the thing'; it is not a false front. The fact that it says more than it says is more important than any one thing that it might be made to say through the process of interpretation" (Sandford 2016, 32). As I discuss below, this would bring Freud even closer to Benjamin's use of the dream.[6] Benjamin concurrently draws from the "archaeological" model in conceptualising interpretation as a way to bring into consciousness repressed unconscious contents. Moreover, this model itself is split into a strand focused on excavating an underlying fragmented truth (in the non-Romantic sense) and that which aims at constructing a new truth, which is where its emancipatory potential lies. Taken together, both models of interpretation reveal the subject as fractured, and both are important for Benjamin.

UNCONSCIOUS VERSUS BODILY PROCESSES

None of the somatic explanations of dream generation satisfactorily establish a causal link between the stimulus and the dream content for Freud—dream images are overdetermined rather than mimetic. Freud sums up the position of the authors of the somatic school as follows: "Dreams are a reaction to the disturbance of sleep brought about by a stimulus—a reaction, incidentally, which is quite superfluous" (SE4, 78). Freud's account in the "Metapsychology of Dreams" (1915) supplementing and summarising some of his earlier work, theorises the process of the projection of these physical impulses into psychic images in order to perpetuate sleep: "the internal demand which was striving to occupy him has been replaced by an external experience, whose demand has been disposed of. A dream is, therefore, among other things, a *projection*: an externalization of an internal process" (SE14, 223). Crucially, Freud asserts that the somatic theory is unable to satisfactorily account for the specific choice in dream image. Against this, he stresses the importance of interpretation, which is foreclosed by the somatic theorists: "for 'interpreting' a dream implies assigning a 'meaning' to it—that is, replacing it by something which fits into the chain of our mental acts as a link having a validity and importance equal to the rest" (SE4, 96). The "scientific" theories of the dream, in contrast, view dreams as a purely somatic, and thus not psychic, process.

In a passage expanding on the theoretical foundations for his understanding of the nineteenth century as a dream in Convolute K of the *Arcades Project*, Benjamin diverges, at first glance, quite significantly from Freud, in fact ostensibly returning to one of the popular theories for the origins of dreams Freud set out to refute in his *Interpretation of Dreams*: "Attempt to develop Giedion's thesis. 'In the nineteenth century;' he writes, 'construction plays the role of the subconscious'; Wouldn't it be better to say 'the role of bodily processes'—around which 'artistic' architectures gather, like dreams around the framework of physiological processes?" (AP, 391). Benjamin here puts forward an understanding of the genesis of dreams centred around "bodily," "physiological processes," proceeding to characterise sleep as "the macrocosmic journey through [the] body" (AP, 389), and going as far as suggesting this heightened awareness of bodily functions and processes generate "illusion or dream imagery which accounts for them" (AP, 389). These reflections on the relationship between the sub- or unconscious, the body and its processes, and the translation of individual-psychoanalytic concepts to the collective and the status of material and cultural production are to form a central web of questions for Benjamin. On closer examination, we can see several links between Freud and Benjamin on this point. It should be noted, first, that Benjamin's account is not entirely inconsistent with Freud's own account of dream images in the *Interpretation of Dreams*. Freud admits that dreams often reveal unconscious knowledge, which also explains their seemingly "prophetic" character (SE4, 34). Freud allows a role for the physical in dream generation, acknowledging in particular the issue of dreams as hypersensitive to physical illness. In the *Interpretation of Dreams*, Freud notes that Aristotle and Hippocrates both knew the characteristic of "dream life" that betrays the first changes of a physical illness. This is taken up again in the "Metapsychology of Dreams," where Freud conceptualises the dreamer as a hypochondriac, experiencing minor physiological changes as through a magnifying glass. This intrinsic narcissism of the dream, where all cathexes are momentarily withdrawn from the outside world into the self, is what equips it with this diagnostic capacity.[7]

Additionally, Freud allows for "somatic excitations" to make it into the dream under certain conditions, thus integrating the somatic model—whose correctness, he stresses, he does not dispute, merely its adequacy (SE4, 221)—with his theory of the wish-fulfilment of the dream. As "a dream appears to be a reaction to everything that is simultaneously present in the sleeping mind as currently active material" (SE4, 228), it follows that somatic stimulus, too, can enter the dream. When it does, "it means that it has been possible to find ideational material to serve as the content of the dream of such a sort as to be able to represent both kinds of source of the dream—the somatic and the psychical" (SE4, 228). A degree of intensity is necessary for this—in the "extreme case" that it does happen, the somatic forms a kernel or core within the dream-material "a wish-fulfilment is then looked for that shall correspond to this nucleus, just as (see above [p. 228]) intermediate ideas are looked for between two psychical dream-stimuli. To that extent it is true that in a number of dreams the content of the dream is dictated by the somatic element" (SE4, 238). While thus admitting that in some cases the somatic is at the "core" of the dream, what differentiates Freud's position in this text from that of his forebears is that he distances himself from the epiphenomenalism of his predecessors; that is, the notion that it is the body that directly produces "mere" mental side effects.[8] Dreams and other psychic phenomena, for Freud, are overdetermined, generated by stimuli that derive from the psyche as well as from the body. In the *Interpertation of Dreams*, Freud establishes a model where the somatic stimuli are taken up into the psychic, where they are merged with other, psychic "day remainders." Unless they are of unusual intensity, they are "treated like some cheap material always ready to hand, which is employed whenever it is needed, in contrast to a precious material which itself prescribes the way in which it shall be employed" (SE4, 237). What occurs in this passage is a psychologisation of somatic stimuli or excitations in the dream, reasserting the primacy of the psychic. However, it is important to note that Freud did not therefore sideline the role of the body in psychoanalysis, or subscribe to a wholesale split between the two: The bodyimportant as a source of excitation, and thus integrated with the psychic. This holds true for the "normal" development of the ego and its drives, as Freud discusses in *The Ego and the Id* (1923), and in "Instincts and their Vicissitudes," where the drive "appears to us as . . . on the boundary between the mental and the somatic, as the psychic representative of the excitation arising from the inner body that enters into the mind, as a measure of the amount of work imposed to the mind in consequence of its connection to the body" (SE14, 121). This is the conception of drives we also see at play in *Beyond the Pleasure Principle*—the overarching aim is the reduction of excitation, the source of which is somatic, but indivisible from its mediation at the psychic level.

This model also applies to the psychoneuroses: "hysteria, obsessional neurosis and melancholia . . . show us that the body is inseparable from the psyche" (Cohen 2015, 214). From the perspective of the psychoneuroses, then, what the body feels and shows always *means* something, and it is this ascription of meaning that enables Freud to discover the therapeutic value of verbal interpretation. The clinician's task becomes something like a translation to the patient of the unconscious sense of her body's strange and insistent messages (Cohen 2015, 215). Thus, Cohen concludes that "[ps] ychoanalysis does not allow us to think of the body as a raw biological entity, in isolation from the psyche which processes its experiences" (Cohen 2015, 214). As noted above, while this model of neurosis was to be the dominant one for psychoanalysis, Freud also conceptualised the so-called "actual" neuroses, characterised by physical symptoms that "signify only themselves. Where in hysteria such symptoms can be understood as encryptions of memory and fantasy, in 'actual' neurosis the body lacks any metaphoric capacity" (Cohen 2015, 216).[9] As observed above, "it is precisely in their defiance of sense that the 'actual' neuroses prove to be of real import to psychoanalysis" (Cohen 2015, 217), in their broken relationship with the psychic and their entwinement with the psychoneuroses. Again it becomes apparent how Benjamin's reflections on the destabilisation of the boundary between body and psyche are influenced by Freud, who "suggests that rather than being discrete entities, 'actual' and psycho-neuroses may be intimately related to one another. The symbolic meanings of psychoneurosis may wrap themselves around a kernel of untranslatable, 'actual' bodily noise" (Cohen 2015, 227), signifying the point where analysis can go no further.

It is via this account of the interplay between actual and psychoneuroses that we can understand Benjamin's tentative reformulation of Giedion's dictum cited towards the beginning of this section: bodily processes give rise to symptoms, and their mediation by the psyche at times breaks down in modernity. We are thus dealing with two levels of suffering: that of the symptoms themselves and that of being unable to even psychically make sense of the excessive somatic tension. To acknowledge that the "translation" of the material, the somatic, is not always fully successful, and that even in its failure it is again bound up with the psychic, draws close to Freud's recognition of the excess of the dream. Freud describes the moment where the meaning of the dream becomes unintelligible even in analysis as its "navel, the spot where it reaches down into the unknown" (SE5, 525)—the point beyond which meaning remains elusive.

BENJAMIN'S PSYCHIC BODY: FROM INDIVIDUAL TO COLLECTIVE UNCONSCIOUS AND DREAMS

Benjamin draws on the dynamic between psychic and somatic that is present in Freud's thought in his work on dreams in the arcades. Benjamin writes that the "overfull stomach" of the sleeper "does not find its ideological superstructure in the contents of the dream—and it is exactly the same with the economic conditions of life for the collective. It interprets these conditions; it explains them. In the dream, they find their expression; in the awakening, their interpretation" (AP, 854–55). It is obvious that Benjamin is not advocating a return to the somatic model critiqued in the *Interpretation of Dreams* here. While those thinkers use the argument of its physical origin as a way to dismiss it entirely and rob the dream of its "dignity" as a psychic, rather than a physical, process, it becomes clear that Benjamin, following Freud, *does* view the dream as a psychic phenomenon: something to be interpreted. Sigrid Weigel sums this up in noting that "in Benjamin's modus operandi with psychoanalytical figures . . . the corporeal origins, lost in the course of the development of psychoanalytical theory, are brought back more strongly into focus, albeit without reversing the break with the model of a simple and straightforward decipherability of bodily signs" (Weigel 1996, 23). Benjamin thus draws on both the strand of psychoanalysis, more forcefully pursued by Freud, that investigates the psychoneuroses, *and* the earlier, latent path of the "actual" neuroses. As Benjamin puts it in a first sketch for the *Arcades Project*, the dreamer

> has this in common with the madman: the noises emanating from within the body, which for the salubrious individual converge in a steady surge of health and bring on sound sleep if they are not overlooked, dissociate for the one who dreams. Blood pressure, intestinal churn, heartbeat, muscle sensations become individually perceptible for him and demand the explanation which delusion or dream image holds ready. (AP, 389)

Freud notes in the *Interpretation of Dreams* that some of the somatic theorists before him posit that only *pathological* somatic excitation is noted in the dream—a conception to which he here is more favourably inclined. Benjamin follows this theory but modifies it, expanding it to the "dreaming collective": "This sharpened receptivity is a feature of the dreaming collective, which settles into the arcades as into the insides of its own body. We must follow in its wake in order to expound the nineteenth century as its dream vision" (AP, 842). At stake is thus the pathology of the social organism, which is translated by the dreaming collective into dream images. This would seem, at face value, to merely expand the somatic model of dream generation, with the social organism functioning analogously to that of the individual. However, we also see that the intervention of a psyche is presupposed here—the explanation that is provided in the dream image or illusion is demanded from another agency within the dreamer than his body. The analogy between the dreamer/his stomach and the collective/economic conditions becomes possible in the nineteenth century where, due to specific historical developments of capitalism, fractured subjects are pulled together in the modern city. Here, the model of dream generation of the individual is thus extended to the "dreaming collective," which "through the arcades, communes with its own insides" (AP, 389).[10] The relationship between inside and outside, that which generates the dream image and that which is generated by it, is further complicated in a variation on this formulation: the methodological injunction to "expound the nineteenth century—in fashion and advertising, in buildings and politics—as the *outcome* of its dream visions" (AP, 389 [emphasis mine]). While what was previously an outcome of the internal workings of the collective, represented in the dream, is now internal to it: "architecture, fashion—yes, even the weather—are, in the interior of the collective, what the sensoria of organs, the feeling of sickness or health, are inside the individual" (AP, 389). What, then, is the "inside" of the dreaming collective, if the fashion, politics, and other cultural products of the nineteenth century, indeed, the century *in toto*, are the *outcome* of the dream visions—and at the same time dreaming signifies a communion with the insides of the dreaming collective? What is the social, collective equivalent of the physical body of the individual to which dream images correspond?

Again Benjamin expands from the individual to the collective, this time using the concept of "consciousness as patterned and chequered by sleep and waking" (AP, 389)[11] and states that the phenomena of the nineteenth century "preserve this unconscious, amorphous dream configuration, they are as much natural processes as digestion, breathing, and the like. They stand in the cycle of the eternally selfsame, until the collective seizes upon them in politics and history emerges" [KI, 5] (AP, 389–90). Weigel suggests that while Benjamin does explicitly refer to psychoanalysis, in the early phases of the *Arcades Project*, "Benjamin does not yet make use of the term or the concept of the unconscious," instead spatialising the "relationship between dream and waking or dream and consciousness" (Weigel 1996, 232). However, here, we are dealing with the dream configuration of the nineteenth century as "unconscious," lending credence to the idea that Benjamin expands the psychic to the somatic rather than subsuming the latter under the former, as his previous formulation might lead us to think.

Analogous to Benjamin's pronouncement on the destabilisation of the sleep-waking dichotomy in psychoanalysis, the distinction between the inside and the outside of the organism, the psyche and the body, are broken down here, so that we seem to deal with a "psychic body." It seems as if Benjamin, rather than undertaking a "somatification" of the psychic, as it first appeared, is proposing a psychologisation of the social body, where the "translation" that takes place in the generation of dream images presupposes something other than merely the "noises and feelings of [the] insides" (AP, 389). This is further stressed in the sentence following Benjamin's methodological announcement that the insights into consciousness of psychoanalysis need to be "transferred from the individual to the collective" (AP 389): the contents of the unconscious are akin to natural processes, but they can—and must—be brought into consciousness, what Benjamin elsewhere terms the "waking mind," and crucially, seized upon "in politics" in order for history to emerge. Benjamin here draws on Freud's model of dream analysis, the making-conscious of what is expressed in the dream-thoughts in analysis. For Benjamin, however, the process of "denaturing" these unconscious contents must also be a *political* act—to be seized collectively rather than merely explored at the level of the individual. This is made possible by the collectivising tendencies of the nineteenth century, the massification discussed in chapter 3: the fracturing of the subject now shows a path towards a different reassembly of the pieces. Benjamin thus radicalises the individual focus of psychoanalytic praxis by heightening its latent political aspect.

ONTOGENESIS VERSUS PHYLOGENESIS

Benjamin was well aware of the conceptual tension between the individual and the collective psyche. A passage from an article in surrealist journal *Minotaure* by writer and medical doctor Pierre Mabille, which Benjamin quotes in the *Arcades Project*, sheds some light on Benjamin's thinking on the issue. Here, the unconscious is conceptualised as phylogenetically structured, that is, containing "the mass of things learned in the course of the centuries and in the course of a life," a "[v]ast submarine fund, in which all cultures, all studies, all proceedings of mind and will, all social uprisings, all struggles are collected in a formless mire." Over the course of their "sedimentation" in history, "The passional elements of individuals have receded, dimmed. All that remain are the givens of the external world, more or less transformed and digested. It is of the external world that this unconscious is made" (AP, 396). These unconscious contents rupture into visibility "above all at moments of crisis or of social upheaval; it forms the great common ground, the reserve of peoples and individuals. Revolution and war, like a fever, are best suited to get it moving" (AP, 396–97). This passage contains many of the elements of Benjamin's dream theory: Dreams as a repository of past forms, the unconscious as composed of the external world, the collectivisation of the psychic, its cathexis to times of crisis, and finally the crucial formulation that further links the somatic and the psychic in the metaphor of "digestion" and "circulation" in the "depths" of something that lies beyond the merely-psychic, merely-somatic—a kind of primal, "subterranean" force. We see this model at play throughout the *Arcades Project*. Here, too, the psyche itself is revealed as not only socially constructed, but composed of "givens of the external world," a subterranean fundus of transhistorical unconscious data that erupts in dreams and specifically at times of social strife. This version of the unconscious is associated with "oblivion"; that is, it is not consciously registered as apperception, nor can it be made fully conscious after the fact, but erupts to the surface from the depths—or is discovered when one digs into its substratum; a model consistent with Freud's. This is true for the individual as well as the collective—but Benjamin is interested more in the latter, consistent with Mabille's pronouncement that "the psychology of the individual is now outmoded" (AP, 397). Suspended in the confrontation between the "visceral unconscious" and the "unconscious of oblivion" (AP, 396)—the first of which is predominantly individual, the second predominantly collective—the subject is revealed as a historical anomaly: not only is the individual psyche divided within itself, it is also riven further by the eruption of "subterranean" contents external to itself.

On the issue of the primacy of phylogenesis and the collective unconscious over ontogenesis and the individual, Benjamin was accused by some of drawing close to Jung. First and foremost among these critics is Theodor Adorno. However, Benjamin was not blind to the reactionary dimension of this concept in Jung, as is made clear in his correspondence. As he wrote to Fritz Lieb on July 9, 1937, "I had intended to write a critique of Jung-ian psychology, whose Fascist armature I had promised myself to expose" (C, 541). Instead of pursuing this project, Benjamin dedicated himself to the Baudelaire essay; however, it is implicit in Benjamin's approach to the concept of the collective unconscious. Compare a letter to Scholem from August 5, 1937: "I have begun to delve into Jung's psychology—the devil's work through and through, which should be attacked with white magic" (C, 543). This "attack with white magic," the critique of the fascist elements of Jung's thought, shines through in Benjamin's politicised use of the concept. It serves to highlight that Capitalist society of the nineteenth century functions as an organism that is asleep, that is, not in control or even fully aware of its products. After all, one of the central theoretical premises of the *Arcades Project* is that "a work of literature, an imaginative composition, could arise from repressed economic contents in the consciousness of a collective, as Freud says it can from sexual contents in an individual consciousness" (AP, 540). Where the individual psyche produces thoughts, production of the collective one is to be thought economically, insofar as all material production under capitalism falls under the category of the economic. The scope of its unconscious, too, is material, and vast—it draws on all of human history. A critique of Jung's enthusiastic espousal of this archaism of the collective unconscious thus also serves to draw on the specificity and contingency of this form of socio-economic organisation: Specific images resonate at specific times and serve a specific function—that of perpetuating the sleep of capitalism. As Margaret Cohen points out, Benjamin's project was far removed from "the antihistorical Jung from whom Benjamin was careful to dissociate himself" (Cohen 1993, 43). Weigel is thus right to observe that "[t] he dismissal of archaic images is evidence of the distance between Benjamin and Jung, with whose model of the 'collective unconscious' Benjamin's talk of the 'unconscious of the collective' has nothing to do" (Weigel 1996, 297). For Benjamin, Jung's archaism serves as another instance of the repetition-compulsion of attempting a return to an imaginary golden age. Its historical and political function are clear: Where for Benjamin, "The now of recognizability is the moment of awakening," "Jung would like to distance [literally 'keep away'] awakening from the dream" [NI8, 4] (AP, 486).

Fortunately, Benjamin didn't have to turn to Jung for a conception of a phylogenetic repository of symbols and a collective psyche: It is to be found in Freud, who wrote in "Analysis Terminable or Interminable" that "even before the ego exists, its subsequent lines of development, tendencies and reactions are already determined . . . analytic experience convinces us that particular psychic contents, such as symbolism, have no other source than that of hereditary transmission." Further, "research in various fields of folk-psychology seems to justify the assumption that in archaic inheritance there are other, no less specialized, deposits from primitive human development." Thus, "when we recognize that the peculiarities of the ego which we detect in the form of resistances may be not only acquired in defensive conflicts but transmitted by heredity, the topographical differentiation between ego and id loses much of its value for our investigations" (SE23, 240–41). Freud here expands on the theory of the id as a remnant of phylogenetic development to encompass certain contents of the ego—blurring the lines between ego and id, inherited and acquired characteristics, and individual and collective. Benjamin follows him in this in all respects in his reading of the nineteenth century in the *Arcades Project*, which, he states, are "structures in which we relive, as in a dream, the life of our parents and grandparents, as the embryo in the womb relives the life of animals" [D2a, 1] (AP, 106). Thus, Benjamin undertakes a dream-narration of the nineteenth century in the *Arcades Project* in order to dispel the phylogenetic weight of tradition that prevents the truly new from coming to the fore. Benjamin modifies Freud's concept of the phylogenetic element of the unconscious in historicising the re-emergence of the mythic[12]: *Urgeschichte*, the primal, surfaces in the nineteenth century under specific conditions—and it is a specific version of *Urgeschichte*, mediated by tradition, specifically that of the most recent generations, whose legacy is the most strongly felt. It is the culture of the generation dominant at a given point in time that must be overcome. In this, there perhaps appears to be an echo of the Freudian "killing of the father" at play.[13] However, where for Freud in *Totem and Taboo*, this murder haunts humanity and forms the moment at which morality is introduced, Benjamin instead aims at a decisive break with the world of the parents. Just as Freud posits analysis as a means of overcoming hereditary psychic resistances and interrupting the psychic temporality where unconscious, "primitive" contents are acted out in the present, Benjamin looks to an awakening from the dream-sleep of the nineteenth century. This concept of awakening is not without its complications and dangers. I will turn to these first, before examining "true" awakening in the next and final chapter.

NIGHTMARES

While dreams are sites of wish-fulfilment, they are also sites of the iteration of trauma. With regard to the repetition of trauma in dreams, Freud notes in *Beyond the Pleasure Principle* that an exception exists to the principle that the dream is a wish-fulfilment: the dreams "which occur in traumatic neuroses," and "the dreams during psycho-analyses which bring to memory the psychical traumas of childhood." These categories of dreams "arise, rather, in obedience to the compulsion to repeat, though it is true that in analysis that compulsion is supported by the wish . . . to conjure up again what has been forgotten and repressed" (BPP, 26). This shapes both Benjamin's conceptualisation of the nineteenth century as a dream-filled sleep, and of its dreamwork. On this understanding, it is not just repressed wish-images, but also repetition-compulsion that is displayed in the dream. The analyst's task becomes disentangling these and to look beyond both—to understand how to break the repetition of trauma and to distil from the dream-thought the underlying wish, which only finds a false, compensatory fulfilment in the dream in order to perpetuate sleep.

Lindner states that Benjamin misreads Freud's wish-fulfilment theory, quoting Benjamin's claim that Freud credited the dream with contrasting in such a way with waking life that it made the latter more bearable (Lindner 2008, 152). This would explain nightmares, for, as Benjamin wrote in a fragmentary note, "These dreams fulfil our wish to be consoled for the inconveniences with which awakening presents us. Awakening from them, we find a situation that is bearable compared to that of the dream" (GS6, 209, transl. mine). Strikingly, Benjamin's account of Freud's statement seems to run directly counter to the actual description of the mechanism of wish-fulfilment in dreams in the *Interpretation of Dreams*, reprised again in the "Metapsychology of Dreams": the wish-fulfilling capacity of the dream (or other hallucination) is not just a diagnostic one, but shows us the latent wish as already fulfilled. This is grounded in the dreamwork's requirement of presentability.

We might argue that Benjamin's claim is still compatible with the idea of dreams as wish-fulfilment since, as Freud reminds us, the manifest mood of the dream is not necessarily the same as the latent one, and affects, just like dream symbols, are often revealed as their opposite only on analysis. Thus, to awaken and find one's situation preferable to that experienced in the dream does not conflict with the latter's wish-fulfilling quality. An obvious objection is that neither does it account for it. However, Freud acknowledges in the 1911 revision to the *Interpretation of Dreams* that his theory of dreams as distorted wish-fulfilment is challenged by a class of dreams that, while not traumatic iterations as established in *Beyond the Pleasure Principle*, nevertheless seem to originate in no discernible wish and are unpleasant or torturous. Benjamin was probably referring to this passage, in particular the anecdote related by Freud to illustrate this caveat: the case of the poet Peter Rosegger, who for years dreams of being a tailor's apprentice every night. The dull routine of his subordinate position and the manual labour he performs in his dream contrasts with his comfortable bourgeois waking life in such a way that the latter seems even more rewarding. Freud admits that "In this series of dreams dreamt by an author who had been a journeyman tailor in his youth, it is hard to recognize the dominance of wish-fulfilment. All the dreamer's enjoyment lay in his day-time existence, whereas in his dreams he was still haunted by the shadow of an unhappy life from which he had at last escaped." He explains the occurrence of these dreams as grounded in the "conflict between a parvenu's pride and his self-criticism" (SE5, 475) and that, in the service of the latter, it points to the existence of a class of "punishment dreams." How, then, is wish-fulfilment to remain the universal driver of the dream, if a dream can seemingly also be punitive? Freud solves this problem by introducing a masochistic tendency which *yearns* for punishment, thereby turning it into the fulfilment of a wish. In an addendum from 1930, Freud also points out that since his analysis of the personality into ego and superego in *Group Psychology and the Analysis of the Ego* (1921), it has become possible to see these dreams as wish-fulfilments of the superego (SE5, 476). On this later model, the superego is thus identified as the agency that creates a wish for punishment This tendency, however, is already noted in 1900.[14]

In the *Interpretation*, Freud also allows space for ostensibly painful or frightening dreams to fulfil a compensatory function:

> They are dreams of consolation for another kind of anxiety felt in sleep—the fear of dying. "Departing" on a journey is one of the commonest and best authenticated symbols of death. These dreams say in a consoling way: "Don't worry, you won't die (depart)," just as examination dreams say soothingly: "Don't be afraid, no harm will come to you this time either." The difficulty of understanding both these kinds of dreams is due to the fact that the feeling of anxiety is attached precisely to the expression of consolation. (SE5, 385)

Benjamin, then, links these different strands of dreams in Freud. Continuing after the above passage contested by Lindner, Benjamin speculates that the terror is grounded in a fear of death, which is compensated by projecting it onto objects that, while holding an even deeper terror, are nevertheless less certain to occur. Crucially, the compensatory function is sometimes expressed precisely in their nightmarish quality. Displacing wishes, compensation for real suffering, and traumatic repetition—the threefold function of the dream in psychic life we have encountered in both Freud and Benjamin so far.

"THE KEEPER OF SLEEP"

In the *Interpretation of Dreams*, Freud repeatedly stresses the overwhelming wish of consciousness to remain asleep. This runs counter to any unconscious wishes that might surface in the course of dreaming, and likewise, as we have seen, to any somatic excitation: If the "soul" is forced to acknowledge impulses during sleep, "it seeks for an interpretation of them which will make the currently active sensation into a component part of a situation which is wished for and which is consistent with sleeping. The currently active sensation is woven into a dream *in order to rob it of reality*" (SE4, 234). Dreaming thus functions as a counter to awakening, a defense mechanism of the sleeping organism. Benjamin follows Freud in this when he makes a note on the back of a manuscript for his Kafka essay about "[t]he efforts of the dreamer, who wants to move his little finger and who would in reality, if he accomplished this, awaken" (GSII, 1259, transl. mine). What demarcates the threshold between dreaming and waking life is thus the actual carrying out of an intention, in this instance of a physical movement.

In the dream, any psychic conflict arising from unfulfilled wishes is presented as *already* resolved, and thus made to disappear. Freud writes that

"All dreams are in a sense dreams of convenience: they serve the purpose of prolonging sleep instead of waking up. *Dreams are the* GUARDIANS *of sleep and not its disturbers*" (SE4, 233). Thus it follows that the dream repels awakening. This protective-repellent function is also at play in secondary revision for Freud:

> When the thought "this is only a dream" occurs during a dream . . . it is aimed at reducing the importance of what has just been experienced and at making it possible to tolerate what is to follow. It serves to lull a particular agency to sleep which would have every reason at that moment to bestir itself and forbid the continuance of the dream . . . It is more comfortable, however, to go on sleeping and tolerate the dream, because, after all, "it *is* only a dream." (SE5, 488)

The realisation within the dream that one is dreaming, even more than the other aspects of dreamwork, thus has a conservative function: its aim is to represses the stirrings of consciousness in the act of awakening by encouraging censorship to tolerate the dream. Where secondary revision fails to make the dream appear logical, it thus pursues the opposite track in highlighting the "unreal" nature of what is dreamt. It can even go as far as performing interpretation from within the dream, which is only later, on waking analysis, revealed as forming part of the dream itself (SE5, 490). Thus dreamwork seeps beyond the act of sleep into awakening, infiltrating the first waking thoughts, and provides a substitute interpretation of the dream in order to prevent a conscious analysis (SE5, 446). Dreams may thus have been interpreted already—but, crucially, wrongly.[15]

Where Sandford (2016, 33) conceptualises the possibility of this interpretation from within the dream as "the absolute point of indifference between dream-work and interpretation," Benjamin draws from Freud's archaeological model as it allows him to assume a vantage point from which to analyse the nineteenth century. We can perhaps speak of a primary and a secondary interpretation. The first occurs within the dream, where the *Leibreiz* is psychologised, that is, taken up by the psyche and connected with a previously existing, infantile wish, or when secondary revision intervenes and forces a false interpretation on the newly awakened mind. The second interpretation, in the "archaeological" model, where the waking mind only has access to the unconscious in the form of fragments, or ruins of the dream-world, and requires the perspective "from the far bank" (SW1, 444), as Benjamin puts it in his aphorism "Breakfast Room" from *One-Way Street.* The aim is to arrive at a true analysis that allows the dream-thoughts to become "etwas durchdrungene[s]," something permeated, as Benjamin puts it in the "Materials for the Expose of 1935." Here, Benjamin reiterates his theoretical understanding of the nineteenth century as dream-world: "First dialectical stage: the arcade changes from a place of splendour to a place of decay. Second dialectical stage: the arcade changes from an unconscious experience to something consciously penetrated" (No 8).[16] At stake is thus the making-conscious of experience in the arcades, enabled by their decay into ruin. On this, Alexander Gelley refers to *Benjamins Begriffe*, where Heiner Weidmann lays out the problematic as follows: "What is involved is the possibility of modernity as a historical discontinuity: How, historically, is a truly epochal new beginning, a revolutionary reversal at all conceivable that would not merely—undialectically—consist in a bad negation of the antecedent condition and thus remain merely illustrative?" (Gelley 2015, 184). Especially when, as Benjamin notes, "The first tremors of awakening serve to deepen sleep" (AP, 863)? In what follows, I shall examine two "bad negations": Art Nouveau and Surrealism.

FALSE AWAKENINGS: ART NOUVEAU AND SURREALISM

In a fragment from his "Materials for the Expose of 1935," Benjamin writes "Epitome [Type] of the false redemption: Jugendstil. It proves the law according to which effort brings about its opposite" (AP, 908) and, in an alternative to this formulation which made its way into the *Arcades Project*,

> the law according to which an action brings about an opposite reaction holds true for Jugendstil. The genuine liberation from an epoch, that is, has the structure of awakening in this respect as well: it is entirely ruled by cunning. Only with cunning, not without it, can we work free of the realm of dream. But there is also a false liberation; its sign is violence. From the beginning, it condemned Jugendstil to failure. Dream Structure. [G1, 7] (AP, 173)

This use of the "law" carries echoes of a mechanical understanding of dialectics. Operating within the causal temporality of the nineteenth century, Art Nouveau only dreams of a liberation and lacks the ruse, or "cunning," necessary for true liberation to succeed, for a true awakening to take place. In this, we see the influence of Freud's concept of the inversion of all psychic values in the dreamwork's disfigurement, and inversion of the dream-wish. This inversion serves the twin purposes of representability and bypassing psychic censorship. However, at the same time, the inversion aids the purposes of censorship in "paralysing" the dream's intelligibility. Labouring within the realm of the dream, like the attempt to interpret the dream in secondary revision, Jugendstil cannot but express the opposite of what it aims at. Benjamin links the dangers of not awakening to a historical oversleeping on the part of the ruling class: "The notion of eternal return appeared at a time when the bourgeoisie no longer dared count on the impending development of the system of production which they had set going. The thought of Zarathustra and of eternal recurrence belongs together with the embroidered motto seen on pillows: 'Only a quarter hour'" (AP, 117). The stasis of the bourgeois class is thus linked to its philosophy of history and expressed in the interior of the bourgeois home, on a pillow whose motto functions a knowing wink—its sleep will last considerably longer than proclaimed.

A second movement Benjamin examines for its relationship to sleep, dreaming, and awakening is Surrealism. Benjamin was initially drawn to it for its insight into alternative modes of perception and cognition, its taking seriously the critical potential of material objects, and its recognition of the energies stored in the outmoded. Benjamin credits Breton with the discovery of the "revolutionary energies that appear in the 'outmoded'—in the first iron constructions, the first factory buildings, the earliest photos, objects that have begun to be extinct, grand pianos, the dresses of five years ago, fashionable restaurants when the vogue has begun to ebb from them" (SW2.1, 210). In stressing the discovery of the importance of the outmoded, it is clear that Benjamin is valorising Surrealism's contribution to his own thought. Similarly, the passage on "being on the track of things" rather than of the psyche, which appears in the *Arcades Project*,[17] is identified with the surrealists in "Dream Kitsch." Crucially, the surrealist mode of apperception and experience was capable of decentring the subject: "Language takes precedence. Not only before meaning. Also before the self [*vor dem Ich*]. In the world's structure dream loosens individuality like a bad tooth. This loosening of the self by intoxication is, at the same time, precisely the fruitful, living experience that allowed these people to step outside the domain of intoxication" (SW2.1, 208). At stake in Surrealism and intoxication, as in the dream, is a state of being that allows for the constraints of individuality to become undone. However, Surrealism for Benjamin ultimately proved incapable of remaining outside of the altered state of intoxication. This is where Benjamin, who was looking for a moment of truth in dream states, rather than seeing them as a resolution in and of themselves,[18] diverged from the surrealists.

Of the genesis of Surrealism, Benjamin writes in the *Arcades Project*: "The father of Surrealism was Dada; its mother was an arcade" [01, 3], and "Surrealism was born in an arcade. And under the protection of what muses!" [01, 2] (AP, 82), among which he numbers "libido." Thus, Benjamin links Surrealism to the unanalysed psychic process, as well as the arcade, the epitome of nineteenth-century capitalism. This is also revealed in its connection to fashion, in whose "mute impenetrable nebula . . . where the understanding cannot follow," "the collective dream energy of a society has taken refuge with redoubled vehemence." Thus, "Fashion is the predecessor—no, the eternal deputy—of surrealism" (AP, 64). To link surrealism to fashion in this way is to consign it to the status of yet another outgrowth of the "dialectics of the new and the ever-same" characteristic of nineteenth-century capitalism. Thus Benjamin quickly became invested in a conceptual liquidation of the surrealist inheritance. He wrote to Scholem: "The work represents both the philosophical application of surrealism—and thereby its sublation *[Aufhebung]*—as well as the attempt to retain the image of history in the most inconspicuous corners of existence— the detritus of history" (C, 505). The stress here is on the *philosophical* use of Surrealism—that is, to derive from its methods and modes of experience and presentation something that Surrealism itself could never furnish: meaning and truth. This is because Surrealism, like Art Nouveau, is itself part of the dream-world: "it broke over its founders as an inspiring dream wave, it seemed the most integral, conclusive, absolute of movements. Everything with which it came into contact was integrated. Life seemed worth living only where the threshold between waking and sleeping was worn away in everyone as by the steps of multitudinous images flooding back and forth" (SW2.1, 208). In insisting everything be integrated into its movement, in its attempt at a seamless fusion, Benjamin traces how Surrealism itself once again becomes phantasmagoric and dreamlike, consigned not to the moment of (historical) awakening, but to the continuation of the dream. What is lacking in what Benjamin describes is precisely the intervention of (psycho)analysis, or the critic—"language only seemed itself where, sound and image, image and sound interpenetrated with automatic precision and such felicity that no chink was left for the penny-in-the-slot called 'meaning'"—And no space for truth, which for Benjamin has to enter from without. As Benjamin writes in "Dream Kitsch," Surrealism confuses dream experience with poetic inspiration (SW2.1, 4). It loses the possibility of a moment of awakening and substitutes an enraptured encounter with the dream-state in its stead. As Lindner also points out, the Surrealism essay ends on the image of the alarm clock that rings "60 seconds to a minute"; no awakening takes place, despite its constant ringing (Lindner 2008, 162). Indeed, in the "Materials for the Expose of 1935," Benjamin contrasts this sharply with his own position: "Opposition to Aragon: to work through all this by way of the dialectics of awakening, and not: to be lulled, through exhaustion [tiredly], into 'dream' or 'mythology'" (AP, 908). Lindner concludes that Benjamin did not take Breton's "flirt" with Freud or his "later attempt to unite psychoanalysis and Marxism *in a surrealist perspective*" [emphasis mine] seriously (Lindner 2008, 157). Crucially, it is the Surrealist perspective Benjamin takes issue with, not the combination of Freud and Marx. As Pensky remarks, "Benjamin's later substantial critiques of surrealism . . . consist in essence of his realization that the surrealists were not capable of transposing the 'shock' of the profane illumination from the model of dream to that of waking" (Pensky 1993, 200).

PREMATURE SYNTHESIS

Freud states that the dream does not seem to be able to portray negation, it has no regard for contradictions and opposites, displaying

> a particular preference for combining contraries into a unity or for representing them as one and the same thing. Dreams feel themselves at liberty, moreover, to represent any element by its wishful contrary; so that there is no way of deciding at a first glance whether any element that admits of a contrary is present in the dream-thoughts as a positive or as a negative.[19] (SE4, 318)

This fusion of opposites is another feature of Freud's dreamwork present in the *Arcades Project*, where it takes the form of diametrically opposed class interests. For Freud, the social also irrupts into the psyche with the faculty of censorship, what was later to be named the superego. Social form—specifically hierarchy—emerges as root cause for repression. Once again Freud turns to Shakespeare to illustrate this: "Wherever there is rank and promotion the way lies open for wishes that call for suppression. Shakespeare's Prince Hal could not, even at his father's sick-bed, resist the temptation of trying on the crown" (SE5, 484). The combination of opposites into a unitary appearance also resurfaces in the flattening perspective of the many new vistas offered by nineteenth-century cultural technology as described by Benjamin: panoramas, dioramas, and the view from buses, showing the city and its multitudes as one unified mass. In this falsely unifying perspective that collapses the stratification of classes and oppositional class interests, common to Freud's dream and the nineteenth century, is reflected in many of the art forms of the nineteenth century. Chief among them is Art Nouveau. Benjamin writes that in "[e]xhibitions, regions and indeed, retrospectively, all times, from farming and mining, from industry and from the machines that were displayed in operation, to raw materials and processed materials, to art and the applied arts" a "peculiar demand for premature synthesis, of a kind that is characteristic of the nineteenth century in other areas as well: of the total work of art" becomes visible. Crucially, "these 'premature syntheses' also bespeak a persistent endeavour to close up the space of existence and of development. To prevent the 'airing-out of the classes'" [G2, 3] (AP, 175). The "premature syntheses" thus run counter to the aims of what must come first—analysis, the differentiation of class interests. Synthesis here can be thought not only in terms of a certain (and oft-contested) reading of Hegel, where the model thesis-antithesis-synthesis is posited, but more so in the sense of a Freudian dream interpretation.

Freud names two reasons why a dream analysis may remain incomplete: Respect for boundaries and the limits of what is to be disclosed—guided by one's own unwillingness to unveil the recesses of one's psyche to the last. In particular, he applies this to those of his analysands that are in the public eye. Additionally, however, Freud stresses that there may be more to the dream than is resolved on a first analysis. In the *Interpretation of Dreams* (SE5, 523), he cautions that the task of dream interpretation is not finished when a "complete interpretation . . . which makes sense, is coherent and throws light upon every element of the dream's content" has been performed: "For the same dream may perhaps have another interpretation as well, an 'over-interpretation,' which has escaped." This "over-interpretation" points to an essential multivalence of the dream, as does Freud's acknowledgment that there is, as mentioned above, at least one "spot where it reaches down into the unknown" (SE5, 525) in every dream. Thus, not only are dreams overdetermined in that they are a palimpsest of "day residues," unconscious wishes, and so on. They also themselves branch out into multiple directions, which Freud calls "the mycelium of thought" (SE5, 525). Even a seemingly complete interpretation is not truly finite; further interpretations may follow. This serves as a cautionary note against accepting any analysis as the "final" or "true" one, lest an analysis later recognised as partial obscures more than it reveals. This insight goes beyond dream analysis and extends to psychoanalysis as a whole. As Freud writes in "Analysis Terminable": "Analytic experience has taught us that the better is always the enemy of the good and that in every phase of the patient's restoration we have to combat his inertia, which disposes him to be content with a partial solution of his conflicts, as they will surely lead to a relapse and recurrent of the worst symptoms, as the underlying conflicts remain unresolved" (SE23, 231). Thus, just like the people of the nineteenth century whose art forms present a semblance of resolution or liberation—a false awakening—Freud's patients are prone to content themselves with a partial, and thus ultimately false, resolution of their conflicts. The analyst should thus not be too hasty to present a "premature synthesis" as what is at stake is the success of the analysis.

NOTES

1. The full quote reads "as long as the Marxist doctrine of the superstructure is not supplemented by the direly necessary one of the development of false consciousness, it will be all but impossible to answer the question 'how does an inappropriate consciousness of an economic situation emerge from its contradictions?' in any way but following the schema of repression. The products of false consciousness resemble puzzle pictures, in which the main thing barely peer out from clouds, fallen leaves and shadows" (GS3, 223, translation mine). This suggests that, rather than pursue the question of false consciousness directly, the psychoanalytical concept of repres-

sion serves as a useful tool for the analysis of capitalism. Even if false consciousness cannot (yet) be understood, then, its unconscious can be accessed through the decoding of its products, the *Vexierbilder* that mask what is truly at stake.

2. It should be noted that Freud's model of libido is non-metaphorically an economic one.

3. See also Cohen (1993, 24): "Marx uses dream rhetoric to emphasize that ideological representation is subjective distortion. As Althusser comments on this use, 'Ideology is conceived as a pure illusion, a pure dream, i.e. as nothingness. All its reality is external to it. Ideology is thus thought as an imaginary construction whose status is exactly like the theoretical status of the dream among writers before Freud' (. . .) When Benjamin, in contrast, characterizes the products of the superstructure as dream, he brings to collective constructions what, echoing Althusser echoing Lacan echoing Freud, we might call Freud's Copernican Revolution (Benjamin too conceives of his historiographical enterprise as a Copernican revolution)."

4. As Cohen (2005, 38) points out, "In the version of 'Paris, the Capital of the Nineteenth Century' sent to Adorno, Benjamin deleted the sentence making explicit the Marxist dialogue in which his collective dream intervenes. Nonetheless, he retains his use of psychoanalytic vocabulary to revise a vision of the superstructure as reflecting the base."

5. Interestingly, Freud also makes reference to the latent wish as a "dream capitalist": "A daytime thought may very well play the part of *entrepreneur* for a dream; but the *entrepreneur*, who, as people say, has the idea and the initiative to carry it out, can do nothing without capital; he needs a *capitalist* who can afford the outlay, and the capitalist who provides the psychical outlay for the dream is invariably and indisputably, whatever may be the thoughts of the previous day, *a wish from the unconscious*" (SE5, 561). On this striking passage, see Tomšič (2015, 106f). Tomšič posits that Freud's dreamwork functions analogously to Marx's thought, suggesting Freud develops a labour theory of the unconscious (Tomšič 2015, 242f).

6. Sandford's account of Freud's dream as a fragment would also see it draw close to Benjamin's early, romantically inflected concept of criticism, present in, for example, "The Task of the Translator" (1923): "The relation of interpretation to such a complex structure is less an overlay or addition than the 'completion' of one of its threads, just as with the Early Romantic concept of criticism which 'completes' the work. The dream interpretation then becomes a fragment in its own right. Further interpretations make up more fragments, which together make up a system of fragments, which is, again, itself a fragment" (Sandford 2016, 32).

7. Note also the proximity to the processes of mourning and melancholia here.

8. See for example, Geert Panhuysen (1998) for a detailed reconstruction of Freud's early departure from the reductionist stance of his predecessors that would conceptualise psychology *as* neurophysiology. Against many of Freud's mid-twentieth-century critics, Panhuysen maintains that this was not characteristic of Freud's position even in 1895, as he observed that "[p]sychiatric symptoms cannot be reduced to demonstrable changes in the brain. Where changes in the brain can be found, they did not indicate the nature of the symptoms" (Panhuysen 1998, 28). Panhuysen also discusses what he sees as a shift from a "parallelist" to an "interactionist" model of

body and mind in Freud, tracing the way Freud accounts for the specific nature of their interaction and co-conditioning in the pleasure principle and the theory of the drives.

9. See Cohen (2015) and Irma Dosamantes-Beaudry (1997) on the body-self, for a discussion of the different paths of approaching the interrelation of the somatic and the psychic self taken by subsequent schools of psychoanalysis following Freud.

10. The conceptualisation of a psychologised body reprises Benjamin's early "Schemata zum psychophysischen Problem" (1922–1923), which begins the first section "Geist und Leib," with the statement that "they are identical, distinct merely as ways of perceiving, not as objects" (GS6, 78, transl. mine). The formulation "Geist-Leib" is also to be found in Benjamin's note "Über das Grauen I" [On Horror I] (GS6, 76) where their identity is stressed once more. With the aid of Freud's concepts of the unconscious and the psyche, Benjamin elaborates on this early concept in the *Arcades Project*, elucidating its relationship to the "dreaming collective" of the nineteenth century.

11. "It is one of the tacit suppositions of psychoanalysis that the clear-cut antithesis of sleeping and waking has no value for determining the empirical form of consciousness of the human being, but instead yields before an unending variety of concrete states of consciousness conditioned by every conceivable level of wakefulness within all possible centers" (AP, 389).

12. Lindner (2008, 165) also notes this, remaining ultimately undecided whether Benjamin is successful in this.

13. This theme is carried over from Benjamin's early engagement with the Youth Movement. See J. Steitzinger, *Revolte, Eros und Sprache. Walter Benjamin's "Metaphysik der Jugend"*(Berlin: Kadmos, 2013).

14. Additionally, it is possible to interpret Rosegger's dream as a case of the traumatic repetition later identified in *Beyond the Pleasure Principle*, if we assume it is grounded in a traumatic episode in the poet's early life.

15. Sandford notes that "Explicitly, Freud identifies secondary revision with what we might call bad interpretation, which for him means misinterpretation. It has, he writes, the function that 'the poet maliciously ascribes to philosophers; it fills up the gaps in the dream-structure with shreds and patches'" (V, 490). Against this, Sandford takes the position that this model of interpretation grounded in "secondary revision—cutting across the distinction between dream and waking thought, across dream construction and interpretation, across 'work' and 'criticism'—refers us to a much richer concept of interpretation" (Sandford 2016, 33).

16. Although the German reads "etwas durchdrungenem" and does not explicitly mention the word "conscious," its insertion in the translation only serves to further clarify the meaning of this quote.

17. See chapter 3 for a discussion of this passage.

18. Already in 1928, Benjamin wrote to Scholem: "In order to lift the work [the *Passagen-Werk*] out of an all too ostentatious proximity to the *mouvement surrealiste* that could become fatal to me, as natural and well-founded as it is, I have had to expand it more and more in my mind, and make it so universal in its most particular, tiniest frameworks that it would enter upon the inheritance of surrealism

even in a purely chronological respect and precisely with all the absolute powers of a philosophical Fortinbras" (C, 342). In addition to the point about Surrealism, we see here once again Benjamin's identification of Shakespeare's monarchical figures with baroque sovereignty.

19. In a footnote Freud here points to his 1910 "Gegensinn der Urworte," where he speculates on *Ur-*, that is, originary or primitive language as having only one word for opposite pairs, pointing to an essential ambivalence rooted in thought and language.

Chapter Six

Awakening

In this chapter, I examine Benjamin's transposition of awakening from the individual to the collective. In the context of true awakening, childhood emerges as a locus of the possibility of a cognition that runs counter to some of the fallacies of subjectivity. It will become clear that the concept of memory, as remembrance, is crucial. I then look to the question of a proximity between Benjamin and Freud on the issue of a therapeutic politics. Last, I examine Benjamin's "Destructive Character" in connection with Benjamin's own dream for the possibility of a disruption of the dream-sleep of the nineteenth century.

THE FAR BANK

In section VI.A "The Work of Condensation" of *The Interpretation of Dreams*, Freud contests the notion that a dream is reproduced most accurately if it is remembered soon after awakening. Rather, just like dream-formation, which begins during the dream-day preceding the sleep in which the dream is experienced, dream analysis is an ongoing process, with new aspects and explanations arising throughout the course of the day and indeed throughout a life. Just as dreams can sometimes be the fulfilment of wishes that arose decades before, and indeed can be traced back to infantile wishes in the last instance, dream analysis disrupts linear temporality and the notion of an originary, authentic, and complete truth of the dream to be accessed most directly in its immediate aftermath. There is thus an implicit danger in narrating dreams "too soon"—both in terms of assuming their authenticity and regarding a too-hasty acceptance of the immediacy of the manifest content.

181

In "Breakfast Room," from *One-Way Street*, Benjamin, following Freud, describes dream-narration first thing in the morning, "on an empty stomach," as a perilous undertaking. This is because the recently awakened sleeper "remains under the spell of the dream" (SW1, 444): a too-hasty engagement with the dream risks merely reproducing, rather than analysing it. Dreams may be mentioned only "from the far bank" (SW1, 445), once the sleeper is fully awake, that is, once he has eaten. At stake is the detachment from the dream, for which Benjamin offers two possibilities. The first is the "combustion of the dream in a concentrated morning's work [*Morgenarbeit*], if not in prayer" (SW1, 445). Linder (2008, 140) reads this passage as indicating the dream must be forgotten. However, does the term "*Morgenarbeit*" not also have an echo of the dreamwork, to which it forms the oppositional pole?

And indeed, Benjamin writes in the 1935 Expose that "Die Verwertung der Traumelemente beim Erwachen ist der Schulfall des dialektischen Denkens" (GS5, 59).[1] The dream is being used up, *verwertet*, functioning as fuel in the morning-work of awakening.[2] Benjamin is here working with the model of a psychic economy: The dream energy, *Traumkraft*, lingers and must be "burned" or used up in another activity. It will not go away of its own accord and cannot simply be forgotten.[3] Lindner (2008, 141) continues with the second possibility of detachment from the dream: breaking one's fast in order to "cleanse" oneself of the dream, not because the dream is dirty, but because dream and waking life must not be commingled in an unmediated—or rather, unanalysed—fashion. He concludes that "first, the dreamer must reach a 'beyond the dream'" (Lindner 2008, 141, transl. mine), which is possible through eating. At stake is thus a physical and spiritual grounding of the self in an activity that either uses up the dream energy: intellectual, physical, or spiritual labour, all of which require concentrated focus—or else fills it with something else: the intake of food. Both make it possible to break with the world of the dream and thus analyse it beyond its sway. When we link this passage from *One-Way Street* to the false awakenings of Art Nouveau and Surrealism discussed previously, thus transposing the process to the collective, we come to see that what is at stake is true—historical—awakening that manages to disrupt the dream cycle and the semblance of dream analysis from within the "*Bannkreis*" of the dream.

BOREDOM AND ITS INSIDE

In "Dream Kitsch" (SW2.1, 3), Benjamin writes that "The dream has grown gray. The gray coating of dust on it is its best part. Dreams are now a shortcut to banality." Precisely in becoming banal, stereotypical, kitsch; in losing the appeal to the transcendental figure of longing—"No one really dreams any longer of the Blue Flower"—the dream, like baroque allegory, has become immanent. This picks up on Benjamin's focus on the trivial, the banality of life in the nineteenth century in the *Arcades Project*. Like everyday objects and habits, dreams store meaning precisely because they are thoroughly everyday and "of their time." However, the dream-world of the arcades, like the individual dream, reveal their stored-up meaning only on analysis. This assessment constitutes an appraisal of the historical possibilities and uses of dreams in modernity. Benjamin writes in the *Arcades Project* that "Boredom is always the external surface of unconscious events" [D2a, 2] (AP, 106). Here Benjamin draws from Freud, for whom the seemingly banal is revealed only in analysis as anything but: it is registered and cathected in the unconscious in such a manner that it surfaces in dreams or compulsions, thus it holds meaning, but this, too, is situated in the unconscious. In the dream-work mechanism of displacement, "ideas which originally had only a weak charge of intensity take over the charge from ideas which were originally intensely cathected and at last attain enough strength to enable them to force an entry into consciousness" (SE5, 177). Thus, one of Benjamin's programmatic announcements in the *Arcades Project* is that "the theory of awakening" is "to be developed on the basis of the theory of boredom" (AP, 908) as, following Freud, boredom for Benjamin signals repressed, unconscious energies which contain an unconscious truth beyond their immediate appearance. Following Freud's dream interpretation, the unconscious truth of dreams can only become visible from outside the dream.[4] Upon awakening, the boring, grey, banal "external surface," the manifest appearance of the underlying unconscious event, is to be turned inside out in the process of interpretation:

> Boredom is a warm gray fabric lined on the inside with the most lustrous and colourful of silks. In this fabric we wrap ourselves when we dream . . . But the sleeper looks bored and gray within his sheath. And when he later wakes and wants to tell of what he dreamed, he communicates by and large only this boredom. For who would be able at one stroke to turn the lining of time to the outside? Yet to narrate dreams signifies nothing else. (AP, 105–6)

Andrew Benjamin, focusing on the "lining of time," relates this passage to Benjamin's other pronouncements on boredom as conditioned by waiting. This relationship to time contains within it the potential for its overcoming: "Awaiting and expectation—as necessitating the transformation of time—a transformation in which the future becomes a condition of the present, rather than the present being a series of empty moments awaiting a future, would mean that there is another mood" (Benjamin 2005, 167). Another mood than that of boredom, revealed by and contained within boredom itself. As with

"Dream Kitsch" and the ephemera of nineteenth-century culture, it is the mood of boredom of the dream that points to this possibility: "The coat turning with a rapidity within which both the grey and the colour in an instance—the instance as 'standstill'—become the opening where 'great deeds' will occur. The grey and the lustrous are brought into play" (Benjamin 2005, 168).[5] If we read Benjamin's comments in relation to his use of Freud, it becomes clear that this standstill, the "one stroke," which occurs suddenly in the act of dream narration, is a moment where the unconscious is made conscious.

Betancourt comments on this passage that the act of dream narration is unsatisfactory at first, as it only manages to show the grey outside: "we only communicate the boredom of the dream, the manifest content that overcame our defense" (Betancourt 2008, 28). He asserts that there is a dialectical movement at play in a dream analysis that manages to make visible the unconscious:

> Latent content will be discovered, revealed: the colourful inside of a grey outside will be turned inside-out not once but many times until we see the constitutive tension . . . The dialectic of it escapes us, it is no longer at a standstill, but we go back to it, from another perspective: this motion is philosophically eternal, only politically [can we] take hold of it. (Betancourt 2008, 28–29)

Dream narration is an attempt to make visible the colourful "arabesques" of the unconscious wish contained within the manifest "grey," banal appearance of the dream. However, something more is revealed: Crucially, the grey boredom that is communicated is not merely appearance, but expresses a truth about the nineteenth century—its structural boredom.

The potentiality of dreams, of boredom, to configure things differently—to envisage another mood, another experience, another structure—enables their political use. As I discuss below, this "political seizing" of the dream is indeed Benjamin's ultimate aim. To him, "Arcades are houses or passages having no outside—like the dream" [L1a, 1] (AP, 406). Thus, we need to break out of arcades, awaken from dream: "Just as Proust begins the story of his life with an awakening, so must every presentation of history begin with awakening; in fact, it should treat of nothing else. This one, accordingly, deals with awakening from the nineteenth century" [N4, 3] (AP, 464). To this end, the aim of the *Arcades Project* is the narration of the nineteenth century as a dream: "in no other way can one deal with the arcades—structures in which we relive, as in a dream, the life of our parents and grandparents, as the embryo in the womb relives the life of animals. Existence in these spaces flows then without accent, like the events in dreams" [D2a, 1] (AP, 106). Benjamin follows Freud in equating dream perception with dream experience—and we see again his transposition of the dream to the collective in this passage.

"EACH EPOCH DREAMS THE ONE TO FOLLOW"

This dictum by French historian Jules Michelet, quoted by Benjamin in the *Arcades Project*, encapsulates Benjamin's own position: the historical reality of an epoch is formed by the unconscious dream-processes of previous ones. The formulation of a dreaming "epoch" also hints at the collective nature of dreaming in the arcades—it is the social organism as a whole that expresses its repressed wishes in the dream-world of the arcades. However, as we have seen, expression is deformed by the censorship imposed in order to keep the collective from awakening. In transposing this process of dream-formation to the collective, Benjamin politicises it—as Buck-Morss points out, "Class differentiations were never lacking in Benjamin's theory of the collective unconscious," and thus, "the collective dream manifested the ideology of the dominant class" (Buck-Morss 1993, 281). Far from being "ideological" in the sense of a fully deliberate manipulation on the part of the bourgeoisie, the introduction of Freudian dream theory allows Benjamin to demonstrate that this process of deformation and censorship is itself unconscious. "In the dream," Benjamin writes of the "economic conditions of life" of the collective, "they find their expression; in the awakening, their interpretation" (AP, 855). Following Freud, the manifest content of the dream can become intelligible only once worked through by the waking mind. In what follows, I will examine how Benjamin conceptualises this "awakening" of the collective. Benjamin here once again links dreaming to phylogenetic development, in which we relive the lives of previous generations. This repetition is characteristic of nineteenth-century Paris, in which the flaneur experiences the urban street as the proverbial memory lane: "For the flaneur, a transformation takes place with respect to the street: it leads him through a vanished time . . . for him, every street is precipitous. It leads downward—if not to the mythical Mothers, then into a past that can be all the more profound because it is not his own, not private" (AP, 416).[6] This is precisely the conception of history that Benjamin aims to break with in his theory of awakening: the phylogenetic determination of life and the semblance of eternal return must be interrupted. At the same time, the flaneur's experience of the inevitability of a return into the past makes this repetition-compulsion of the nineteenth century visible—a first stage in the movement towards its resolution. There is a second aspect to the flaneur's downward precipitation: it reveals something about the specificity of childhood and youth in the movement of dream and awakening, as "it always remains the past of a youth . . . it is not a past coming from his own youth, from a recent youth, but a childhood lived before then that speaks to him, and it is all the same to him whether it is the childhood of an ancestor or his own" (AP, 416).[7] The fact that this is a shared past is crucial—collectively, an awakening from this past can take place. Thus, Benjamin opens Convolute K with the words

> Awakening as a graduated process that goes on in the life of the individual as in the life of generations. Sleep its initial stage. A generation's experience of youth has much in common with the experience of dreams. Its historical configuration is a dream configuration. Every epoch has such a side turned toward dreams, the child's side. For the previous century, this appears very clearly in the arcades. [K1, 1] (AP, 388)

Linking the experience of dreams to childhood and youth, individually and collectively, introduces awakening as a gradual development that occurs in stages and introduces the issue of pedagogy. This developmental metaphor— at an individual and social level—is in keeping with Freud's statement that "the work of analysis aims at inducing the patient to give up the repressions (using the word in the widest sense) belonging to his early development and to replace them by reactions of a sort that would correspond to a psychically mature condition" (SE23, 257). At stake for Benjamin is a collectivised form of this pedagogical task of psychoanalysis. Benjamin continues his reflection on the process of awakening by pointing to a break in modernity:

> whereas the education of earlier generations explained these dreams for them in terms of tradition, of religious doctrine, present-day education simply amounts to the distraction of children. Proust could emerge as an unprecedented phenomenon only in a generation that had lost all bodily and natural aids to remembrance and that, poorer than before, was left to itself to take possession of the worlds of childhood in merely an isolated, scattered, and pathological way. (AP, 388)

Education is conceptualised here as the "explanation of dreams," that is, an interpretation of the unconscious wish via tradition or religion, a process which has been broken in modernity—replaced by the "distraction of children." Benjamin then performs a movement from dreams to remembrance, demonstrating that the two are intimately linked. In contrast with the impoverished generation of the nineteenth century, this passage implies previous modes of remembrance as characterised by richness; a focused, collective, healthy activity. Having reached this impasse in collective memory, which as we saw in the previous chapter has become an impossibility over the course of modernity, Benjamin insists on the need to awaken, which is equated with "An attempt to become aware of the dialectical—the Copernican—turn of remembrance" (AP, 388). Together with the Michelet quote above, this introduces a generational aspect to the dream and its end: awakening is premised on interrupting the sequential flow of dreams; it must occur at—or precipitate—an epochal break, as an awakening from the dream of a specific epoch. In the case of Benjamin's own age, that is recent past of the nineteenth century, which laid the groundwork for what was to come in the twentieth, and cannot awaken from itself. This awakening must thus occur at a later time.

Thus Benjamin notes in the materials for the 1935 Expose: "We have to wake up from the existence of our parents. In this awakening, we have to give an account of the nearness of that existence" (AP, 908). In particular, it is the recent past and its tradition—the world of the parents—that must be ended in this awakening. For Freud, the psychic life of the individual is structured by infantile experiences and traumas, most centrally those experienced in relation to the parents, which are to be reworked in psychoanalysis. Benjamin expands this to "generations," or "epochs"; that is, once again, a collective at a specific historical point. Just as in Freudian dream analysis, the dream's proximity and influence on waking consciousness has to be acknowledged, Benjamin expands on this aspect of awakening by adding that this "new, dialectical method of doing history teaches us to pass in spirit—with the rapidity and intensity of dreams—through what has been, in order to experience the present as waking world, a world to which every dream at last refers" (AP, 884). Without this making-conscious of the ongoing influence of the dream, we risk merely reproducing it, remaining under its sway, as happens in the incomplete breaks of Art Nouveau and Surrealism. Benjamin thus conceptualises the *Arcades Project* as "an experiment in the technique of awakening" which, as we saw above, signifies "[a]n attempt to become aware of the dialectical—the Copernican—turn of remembrance" (AP, 388). The technique of collective awakening is to be altered, experimented on, by including the movement of remembrance within it.

CHILDHOOD

There exists a tension between two versions of childhood in the process of dreaming and awakening for Benjamin. On the one hand, childhood's particular relationship to the past and to the dream situates it at the cusp of awakening, signaling a moment of open-ended possibility. On the other, it is characterised by attempts at the foreclosure of present and future through tradition and the theory of eternal return. The latter, as we have seen, forms the philosophical complement to Freud's concept of repetition-compulsion, which as discussed Benjamin drew on extensively in his work on the nineteenth century. It also manifests in Freud's treatment of childhood in the *Interpretation of Dreams* and in particular his thought on regression. Of interest in this context is the analysis Freud provides of one of his own dreams, where he concludes that the dream's condensation of people he knew at different times in his life implies the latent thought that "No one is irreplaceable! There are nothing but *revenants*: all those we have lost come back!" (SE5, 486). He traces this thought to the names of his children, chosen in memory of lost loved ones—and in this custom, "their names made the children into revenants. And after all . . . is not having children our only path to immortality?" (SE5, 486). Childhood and new life emerge here as overdetermined by the present generation of parents, and, mediated by them, by further reaches of past generations. This is expressed in Benjamin's injunction to wake up from the existence of our parents.

Against this foreclosure of possibility by the past, Benjamin posits a second vision of childhood when he writes in "Dream Kitsch" that children are not yet engaged in an "agonized protest" (SW2.1, 4) against the world of their parents, but are superior to it by refusing to enter into the dialectical unfolding of thesis and antithesis. Thus they break out of the continuum of the dream, not by reacting against it from within it, but by managing to remain outside of its all-encompassing reach. Salzani notes that the figure of the child "represents a condition preceding the Fall into bourgeois modernity, still immune to the phantasmagoria of the city and of the commodity, and is thus related to pre-modern *Erfahrung*; [and] epitomises the state of *waiting*, which is for Benjamin the fundamental threshold into a revolution of experience" (Salzani 2009, 140). The child's boredom is different from that of adults; the habit of children's play is different to the habituation of factory labour and other modern habits that are more rightly characterised as repetition-compulsion, such as gambling: "repetition that still construes habits, but not as the *wieder-tun* of the child's play, a 'doing again' which is active creation [*schaffen*] (*GS* 3:131-2/*SW* 2:120). Rather, these new habits are a *Wieder-kehr*, a passively suffered *return* of the same as a numbing anaesthetic" (Salzani 2009, 132). Children, as Salzani also notes, dwell on the threshold. Their experience is not yet fully overdetermined by the fractured subjectivity of modernity, as they are still practicing creativity in play.

As discussed, Benjamin follows Freud in positing two psychic agencies, with dream- consciousness intransparent to itself and only able to be illuminated from the vantage point of the other, waking mind. Benjamin expands on this in "On the Image of Proust," where he writes "The similarity of one thing to another which we are used to, which occupies us in a wakeful state, reflects only vaguely the deeper similarity of the dream world in which everything that happens appears not in identical but in similar guise, opaquely similar to itself" (SW2.1, 239). It is intransparent to itself because the dream cannot rightfully analyse itself—as discussed above, interpretation within the dream results not in a resolution, but forms a "bad" interpretation. A true analysis is premised on awakening. Children, however, are uniquely able to perceive from *both* in- and outside of the dream. Thus, Benjamin continues, they "know a symbol of this world: the stocking which has the structure of this dream world when, rolled up in the laundry hamper, it is a 'bag' and a 'present' at the same time" (SW2.1, 239–40). In the perception of children, the unconscious associations characteristic of the dream is transposed into their waking life and manifests in play. The stocking has the "structure of the dream-world" in being subject to condensation, that which allows it to be both a bag and a present. This perception is able to move back and forth quickly, in one move, between the waking world and the dream-world, seeing the object as both literal and metaphorical and being able to move between both modes of perceptions quickly.

This ability is where for Benjamin the similarity to Proust appears. Like children metamorphosing the bag and that which is inside it back into a sock, "Proust could not get his fill of emptying the dummy, his self, at one stroke in order to keep garnering that third thing, the image which satisfied his curiosity—indeed, assuaged his homesickness" (SW2.1, 240). The ego [*das Ich*] is here likened to the sock of children's play, in being something that is entangled with itself, its insides and outsides blurring, simultaneously vessel and content. In Proust's last sleight of hand, they are both turned back into an image. This image provokes homesickness for the dream-world—of childhood, of intoxication, in which the world is "disfigured" in its similitudes, which reveals the "true surrealist face" of being, in which all its possible identities are visible at the same time. Benjamin's formulation of "the dummy, his self" has a further dimension to it: Once again the subject is fractured, revealed as comprising an ego that is nothing but a prop. Thus, at stake is an overcoming of the semblance of the subject through the revelation of its constitutive fracture.

PRIMARY NARCISSISM

In a 1938 note published as "Ergebnisse, Ideen, Probleme," Freud summarises his earlier insights on the process where children lose the ability of identification over the course of their development, first discussed in his 1914 "On Narcissism": "The child favours expressing object- relations through identification: I am the object. Having is the later relation, and falls back into being following the loss of the object. The pattern: Breast. The breast is a part of me, I am the breast. Later only: I have it, i.e., I am not it" ([June 1938] GW17, 151, transl. mine). The wholeness of primary narcissism is thus unattainable once a differentiation between self and world, between having and being, are introduced. This is precisely what Benjamin refers to as "Freud's brilliant interpretation of the superiority of the child (in his study on narcissism)" (GS3, 273, transl. mine). In asserting that it is experience that proves the very opposite of this infantile superiority, Benjamin follows Freud's account of the development away from primary narcissism.8 This overestimation of the reach of the self is then repressed as a loss, and thus committed to the unconscious. This is at the heart of Proust's violent affect of "homesickness" associated with this experience of the inaccessibility of childhood; that is, ultimately, the inaccessible experience of wholeness of the subject in primary narcissism. It gives rise to an attempt at a re-enactment both of the state of primary narcissism and of the moment of its loss. Benjamin explicitly links the "law of repetition" governing play to Freud's concept of repetition-compulsion: "The obscure urge to repeat things is scarcely less powerful in play, scarcely less cunning in its workings, than the sexual impulse in love. It is no accident that Freud has imagined he could detect an impulse 'beyond the pleasure principle' in it" (GS2, 120). Benjamin, writing in 1928, is thus alert to the entanglement of desire and trauma in repetition and presupposes an "Ursituation" to which both strive to return: "every profound experience longs to be insatiable, longs for return and repetition until the end of time, and for the reinstatement of an original condition from which it sprang" (GS2, 120).9 Child's play, as we have seen, manages to recreate the experience in a way that is inaccessible to the subject in later life. Lindner comments that the connection of the motifs of dream and childhood in the early stages of the Arcades Project are "not merely an indicator of the as yet unresolved difference between autobiography and historiography . . . but simultaneously a reference to a specific, irretrievable access to history" present in childhood (Lindner 2008, 156, transl. mine). As Werner puts it in her analysis of memory in the Berlin Childhood Around 1900, "Remembrance [Erinnerung] may attempt to counteract irretrievability, but this effort only serves to demonstrate even more clearly that lived moments cannot be brought back. Despite, or perhaps precisely because of this insight into the irretrievability of the past, Berlin Childhood aims at a conscious approach to the past" (Werner 2015, 47, transl. mine). This is characterised by a specific way of engaging nostalgia: Benjamin writes in the book that he "sought to limit its effect through insight into the irretrievability—not the contingent biographical but the necessary social irretrievability—of the past" (SW3, 344). Read together with the theme of awakening as historical change or interruption, the importance of safeguarding against nostalgia is another way to approach the question of the movement from the nineteenth into the twentieth century as a move against melancholia. But how does the dreaming collective avoid becoming a "historical re-enactment society" in its dual move of remembrance in awakening? How do we move beyond melancholia and regression?

THE MOVEMENT OF AWAKENING: REMEMBRANCE AND THE FLASH OF AWAKENED CONSCIOUSNESS

As Freud outlines in "Remembering, Repeating and Working-Through," compulsive repetition, the acting out of the past can be overcome in turning it into remembrance; that is, something consciously processed and verbalised within analysis. This insight into the ongoing influence of the repressed, which must be made conscious in order to be overcome, is at the heart of Benjamin's thought on awakening. Indeed, for him "Awakening is the exemplary case of remembering" (AP, 908). To make the nearest, "most obvious" actually visible requires a change in perspective, which is to be attained via remembrance. In opposition to Max Horkheimer's position that history is finite, that the past is past and "the slain are really slain" (AP, 471), Benjamin stresses the transformative potential of remembrance, "'*Eingedenken*.' What science has 'determined,' remembrance can modify. Such mindfulness can make the incomplete (happiness) into something complete, and the complete (suffering) into something incomplete" (AP, 471). Remembrance thus modifies the past not only epistemologically (that is, in terms of how the past is understood and accessed) but ontologically—it renders the complete incomplete, capable of dissolving past suffering with its rupturing force. Benjamin acknowledges that this places remembrance's reach into the theological, even if it is not to be grasped with "immediately theological concepts" (AP, 471).[10] However, it is also a psychoanalytic insight: placed in a different, therapeutic context, the return of repressed memory can function as liberating. The incompleteness of history, revealed in remembrance, thus indicates that it is "capable of change," through transformative memory. With Cathy Caruth, we can perceive a specific closeness to Freud on this point: Caruth draws attention to Freud's conceptualisation of monotheism as an awakening in *Beyond the Pleasure Principle* and suggests that "[t]he belated experience of trauma in Jewish monotheism suggests that history is not the passing on of a crisis but also the passing on of a survival that can only be possessed within a history larger than any single individual or any single generation" (Caruth 1996, 71).[11] But how is this remembrance to be conceptualised, if, as we saw in chapter 3, the path to remembrance is blocked in modernity? The answer lies in the specificity of Benjamin's concept of awakening: in a thorough rupture with the world of the nineteenth century and its forms, laying bare both its underlying unconscious, repressed, deformed dream-wishes and past traumas. Benjamin speculates that "All insight to be grasped according to the schema of awakening. And shouldn't the 'not-yet-conscious knowledge' have the structure of dream?" (AP, 907), and thus be in need of interpretation. Benjamin conceptualises this as a process of making visible and becoming-conscious: the "Knowledge of what has been as a becoming aware [making conscious for oneself—*Bewusstsichmachen*], one that has the structure of awakening . . . on the part of the collective" (AP, 907). This is to be understood as the "dissolution of 'mythology' into the space of history" (AP, 458)—the caesura in the temporality of myth, of the dream, where the not-yet becomes the "now" of consciousness and its unconscious, compulsive force is thus broken. Benjamin describes the experience of awakening as a uniquely "dialectical" one "which 'refutes everything "gradual" about becoming' and shows all seeming 'development' to be dialectical reversal" (AP, 389), the "flash of awakened consciousness" (AP, 388). This seemingly runs counter to Benjamin's other conceptualisation of "awakening as a graduated process" (AP, 388). Lindner takes the view that Benjamin sees awakening only as such an instantaneous event: "Benjamin wanted to charge that which has been [*das Gewesene*] with the flash-like intensity of the dream and see it suddenly reverse into the present as the waking world" (Lindner 2008, 167, transl. mine).

Perhaps we can make sense of these apparently contradictory temporalities if we remember that when Benjamin speaks of the "graduated" process of awakening, he refers to different stages, the first of them characterised, paradoxically, by sleep. This earlier stage is still under the sway of the dream. True historical awakening, conversely, can occur only as a flash, rather than as the certain outcome of a gradual movement of becoming conscious over time. Benjamin is here refuting the bourgeois philosophy of progress in his model of awakening. If we read him with Freud, we come to see that the occurrence of these flashes can nevertheless happen over a period of time, embedded in a process of interpretation. Freud writes that

> [t]he interpretation of a dream cannot always be accomplished at a single sitting, When we have followed a chain of associations, it not infrequently happens that we feel our capacity exhausted; nothing more is to be learnt from the dream that day. The wisest plan then is to break off and resume our work another day: another part of the dream's content may then attract our attention and give us access to another stratum of dream-thoughts. This procedure might be described as "fractional" dream-interpretation. (SE5, 523)

This "fractional" dream interpretation, which Benjamin draws on,[12] relies not on a certain disclosure of the dream within a fixed timeframe, but on a movement of return and re-examination, interspersed with sudden flashes of recognition. Thus, there exist striking similarities between Benjamin's notion of a process of "advancement . . . of a not-yet-conscious knowledge of what has been" (AP, 389) and the role of awakening in the Freudian model:

awakening as suspended between the dream-world and the waking mind, secondary revision and the beginning of dream analysis, from the vantage point of being outside the dream but bringing its elements into consciousness, reordering and "working through" them in the process.

THE DIALECTICAL IMAGE, THE HISTORIAN, THE COLLECTIVE

At the same time, recognition for Benjamin can occur only in a specific moment in connection—constellation—with a specific moment of the past. This is at the root of his pronouncement in "Capitalism as Religion" that "[w]e cannot draw closed the net in which we are caught. Later on, however, we shall be able to gain an overview of it" (SW1, 288). In the materials for the 1935 Expose, Benjamin conceptualises this as follows: "The dissolution of historical semblance must follow the same trajectory as the construction of the dialectical image" (AP, 918). The processes of dissolution and construction are thus intertwined. As Pensky points out, "[d]estruction is the necessary but not sufficient condition for the appearance of the dialectical image." Rather, "Only by the constructive act of materialist historiography does the dialectical image appear as monadological; that is, not as the archaic image, but represented through the details, fully concrete and historically determinate yet also monadically containing its entire pre- and post-history within it." (Pensky 1993, 223). As Freud notes, the dream does not reveal itself at once, it may take days, or weeks. Additionally, wishes don't always find their fulfilment in dreams in any temporal proximity to their generation. Freud recounts events where wishes from decades before are fulfilled in a dream once the circumstances of the dreamer's life have changed so as to make this wish no longer actual. Beneath this layer of wishes that arise throughout life, there is another layer of infantile wishes that persists and will be reawakened again and again. Benjamin notes that "the overdetermined elements of the dream in Freud are capable of being interpreted two, three or more times" (GS3, 588, transl. mine), showing he knew Freud's dream theory well and carried over its troubled temporality into his own theory of dreaming in proposing just such a process of recognition at specific points in time:

> In the dialectical image, what has been within a particular epoch is always, simultaneously, "what has been from time immemorial." As such, however, it is manifest, on each occasion, only to a quite specific epoch—namely, the one in which humanity, rubbing its eyes, recognizes just this particular dream image as such. It is at this moment that the historian takes up, with regard to that image, the task of dream interpretation. [N4, 1] (AP, 464)

Awakening is identified as the moment where the dialectical image is constructed, and thus where historical semblance is dissolved. This is at stake in Benjamin's figure of the historian who takes up "the task of dream interpretation"—to deconstruct historical semblance in interpretation, by constructing the dialectical image from out of the dream elements. However, for Benjamin there is a further step involved: to decode the wish images contained in the dream, but also to take the insights of the analysis into the realisation of the fundamental motivators behind them—as Benjamin writes, "The realization of dream elements in the course of waking up is the canon of dialectics. It is paradigmatic for the thinker and binding for the historian" [N4, 4] (AP, 464). In the figure of the historian—or, variously, the historical materialist—the repressed, unconscious "dream-elements" thus find both their interpretation and their realisation. Awakening mediates between dreams and remembrance—carrying over elements of the dream to be realised into waking life. As Elissa Marder observes, "Benjamin declares that the work of the historian is not to recount history, but to interrupt its course" (Marder 2006, 191).

Crucially, the historical materialist/historian is not to become a substitute for the collective—as Wohlfarth notes, separating the dialectical from the "archaic" image is a practical, collective task (Wohlfarth 2011, 262). Awakening, just like this process of separation, then, is both an individual and a collective task. In an unpublished, handwritten note, Benjamin draws the contrasting points up in the following way: "Thus on the one hand: Not-yet-conscious knowledge of what has been (phylogenetically and ontogenetically) (Freud: Beyond the Pleasure Principle), On the other: the presently happening perceived as memory. Is the first, objective view correct, or the second, subjective one? Or is there a synthesis?" (WBA 618/3, WBA Ms 646, transl. mine).[13] Benjamin here identifies apperception, the "flash of recognition" in the now-time, with a "subjective" point of view. By the time of producing preliminary sketches for the *Arcades Project*, however, Benjamin asks "wouldn't it be possible, furthermore, to show how the whole set of issues with which this project is concerned is illuminated in the process of the proletariat's becoming conscious of itself?" (AP, 863). Perhaps we get the closest to the "synthesis" Benjamin seeks between individual and collective in the "Materials for the expose of 1935," No 8: "We conceive the dream (1) as historical phenomenon, (2) as collective phenomenon. Efforts . . . to shed light on the dreams of the individual with the help of the doctrine of the historical dreams of the collective" (AP, 908–9). And just as the dream is a collective, historical phenomenon, and the dreams of the individual can be explained via the collective repressed wishes manifested in a specific historical moment, "Here the question arises: In what different canonical ways can man [der Mensch] behave (the individual man, but also the collective) with regard to dreaming? And what sort of comportment, at bottom, is adequate to the waking being?" (AP, 907). This points beyond the dream, and the moment of awakening, towards being truly awake. At stake is action in the world—individual, as much as collective, political action. Dream interpretation can thus serve as a model for historical materialist philosophy of history—just as dreams can be analysed only when put into the context of a particular life and its circumstances, as well as the repressed wishes of the dreamer, so history can be made sense of only at particular moments in time, when it becomes possible to recognise the particular dream image, that is, as particularity, torn out of its original context of meaning and revealed as speaking of something other than its manifest content. Together, psychoanalysis and historical materialism furnish Benjamin with the insights and the tools to both get at the unconscious knowledge and actualise it.

THERAPEUTIC HISTORIOGRAPHY

We have already seen the influence of Freudian dream interpretation on Benjamin's theory of dreaming and awakening: Only on analysis can the false dawn of the compensatory fantasy of nineteenth-century utopianism be revealed; the dream needs to be interpreted. In collectivising this praxis, Benjamin also draws from the psychoanalytic situation more generally. What is specific about the psychoanalytic situation for Freud is that it provides a space outside of the continuum of the patient's normal life, where thoughts are made conscious and verbalised without censorship. The psychoanalyst may interrupt and probe certain aspects of the patient's narration and provide a construction which confronts the patient with a conjecture about the originary trauma and its ongoing influence.

Cohen sees " Benjamin's fascination with the wish images of a collective" as "exemplary of the therapeutic dimension to his notion of praxis." This therapeutic dimension also manifests itself in his notion of "the dialectical image" that is a "dream image" (Cohen 1993, 37–38). She links Benjamin's dialectical image to Freud's "constructions of analysis in the curious objectivity that Benjamin attributes to it," an objectivity that is revealed not as a truth as measured by the actually occurring past, "but also its therapeutic effectiveness in the present; Freud simultaneously stresses that this gauge is far from confirming that the construction ever existed as such" (Cohen 1993, 47). At stake is not authenticity, but effectiveness—and indeed, this is close to Benjamin's attempt to make the past something that is recognised in the present rather than something to be reconstructed as it "really was" (SW4, 391).

Freud emphasises that dreaming and waking thought are ultimately not that different from each other. Both aim at wish-fulfilment, the former merely needing to be decoded—interpreted—to be inserted into the sequence of waking thought. At the same time, as we have also seen, the unconscious determines action far beyond the reaches of the dream, in psychopathology as much as in everyday revelations such as slips of the tongue. Psychoanalysis can serve to make this unconscious influence visible and, if successful, interrupt it. This brings us close to Benjamin's thought on awakening as an interruption of the dream-continuum of the nineteenth century, the arrest of thinking that allows the dialectical image to "flash" up. The arrest of thinking is also what is at stake in psychoanalytic praxis—interrupting the flow of thoughts and associations, allowing psychic contents to be broken out of their usual context and reinserting them in a different one. With Benjamin, we can thus conceptualise psychoanalytic insights as dialectical images, "a configuration pregnant with tensions." With Freud, we can understand Benjamin's temporality of interruption as a collective therapeutic moment, to be carved out of life, in its arrest. This also entails a new, psychoanalytically inflected philosophy of history, that unveils its revolutionary moments, against the bourgeois conception of (art) history which "seeks the establishment of a continuity. It sets store only by those elements of a work that have already emerged and played a part in its reception. The places where tradition breaks off—hence its peaks and crags, which offer footing to one who would cross over them—it misses" [N9a, S] (AP, 474). Benjamin thus positions his approach against the bourgeois one, putting his hope in the "peaks and crags" overlooked by its smoothing gaze. Benjamin writes of the "destructive or critical momentum of materialist historiography" that it "is registered in that blasting of historical continuity with which the historical object first constitutes itself" (AP, 475). Materialist historiography explodes historical objects out of the continuum of history.

For Freud, contents of the unconscious are likewise exploded out of their normal constellation in analysis, made conscious, and thus become malleable. Drawing explicitly on Freud's theory of drives in "Central Park," Benjamin writes "The labyrinth is the habitat of the dawdler. The path followed by someone reluctant to reach his goal easily becomes labyrinthine. A drive, in the stages leading to its satisfaction, acts likewise. But so, too, does a humanity (a class) which does not want to know where its destiny is taking it" (SW4, 171). Class struggle itself here functions as a "beyond the pleasure principle," with the "self-abolishing" class of the proletariat acting like the drive in delaying its gratification. Like the suffering of psychopathology for Freud, the labyrinth this delay constructs in the forms of nineteenth-century capitalism is self-made, but not consciously so. Thus arises the need to shock "humanity (the class)" out of this, as the course of history, conceptualised as progress, is itself the catastrophe: "It is not an ever-present possibility but what in each case is given. Strindberg's idea: hell is not something that awaits us, but this life here and now" (SW4, 184–85). Thus, like Benjamin's grasping for the "peaks and crags" of history, "Redemption depends on the tiny fissure in the continuous catastrophe" (SW4, 185). The hellish, traumatic continuum of time in capitalism must be interrupted. This interruption requires a shock: In the original preface to the *Trauerspiel* study, Benjamin writes of the echo of a slap (rather than a kiss) that awakens Sleeping Beauty in his renarration of the fairy tale (GS1.2, 901–2). And indeed, this thought remains in the *Arcades Project*: "To the process of rescue belongs the firm, seemingly brutal grasp" [N9a, 3] (AP, 474). Much like Sleeping Beauty, the sleeping collective must be shocked out of its dream. In this, Benjamin's method follows not just Marx and the figure of revolution, but also Freud, who as we have seen acknowledges that the process of psychoanalysis is sometimes apparently cruel to the patient, ostensibly deepening suffering in order to truly ease it.

On the possibility of a "benign" shock for Freud, from which she observes Benjamin draws, Wiegmann states that true liberation presupposes a recognition of hitherto-existing helplessness, as "in the recognition of its helplessness, the individual receives such a shock that it manages to overcome it" (Wiegmann 1989, 35–36, transl. mine). She suggests that Freud hints at the empowering dimension of this making-conscious of suffering and the shock it provokes, overcoming the helplessness and becoming an "acting subject." A further clue to the possibility of a "positive" shock for the purposes of awakening is given in Freud's example of the poet who becomes a tailor in his dreams. At the moment in the dream where his tailor-master sends him away, the dreamer incurs a fright, or shock, causing him to awaken from the dream. Thus, it is a further shock that interrupts the continuum of traumatic repetition. For Freud as for Benjamin, awakening is a struggle against the wish to remain asleep—and one of the things to be mobilised in this struggle is cunning (*List*). The temptation to link Benjamin's somewhat cryptic references to "cunning" to the Hegelian "cunning of reason" must be resisted, as this concept is too determinist to be compatible with Benjamin's focus on interruption. Rather, we can find a clue to it in Freud, who warns that not every dream can be successfully interpreted, as

in interpreting a dream we are opposed by the psychical forces which were responsible for its distortion. It is thus a question of relative strength ["*eine Frage des Kräfteverhältnisses*," a question of the balance of power] whether our intellectual interest, our capacity for self-discipline, our psychological knowledge and our practice in interpreting dreams enable us to master our internal resistances. (SE5, 524–25)

In this battle for mastery of the dream, an agonistic intrasubjective relationship between the different psychic faculties is suddenly made visible. Freud theorises that the body has to be "tricked" into waking up, because of the strength of the sleep-wish, where the momentary return to the inorganic seeks not to be interrupted. Benjamin picks up on this feature of Freudian awakening, writing that "[t]he dream waits secretly for the awakening; the sleeper surrenders himself to death only provisionally, waits for the second when he will cunningly wrest himself from its clutches. So, too, the dreaming collective" [K1a, 2] (AP, 390). Transposed to the political arena of the nineteenth century, this represents a struggle between classes: the stasis of the ruling class, comfortable in the dream-world of capitalism, and the impulse towards awakening on the part of those that are striving to "wake up from the existence of our parents." This is also one of the ways in which Benjamin conceptualises the function of the *Arcades Project*: it is to imitate the "trick" awakening uses in the physiological sense, to overcome the organism's wish to return to the inorganic.

In his notes for the *Arcades Project*, Benjamin asks "Didn't Marx teach that the bourgeoisie, as class, can never arrive at a perfectly clear awareness of itself? And if this is the case, isn't one justified in annexing to Marx's thesis the idea of the dream collective (that is, the bourgeois collective)?" [0°, 67] (AP, 863). In this, Lindner sees Benjamin as taking a more radical stance than Marx on the question of the collective dream and awakening, in that his "speculative use of theory consisted in the assumption that capitalism as a collective dream sleep had overcome modernity, and blocks historical memory" (Lindner 2008, 166, transl. mine). At stake is the question of the possibility of a real awakening in the face of such a blockade of memory. This has to be premised on the end of the dreaming collective in the moment of awakening—it cannot remain once the dream is dissolved and must itself become something else. Gelley suggests that "the dreaming collective remains suspended at the moment of awakening" (Gelley 2015, 91). This is at the heart of Benjamin's interest in the threshold, liminal spaces, in the *Arcades Project*: Awakening itself is a threshold. It is in the in-between space, not yet in the waking world and no longer in the dream—that re/cognition is possible. Benjamin writes that "[f]alling asleep is perhaps the only [threshold] experience that remains to us. (But together with this, there is also waking up . . . The threshold must be carefully distinguished from the boundary. A *Schwelle* (threshold) is a zone. Transformation, passage, wave action are in the word *schwellen*, swell" [O2a, I] (AP, 494). Thresholds are thus differentiated from boundaries as they signify an experience of change, or at least the potential for change, within a "zone," a space of possibility, while boundaries are closed off, sharply demarcated lines. This is why, as Weigel notes, thresholds have "paradigmatic significance" in the *Arcades Project* and present its most "prominent location" (Weigel 1996, 48).

Gelley conceptualises awakening as "a solicitation, a call to a collectivity to come . . . a reaching out to a virtual collective to be constituted by awakening" (Gelley 2015, xii). Developing Ranciere's argument, Gelley terms this Benjamin's "retrograde temporality," conceived of as "not some inversion of historical sequence but rather a need to revise our relation to history, to assume 'the past' as relevant only to the present" (Gelley 2015, 188). Breaking out of the arcades and awakening from the dream-sleep of the nineteenth century is thus premised on the dissolution of the dreaming collective, which "knows no history. Events pass before it as always identical and always new. The sensation of the newest and most modern is, in fact, just as much a dream formation of events as 'the eternal return of the same'" [S2, 1] (AP, 546). Against this dreamlike mode of perception and its stasis, Benjamin posits a temporality that breaks with this flow of events and introduces one in which everything, even truth, is thoroughly temporalised: "'The truth will not escape us'. . . the concept of truth with which these presentations take issue" (AP, 463). Truth *can* escape us, must be seized, as it is perceptible as a truth only for a specific moment, the *Jetzt der Erkennbarkeit*. This is Benjamin's concept of actuality, always threatened by its own disappearance. Impending destruction thus functions as catalyst for cognition in the arcades: Quoting Aragon, Benjamin writes that "[i]t is only today, when the pickaxe menaces them, that they have at last become the true sanctuaries of a cult of the ephemeral, the ghostly landscape of damnable pleasures and professions. Places that yesterday were incomprehensible, and that tomorrow will never know . . . but today they can be recognized" [C2a, 9] (AP, 87). This recognition, for Benjamin, is a political act: "The change in fashions, the eternally up-to-date . . . escapes 'historical' consideration; it is truly overcome only through a consideration that is political (theological). Politics recognizes in every actual constellation the genuinely unique—what will never recur" (AP, 543). This political-theological moment of awakening is thus aimed at an engagement with the past that aims, as Agamben puts it, "not to restore its true dignity, to transmit it anew as an inheritance for future generations," but "an interruption of tradition in which the past is fulfilled and thereby brought to its end once and for all" (Agamben 1999, 153).

Freud writes the following on the topic of unequal cultures in *The Future of an Illusion*: "It goes without saying that a civilization which leaves so large a number of its participants unsatisfied and drives them into revolt neither has nor deserves the prospect of a lasting existence" (SE21, 109). Reading Freud with Benjamin, we can see how these infrequent interjections and latent political currents of psychoanalysis can be radicalised. Nevertheless, this is the point where Benjamin and Freud part ways—where the aim of the latter is primarily to provide a cure for the individual, for Benjamin the moment of a "cure," of a "making whole," and of catharsis is always deferred. For Benjamin, history itself, and thus its interruption, is the litmus test for the truth, the success of awakening. This runs counter to the bourgeois, melancholy conception of history, whose "[s] pleen is the feeling that corresponds to catastrophe in permanence" (SW4, 164). This vision of history

> Can actually claim no more attention from thinkers than a child's kaleidoscope, which with every turn of the hand dissolves the established order into a new array. There is profound truth in this image. The concepts of the ruling class have always been the mirrors that enabled an image of "order" to prevail.—The kaleidoscope must be smashed. (SW4, 164)

Alongside this politicised image of a kaleidoscope reflecting the order of the rulers, containing all revolutions *within* it, Benjamin also writes about another kaleidoscope in "On some Motifs in Baudelaire": Baudelaire speaks of a man who plunges into the crowd as into a reservoir of electric energy. Circumscribing the experience of the shock, he calls this man "a kaleidoscope endowed with consciousness" (SW4, 328). We may surmise that this kaleidoscopic mode of subjectivity, too, must be shattered in order to go beyond its already-existing fractures. Pensky writes *a propos* the baroque allegorist that he

> becomes the source of meaning, but this power is also a defeat, since the allegorist's allegories are dedicated not to the creation of meaning, but to its recovery. And the more allegories the allegorist dedicates to this goal, the more the network of allegorical references multiplies and intertwines, the more distant this goal becomes, the more urgently the allegorist works, and the deeper the allegorist plunges into the well of subjectivity. (Pensky 1993, 27)

As we have seen, the problem of baroque subjectivity remains in the nineteenth century. Neither age is capable of producing an allegory that goes far enough in its destruction. Allegorical intention may tear objects out of life, but it is simultaneously "shattered and preserved," and in clinging to this sublation of the dismembered object as ruin, allegory "offers the image of petrified unrest. Baudelaire's destructive impulse is nowhere concerned with the abolition of what falls prey to it" (SW4, 169). Remaining within the dream-world of the nineteenth century, Baudelaire cannot take the final step: of shattering it in awakening.

Against this stands Benjamin's "Destructive Character" (1931) who pursues destruction not for its own sake, or for the sake of the ruins, but for the way leading out of them.[14] We can perhaps read him as another iteration of the "contemporary" that forms an object of Benjamin's speculation in Convolute N: "The contemporary who learns from books of history to recognize how long his present misery has been in preparation (and this is what the historian must inwardly aim to show him) acquires thereby a high opinion of his own powers. A history that provides this kind of instruction does not cause him sorrow, but arms him" (AP, 481). Emboldened by the insights of the historical materialist—that previous history has been a dream, which it is in the interest of the ruling class to perpetuate, and which consequently must be smashed on awakening, its wish-elements "realized" in this moment—the destructive character does not fall back into melancholy, but is spurred to action. As Wohlfarth writes in his seminal article, "The 'destructive character' is no 'character' in the psychological sense. Character is rather one of his targets. What emerges from its effacement is the faceless model of a positively conceived characterlessness" (Wohlfarth 1978, 50). He signifies the overcoming of the types of the nineteenth century, its semblance of subjectivity in its excessive focus on inwardness and the *interieur*—he is the "enemy of the etui-man" (SW2.2, 542), the bourgeois whose main goal is comfort and who is compelled to leave traces wherever he goes. In him, a thoroughgoing awakening from the dream-world that does not remain attached to its ruins is to be realised—"[t]he destructive character obliterates even the traces of destruction" (SW2.2, 542). He stands against those who "pass things down to posterity, by making them untouchable and thus conserving them" (SW2.2, 542)—bourgeois historiographers. The destructive character does have a relationship to historical transmission: He "has the consciousness of historical man"; "sees nothing permanent. But for this very reason, he sees ways out everywhere" (SW2.2, 542). What he is alert to is the possibility of change in history, at a specific moment: "liquidating" the potential of situations, breaking the transmission of trauma and rupturing the continuum of myth and mourning.

WALTER BENJAMIN'S DREAM

In "Number 113—Cellar" from One-Way Street, Benjamin recounts one of his own dreams, bringing together the themes of dreaming, awakening, and the question of a humanity beyond the vicissitudes of the bourgeois subject. Drawing on dream symbolism of the house as a stand-in for the dreamer's life as a whole, Benjamin begins his narration with "enemy bombs" striking the house, reducing it to rubble and unearthing "perverse antiquities" in its underground foundations (SW1, 445). These otherwise hidden depths function as the unconscious, much as the "chtonic depths" of Paris do in the Arcades Project. It is at this moment of danger that the repressed, forgotten, ritualistic dimension of everyday habit is violently unearthed.

Suddenly, in this "night of despair," Benjamin's unnamed first childhood friend[15] appears in a manner reminiscent of a dream of Freud's own narrated in the *Interpretation*. Freud here describes the appearance of the first close friend of his childhood in various guises throughout his waking and dreaming life as a *"revenant"* (SE5, 486). Benjamin ardently renews their friendship and fraternal bond. This compensatory moment does not survive the moment of awakening, however, and neither does the dream image of his friend: "when I awoke, it became clear that what despair had brought to light like a detonation was the corpse of that boy, who had been immured as a warning: that whoever one day lives here may in no respect resemble him" (SW1, 445). Despair is recognised on awakening to function as a "detonation," which, like the enemy bombs, make visible that humanity of the future must follow a break with the return of the repressed, with the semblance of the bourgeois subject—it must not resemble the revenant in any way. In this, it goes beyond even the destructive character, but is implied in his "clearing up," making space: like the destructive character, Benjamin does not need to know what the subject will be like in future, whether there will be one, and does not name this future being. What will appear in the stead of the fracture, the ruin of that which has been destroyed, is "First of all, for a moment at least, empty space—the place where the thing stood or the victim lived. Someone is sure to be found who needs this space without occupying it" (SW2.2, 541). Someone who will inhabit without possessing—beyond melancholia, beyond narcissism, beyond the dream and awakening, beyond the revenant, beyond the likeness of those who came before, this is Benjamin's negative foil of the fractured subject.

NOTES

1. The Selected Works translation renders this as "The realization of dream elements, in the course of waking up, is the paradigm of dialectical thinking" (AP, 12), which loses the connotations of Verwertung as a using up of something.

2. The translation in the Selected Works reflects this but occludes the close terminological proximity to dreamwork in rendering "Morgenarbeit" as "a morning's work."

3. There is a second aspect to the "using up" of the dreamwork in prayer to be found in Benjamin's note "Über das Grauen I," where Benjamin writes that "Am leichtesten stellt sich Grauen beim Erwachen aus einem Zustand tiefer Kontemplation und Konzentration, wie tiefes Sinnen, Versunkenheit in Musik oder Schlaf, ein." Against this, immersion in the form of prayer is described as "sacred immersion,"

dispelling the threat of this sense of Grauen, that is, immersion in something alien. Benjamin suggests that the ideal-typical case of this Grauen occurs in the recognition of the mother, linking his notion of Grauen with the moment where Freud pinpoints the break with primary narcissism: in recognising that the mother and her breast are not of the self, are an other, thus rupturing infantile one-ness with the world.

4. The same applies to Proust's style: A consequence of his sacrificing of a plot and giving the text up entirely to the dictates of memory is that the result falls back into boredom, the banal. Benjamin quotes contemporary critic Max Unold on Proust's "idle stories—all ordinary dreams turn into idle stories as soon as one tells them to someone" which precisely in their banality form "the bridge to the dream" (SW2.1, 239).

5. The potential of the colour grey can also be found in Benjamin's fragmentary "Notes for a Study of the Beauty of Colored Illustrations in Children's Books": "The gray Elysium of the imagination is, for the artist, the cloud in which he rests and the wall of cloud on the horizon of his visions. This wall opens up for children, and more brightly coloured walls can be glimpsed behind it." (SW1, 265). See also Caygill (1998) for a discussion of the centrality of the optical, and particularly colour, for the conceptualisation of experience in Benjamin's early work.

6. As the editors of the Selected Works note, this is "a reference to Goethe's Faust, Part II, Act 1, in which Faust visits 'the Mothers,' vaguely defined mythological figures, in search of the secret that will enable him to discover Helen of Troy. The phrase has now entered into proverbial speech, evoking the search for the ultimate mysteries of life" (SW2, 266). We can also see a covert allusion to Bachofen's "Sage von Tanaquil" (1870) and Bachofen's work on ancient matriarchy. As Mali notes, Bachofen "spent his life pursuing the most archaic levels of ancient civilization and consciousness, which literally led him to descend into the hidden depths of pre-Roman tombs, and beyond them into contact with the dead, with the Mothers, and thus assumed the form of a mythological journey" (Mali 1999, 179).

7. Mali suggests that, "In the opening scene of the 'Tiergarten' Benjamin realizes that his steps there, which had led him 'downward, if not to the mothers of all being then certainly to the mothers of this garden,' predestined his life to be a quest to regain this lost maternal paradise" (Mali 2003, 258). Mali sees Benjamin draw close to Bachofen's maternal conception of his life here.

8. This appears in a review of Alois Jalkotzy's Märchen und Gegenwart. Das Deutsche Volksmärchen und unsere Zeit (1930), entitled "Colonial Pedagogy."

9. This is also at play in the Imperial Panorama, referenced in Benjamin's description of the Cabinet des mirages (where the scenery is constantly transformed) in the Arcades Project: "A fluctuating light and gentle music accompany the performance, and coming before each transformation is the classic signal of the hand bell, and the jolt, which we recognize from our earliest trips around the world, when, in the Kaiserpanorama, before our eyes that were full of the pain of departure, an image would slowly disengage from the stereoscope, allowing the next one to appear" [R1, 8] (AP, 538).

10. These reflections from Convolute N were, of course, to form the basis of Benjamin's exploration of the interrelation of theology and materialism in his 1940 "Theses on the Concept of History."

11. See also Gelley (2015, 179–80) for a discussion of this passage.

12. Benjamin explicitly references it in GS3, 588; the passage is discussed in more detail below.

13. "Also einerseits: Noch nicht bewusstes Wissen vom Gewesenen (phylogenetisch und ontogenetisch) (Freud: Jenseits des Lustprinzips) Andererseits: das Gegenwärtige, Geschehende als Erinnerung apperzepiert. Ist nun die erste objektive oder die zweite subjektive Ansicht zutreffend? Oder gibt es eine Synthesis?" (also cited in Werner 2015, 50).

14. As Wohlfarth (1978, 57) writes, "There is much evidence to suggest that Brecht was one of Benjamin's models for The Destructive Character, which was written during a period of intense discussion between them."

15. There is good reason to read this figure as Benjamin's friend Fritz Heinle, the youth movement poet who committed suicide at the age of nineteen in protest against the First World War. See D. Pike (1997, 237–43) for a reading of the piece in context with the other No. 113 "rooms," "Vestibule" and "Dining Room." Pike connects the appearance of Goethe in these aboveground, that is conscious, spaces, to Heinle's identity as a poet and concludes: "he embodies the fate of the youth movement (victims of the war) but equally, and inseparably, the difficulty of writing about it, for lyric was killed along with the youth" (Pike 1997, 242).

Bibliography

Adorno, Theodor, Walter Benjamin, and Henri Walter Lonitz (ed.). 1999. *Theodor Adorno & Walter Benjamin: The Complete Correspondence 1928–1940.* Cambridge, MA: Harvard University Press.

Agamben, Giorgio. 1998. *Homo Sacer: Sovereign Power and Bare Life.* Stanford: Stanford University Press.

Agamben, Giorgio. 1999. *Potentialities. Collected Essays in Philosophy.* Stanford: Stanford University Press.

Agamben, Giorgio. 2005. *State of Exception.* Chicago: University of Chicago Press.

Agamben, Giorgio. 2016. "On Benjamin's Baudelaire" in *Walter Benjamin and Theology.* Dickinson, Colby, and Stéphane Symons (eds.). 217-230. New York: Fordham University Press.

Armstrong, Tim. 2000. "Two Types of Shock in Modernity." *Critical Quarterly* vol. 42, no.1, 60–73.

Balibar, Etienne. 2014. "The Subject." In *Dictionary of Untranslateables: A Philosophical Lexicon,* Barbara Cassin et al. (eds.). Princeton: Princeton University Press, 1069–90.

Barbisan, Lea. 2017. "Eccentric Bodies: From Phenomenology to Marxism—Walter Benjamin's Reflections on Embodiment." In *Anthropology & Materialism,* Special Issue 1, 1–14.

Benjamin, Andrew (ed.). 2005. *Walter Benjamin and History.* London: Continuum.

Benjamin, Andrew. 2005. "Boredom and Distraction: The Moods of Modernity." In *Walter Benjamin and History,* Andrew Benjamin (ed.), 156–70. London: Continuum.

Benjamin, Walter, and Heinrich Kaulen (ed.). 2011. *Werke und Nachlass Vol. 13: Kritiken und Rezensionen.* Frankfurt am Main: Suhrkamp.

Bernstein, Richard J. 1998. *Freud and the Legacy of Moses.* New York: Cambridge University Press.

Betancourt, Alex. 2008. *Walter Benjamin and Sigmund Freud between Theory and Politics.* Saarbrücken: VDM Verlag Dr. Müller.

Blättler, Christine, and Christian Voller. 2016. "Einleitung." In *Walter Benjamin: Politisches Denken*, Christine Blättler and Christian Voller (eds.), 9–32. Staatsverständnisse vol. 93. Nomos.

Borch-Jacobsen, Mikkel. 1988. *The Freudian Subject*. Stanford: Stanford University Press.

Brabant, E. et al. (eds.). 1993. *The Correspondence of Sigmund Freud and Sándor Ferenczi*, Vol. 1, 1908–1914. Cambridge, MA: Belknap Press of Harvard University Press.

Bredekamp, Horst. "From Walter Benjamin to Carl Schmitt, via Thomas Hobbes." *Critical Inquiry* vol. 25, no. 2, Winter 1999, 247–66.

Buck-Morss, Susan. 1993. *The Dialectics of Seeing: Walter Benjamin and the Arcades Project*. Cambridge, MA: MIT Press.

Bullock, Marcus, and Michael W Jennings (eds). 2002. *Selected Writings Volume 1*, 1913–1926. Cambridge, MA: The Belknap Press of Harvard University Press.

Butler, Judith. 2003. "Afterword: After Loss, What Then?" In *Loss: The Politics of Mourning*, D. Eng, and D. Kazanjian (eds.), 467–73. Los Angeles: University of California Press.

Butler, Judith. 2012. *Parting Ways: Jewishness and the Critique of Zionism*. New York: Columbia University Press.

Canetti, Elias. 1978. *Crowds and Power*. New York: Seabury Press.

Caruth, Cathy. 1996. *Unclaimed Experience: Trauma, Narrative, and History*. Baltimore: John Hopkins University Press.

Caygill, Howard. 2016. "Benjamin's Natural Theology." In *Walter Benjamin and Theology*, Colby Dickinson and Stéphane Symons (eds.), 144–63. New York: Fordham University Press.

Caygill, Howard. 1998. *Walter Benjamin: The Colour of Experience*. London: Routledge.

Clark, Stuart. 1999. *Thinking with Demons: The Idea of Witchcraft in Early Modern Europe*. Oxford: Oxford University Press.

Cohen, Josh. 2015. "Psychoanalytic Bodies." In *The Cambridge Companion to the Body in Literature*, David Hillman and Maude Ulrika (eds.), 214–29. Cambridge: Cambridge University Press.

Cohen, Margaret. 1993. *Profane Illumination: Walter Benjamin and the Paris of Surrealist Revolution*. Berkeley: University of California Press.

Cohen, Margaret. 2005. "Benjamin's Marxisms." In *Walter Benjamin: Appropriations*, Peter Osborne (ed.), 18–54. London: Routledge.

Comay, Rebecca. 2005. "The Sickness of Tradition: Between Melancholia and Fetishism." In *Walter Benjamin and History*, Andrew Benjamin (ed.), 88–101. London: Continuum.

Comay, Rebecca. 2011. *Mourning Sickness: Hegel and the French Revolution*. Stanford: Stanford University Press.

Conty, Arianne. "They Have Eyes That They Might Not See: Walter Benjamin's Aura and the Optical Unconscious." *Literature & Theology* vol. 27, no. 4, December 2013, 472–86.

Dalle Pezze, Barbara, and Carlos Salzani (eds.). 2009. *Essays on Boredom and Modernity. Critical Studies Vol. 31*. Leiden: Brill.

de Wilde, Marc. "Meeting Opposites: The Political Theologies of Walter Benjamin and Carl Schmitt." *Philosophy & Rhetoric* vol. 44, no. 4 (2011), 363–81.

Dickinson, Colby, and Stéphane Symons (eds.). 2016. *Walter Benjamin and Theology*. New York: Fordham University Press.

Dörr, Georg. 2007. *Muttermythos und Herrschaftsmythos: Zur Dialektik der Aufklärung um die Jahrhundertwende bei den Kosmikern, Stefan George und in der Frankfurter Schule.* Würzburg, Königshausen & Neumann.

Dosamantes-Beaudry, Irma. 1997. "Somatic Experience in Psychoanalysis." *Psychoanalytic Psychology* vol. 14, no. 4, 517–30.

Duettlinger, Carolin. 2007. "Between Contemplation and Distraction: Configurations of Attention in Walter Benjamin." *German Studies Review* vol. 30, no. 1, 33–54.

Edwards, Philip (ed.). 2003. "Introduction." In *Hamlet, Prince of Denmark*, William Shakespeare and Philip Edwards (ed.), 1–70. Cambridge: Cambridge University Press.

Edwards, Philip (ed.). 2003. *Hamlet, Prince of Denmark*. Cambridge: Cambridge University Press.

Eiland, Howard, and Michael W. Jennings (ed.). 2006. *Selected Writings Volume 3, 1935–1938*. Cambridge, MA: Belknap Press of Harvard University Press.

Eiland, Howard, and Michael W. Jennings (ed.). 2006. *Selected Writings Volume 4, 1938–1940*. Cambridge, MA: Belknap Press of Harvard University Press.

Eng, D., and D. Kazanjian (ed.). 2003. *Loss: The Politics of Mourning*. Los Angeles: University of California Press.

Fenves, Peter. 2006. "Ueber das Programm der Kommenden Philosophie." In *Benjamin-Handbuch: Leben—Werke—Wirkung*, Burkhardt Lindner (ed.), 134–50. Stuttgart: J. B. Metzler.

Ferber, Ilit. 2013. *Philosophy and Melancholy: Benjamin's Early Reflections on Theatre and Language*. Stanford: Stanford University Press.

Ferber, Ilit. "Melancholy Philosophy: Freud and Benjamin." *E-REA* vol. 4, no.1, Spring 2006, 66–74.

Ferenczi, Sándor. 2002. *Final Contributions to the Problems and Methods of Psycho-Analysis*. London: Karnac.

Ferris, David S. (ed.). 2004. *The Cambridge Companion to Walter Benjamin*. Cambridge: Cambridge University Press.

Freud, Sigmund. 1953–1974. *The Standard Edition of the Complete Psychological Works of Sigmund Freud in 24 Volumes*. London: Hogarth Press.

Freud, Sigmund. 1961. *Beyond the Pleasure Principle*. New York: W. W. Norton & Company.

Gay, Peter. 1987. *A Godless Jew: Freud, Atheism and the Making of Psychoanalysis*. New Haven, CT: Yale University Press.

Gelley, Alexander. 2015. *Benjamin's Passages: Dreaming, Awakening*. New York: Fordham University Press.

Glatzer, Nahum N. (ed.). 1995. *Franz Kafka: The Complete Stories.* New York: Schocken.

Gozlan, Oren (ed.). 2018. *Current Critical Debates in the Field of Transsexual Studies*. London: Routledge.

Hallward, Peter. "Blanqui's Bifurcations." *Radical Philosophy* 185 (May/June 2014), 36–44.

Hamacher, Werner. 2002. "Guilt History: Benjamin's Sketch 'Capitalism as Religion.'" *Diacritics* vol. 32, no. 3/4, 81–106.

Hanssen, Beatrice. "Portrait of Melancholy (Benjamin, Warburg, Panofsky)" *MLN* vol. 114, no. 5, Comparative Literature Issue (December 1999), 991–1013.

Hanssen, Beatrice. 1998. *Walter Benjamin's Other Histories. Of Stones, Animals, Human Beings, and Angels*. Berkeley: University of California Press.

Hanssen, Beatrice (ed.). 2006. *Walter Benjamin and the Arcades Project*. New York: Continuum.

Hanssen, Beatrice, and Andrew Benjamin (eds). 2002. *Walter Benjamin and Romanticism*. New York: Continuum.

Heidegger, Martin. 1995. *The Fundamental Concepts of Metaphysics: World, Finitude, Solitude*. Bloomington and Indianapolis: Indiana University Press.

Heil, Susanne. 1996. *Gefährliche Beziehungen: Walter Benjamin und Carl Schmitt*. Stuttgart: Metzler.

Hillman, David, and Maude Ulrika (eds.). 2015. *The Cambridge Companion to the Body in Literature*. Cambridge: Cambridge University Press.

Homburg, Phillip. 2018. *Walter Benjamin and the Post-Kantian Tradition*. London: Rowman & Littlefield.

Jennings, Michael W., Howard Eiland, and Gary Smith (eds). 2005. *Selected Writings Volume 2, Part 1, 1927–1930*. Cambridge, MA: Belknap Press of Harvard University Press.

Jennings, Michael W., Howard Eiland, and Gary Smith (eds). 2005. *Selected Writings Volume 2, Part 2, 1931–1934*. Cambridge, MA: Belknap Press of Harvard University Press.

Kafka, Franz. "Poseidon." In *Frankz Kafka: The Complete Stories*, Nahum N. Glatzer (ed.), 434–35. New York: Schocken.

Kahn, Victoria. "Hamlet or Hecuba: Carl Schmitt's Decision." *Representations* vol. 83, no. 1 (Summer 2003), 67–96.

Khatib, Sami. 2017. "'Sensuous Supra-Sensuous': The Aesthetics of Real Abstraction." In *Aesthetic Marx*, Samir Gandesha and Johan Hartle (eds.), 49–72. London: Bloomsbury.

Klein, D. 1985. *Jewish Origins of the Psychoanalytic Movement*. Chicago: University of Chicago Press.

Kracauer, Siegfried. 1995. *The Mass Ornament: Weimar Essays*. Cambridge, MA: Harvard University Press, 331–34.

Leslie, Esther 2000. *Walter Benjamin: Overpowering Conformism*. London: Pluto Press.

Ley Roff, Sarah. 2004. "Benjamin and Psychoanalysis." In *The Cambridge Companion to Walter Benjamin*, David S. Ferris (ed.). Cambridge: Cambridge University Press.

Lindner, Burkhardt (ed.). 2008. *Walter Benjamin: Träume*. Frankfurt am Main: Suhrkamp.

Lockyer, Roger. 1998. *James VI and I*. London: Longman.

Lupton, Julia R., and Kenneth Reinhard. 1993. *After Oedipus: Shakespeare in Psychoanalysis*. Ithaca: Cornell University Press.

Mali, Joseph. 2003. *Mythistory: The Making of a Modern Historiography*. Chicago: University of Chicago Press.

Mali, Joseph. "The Reconciliation of Myth: Benjamin's Homage to Bachofen." *Journal of the History of Ideas* vol. 60, no. 1, January 1999, 165–87.

Marder, Elissa. 2006. "Walter Benjamin's Dream of 'Happiness.'" In *Walter Benjamin and the Arcades Project*, Beatrice Hanssen (ed.), 184–200. New York: Continuum.

Matus, Jill. 2009. *Shock, Memory and the Unconscious in Victorian Fiction*. Cambridge: Cambridge University Press.

Menninghaus, Siegfried. 1986. *Schwellenkunde: Walter Benjamin's Passage des Mythos*. Frankfurt am Main: Suhrkamp Verlag.

Mette, Alexander. 1928. Über Beziehungen zwischen Spracheigentümlichkeiten Schizophrener und *dichterischer Produktion*. Dessau, Dion.

Mette, Alexander. 1931. "Ursprung des deutschen Trauerspiels." *Imago* vol. 7, no. 4, 536–38.

Monagle, Claire, and Dimitris Vardoulakis. 2003. *The Politics of Nothing: On Sovereignty*. London: Routledge.

Mulvey, Laura. "Visual Pleasure and Narrative Cinema." *Screen* vol. 16, issue 3 (October 1975), 6–18.

Nägele, Rainer (ed.). 1988. *Benjamin's Ground. New Readings of Walter Benjamin*. Detroit: Wayne State University Press.

Nägele, Rainer (ed.). 1991. *Theater. Theory. Speculation: Walter Benjamin and the Scenes of Modernity*. Baltimore: Johns Hopkins University Press.

Nägele, Rainer. 1991. "Beyond Psychology: Freud, Benjamin, and the Articulation of Modernity." In *Theater. Theory. Speculation: Walter Benjamin and the Scenes of Modernity*, Rainer Nägele (ed.). Baltimore: Johns Hopkins University Press.

Oberprantacher, Andreas, and Andrei Siclodi (eds.). 2016. *Subjectivation in Political Theory and Contemporary Practices*. London: Palgrave MacMillan.

Osborne, John (ed.). 1998. *The Origin of German Tragic Drama*. London: Verso.

Osborne, Peter (ed.). 2005. *Walter Benjamin: Appropriations*. London: Routledge.

Osborne, Peter (ed.). 2006. "The Dreambird of Experience: Utopia, Possibility, Boredom." *Radical Philosophy* no. 127 (May/June 2006), 3644.

Panhuysen, Geert. (1998). "The Relationship between Somatic and Psychic Processes: Lessons from Freud's *Project*," Annals of the New York Academy of Science, "Neuroscience of the Mind: On the Centennial of Freud's Project for a Scientific Psychology." New York: New York Academy of Sciences, 20–42.

Paul, Joanne. "The Best Counsellors Are the Dead: Counsel and Shakespeare's Hamlet." *Renaissance Studies* vol. 29, no. 3 (June 2015), 1–20.

Pensky, Max. 1993. *Melancholy Dialectics: Walter Benjamin and the Play of Mourning*. Amherst: University of Massachusetts Press.

Pike, David L. 1997. *Passage Through Hell: Modernist Descent, Medieval Underworld*. Ithaca: Cornell University Press.

Porath, Erik. 2005. Gedächtnis des Unierinnerbaren. Philosophische und medientheoretische Untersuchungen zur Freudschen Psychoanalyse. Bielefeld: Transcript.

Rancière, Jacques. 1996. "The Archaeomodern Turn." In *Walter Benjamin and the Demands of History*, Michael Steinberg (ed.), 27–28. Ithaca: Cornell University Press.

Rexroth, Tillmann (ed.). 1991. *Gesammelte Schriften IV*. Frankfurt am Main: Suhrkamp.

Salah, Trish. 2018. "To Return to Schreber." In *Current Critical Debates in the Field of Transsexual Studies*, Oren Gozlan (ed.), 169–80. London: Routledge.

Salzani, Carlos. 2009. "The Atrophy of Experience: Walter Benjamin and Boredom." In *Essays on Boredom and Modernity. Critical Studies Vol. 31*, Barbara Dalle Pezze and Carlos Salzani (eds.), 127–54. Leiden: Brill.

Sandford, Stella. "The Dream Is a Fragment. Freud, Transdisciplinarity and Early German Romanticism." *Radical Philosophy* no. 189 (July/August 2016), 25–34.

Santner, Eric L. 1996. *My Own Private Germany: Daniel Paul Schreber's Secret History of Modernity*. Princeton: Princeton University Press, 1996.

Santner, Eric L. 2001. *On the Psychotheology of Everyday Life: Reflections on Freud and Rosenzweig*. Chicago: University of Chicago Press.

Schmitt, Carl. 1994. *Die Diktatur: Von den Anfängen des modernen Souveränitätsgedankens bis zum proletarischen Klassenkampf*. Berlin: Duncker & Humblot.

Schmitt, Carl. 2006. *Hamlet or Hecuba: The Irruption of Time into Play*. Corvallis: Plutarch Press.

Scholem, Gershom. 1988. "Walter Benjamin and His Angel." In *On Walter Benjamin: Critical Essays and Recollections*, Gary Smith (ed.). Cambridge: MIT Press.

Scholem, Gershom, and Theordor Adorno (eds). 1976. *On Jews and Judaism in Crisis*. New York: Schocken Books.

Scholem, Gershom, and Theordor Adorno (eds). 1981. *Walter Benjamin: The Story of a Friendship*. New York: Schocken Books.

Scholem, Gershom, and Theodor Adorno (eds). 1994. *The Correspondence of Walter Benjamin, 1910–1940*. Chicago: University of Chicago Press.

Shakespeare, William, and Harold Jenkins (ed.). 1982. *Hamlet* (The Arden Shakespeare). London: Routledge.

Smith, Gary (ed.). 1988. *On Walter Benjamin: Critical Essays and Recollections*. Cambridge, MA: MIT Press.

Steitzinger, Johannes. 2013. *Revolte, Eros und Sprache. Walter Benjamin's "Metaphysik der Jugend."* Berlin: Kadmos.

Stewart, E. 2010. *Catastrophe and Survival: Walter Benjamin and Psychoanalysis*. London: Continuum.

Tiedemann, Rolf. 1996. "Dialectics at a Standstill." In *The Arcades Project*, Walter Benjamin and Rolf Tiedemann (ed.), 929–46. Harvard: Harvard University Press.

Tiedemann, Rolf (ed.). 1999. *The Arcades Project*. Harvard: Harvard University Press.

Tiedemann, Rolf (ed.). 1991. *Gesammelte Schriften V*. Frankfurt am Main: Suhrkamp.

Tiedemann, Rolf, and Hermann Schweppenhäuser (eds.). 1991. *Gesammelte Schriften*. Frankfurt am Main: Suhrkamp.

Tiedemann, Rolf, and Hermann Schweppenhäuser (eds.). 1991. *Gesammelte Schriften VI*. Frankfurt am Main: Suhrkamp.

Tiedemann-Bartels, Hella (ed.). 1991. *Gesammelte Schriften III*. Frankfurt am Main: Suhrkamp.

Tomba, Massimiliano. "Another Kind of *Gewalt*: Beyond Law. Re-Reading Walter Benjamin." *Historical Materialism* vol. 17, no. 1 (2009), 126–44.

Tomšič, Samo. 2015. *The Capitalist Unconscious: Marx and Lacan*. London: Verso.

Viesel, Hansjörg. 1988. *Jawohl, der Schmitt. Zehn Briefe aus Plattberg*. Berlin: Gabler & Lutz.

Vischer, Robert. 1994. "On the Optical Sense of Form: A Contribution to Aesthetics." In *Empathy, Form, and Space: Problems in German Aesthetics, 1873–1893*, Harry F. Mallgrave and Eleftherios Ikonomou (eds.). Santa Monica: The Getty Center for History of Art and the Humanities.

Voller, Christian (ed.). 2016. *Walter Benjamin's Politisches Denken*. Nomos: Baden-Baden.

Weber, Samuel. 2008. *Benjamins-abilities*. Harvard: Harvard University Press.

Weber, Samuel. "Genealogy of Modernity: History, Myth and Allegory in Benjamin's *Origin of the German Mourning Play*." *MLN* vol. 106, no. 3 (April 1991), 465–500.

Weber, Samuel. "Taking Exception to Decision: Walter Benjamin and Carl Schmitt." *Diacritics* vol. 22, no. 3/4, Commemorating Walter Benjamin (Autumn–Winter 1992), 5–18.

Weigel, Sigrid. 1996. *Body and Image-Space: Re-reading Walter Benjamin*. London: Routledge.

Weigel, Sigrid. 2016. "Fidelity, Love, Eros: Benjamin's Bireferential Concept of Life as Developed in Goethe's *Elective Affinities*." In *Walter Benjamin and Theology*, Colby Dickinson and Stéphane Symons (eds.), 75–93. New York: Fordham University Press.

Werner, Nadine. 2015. *Archäologie des Erinnerns: Sigmund Freud in Walter Benjamin's Berliner Kindheit*. Gottingen: Wallstein.

Wiegmann, Jutta. 1989. *Psychoanalytische Geschichtstheorie. Eine Studie zur Freud-Rezeption Walter Benjamins*. Bonn (Doctoral dissertation).

Wizisla, Edmund. 2004. *Benjamin und Brecht: Die Geschichte Einer Freundschaft*. Frankfurt am Main: Suhrkamp Verlag.

Wohlfarth, Irving. 2011. "Die Passagenarbeit." In *Benjamin-Handbuch: Leben— Werke—Wirkung*, Burkhardt Lindner (ed.), 251–74. Stuttgart: J. B. Metzler.

Wohlfarth, Irving. "No-Man's-Land: On Walter Benjamin's 'Destructive Character.'" *Diacritics* vol. 8, no. 2 (Summer 1978), 47–65.

Wohlfarth, Irving. "Walter Benjamin and the Idea of a Technological Eros. A Tentative Reading of *Zum Planetarium*." In *Benjamin Studien I* (2002), Geyer et al., 65–110.

Worringer, Wilhelm. 1997. *Abstraction and Empathy: A Contribution to the Psychology of Style*. Chicago: Ivan R. Dee.

Zumbusch, Cornelia. 2012. "Urgeschichte. Erzählungen vom Vorvergangenen bei Herder, Engels, Freud und Benjamin." In *Urworte. Zur Archäologie erstbegründender Begriffe*, Tobias Döring and Michael Ott (eds.), 137–53. Munich.

Index